BATTLESHIPS IN TRANSITION

BATTLESHIPS IN TRANSITION

THE CREATION OF THE STEAM BATTLEFLEET 1815-1860

Andrew Lambert

NAVAL
INSTITUTE
PRESS

© Andrew Lambert 1984

First published in Great Britain in 1984 by
Conway Maritime Press Ltd, 24 Bride Lane,
Fleet Street, London EC4Y 8DR.

Published and distributed in the United
States of America and Canada by the Naval
Institute Press, Annapolis, Maryland 21402

Library of Congress Catalog Card No.
84–61561

ISBN 0–87021–090–4

Manufactured in the United Kingdom

Contents

Acknowledgements

Thanks are due to the staffs of the following libraries and institutions where research for this book was undertaken: The National Maritime Museum; the Public Record Office; the British Library, both the Department of Printed Books and the Department of Manuscripts; the Scottish Record Office; the Bodleian Library, Oxford; the University Library, Cambridge; and the Borthwick Institute, York.

Special thanks are due to David Lyon and the staff of the Draught Room, and to Alan Pearsall and the staff of the Reading Room at the National Maritime Museum; to Franz Bilzer and Erwin Sieche of Vienna; the staff at the Musée de la Marine and the Historical branch of the Ministère de la Defense in Paris, the Rigsarkivet in Copenhagen, the Sjöhistoriska Museum in Stockholm, the Museo Storico Navale in Venice, Stephen S Roberts of Arlington, and Andrzej Mach and Przemyslaw Budzbon in Gdansk. Without the help of these people this book could not have been written. The errors and omissions of the work are, as ever, the sole responsibility of the author.

I cannot close this section without paying tribute to the inspiration and help given by Professor Bryan Ranft and by Robert Gardiner of Conway Maritime Press. Finally I am indebted to Ann Billows for the preparation of the index.

The bare hull of the *Edgar* stripped down to the waterline and with her machinery removed. Behind her are the bows of the partially dismantled *Duke of Wellington* while the as yet untouched *Hannibal* is to the right.
Topham Picture Library

The *Edgar* showing her boilers being dismantled. The iron diagonal riders that were an essential feature of the wooden steam battleship can be clearly seen.
Topham Picture Library

The *Howe* as the training ship *Impregnable* at Devonport.
Conway Picture Library

The *Atlas* as an asylum ship at Chatham, 1884-1904.
Conway Picture Library

Introduction

The object of this study is to fill a major gap in the history of warship development and naval policy. Hitherto there has been no adequate discussion of the transitional stage that separated the sailing ship of the line from the ironclad. Many authors have examined the development of steam propulsion and its naval ramifications, but none have progressed beyond the introduction of the paddle wheel and the screw propeller. The later history of the wooden steamship has been ignored; in consequence the 1850s, a decade of major advances, has been almost forgotten. The accepted view of the wooden steam battleship is that it was the anachronistic product of a conservative tradition. The brief lifespan and transitional nature of these ships has been quoted in ill-informed attempts to dismiss them out of hand. Similarly contrasts are drawn, quite improperly, with the more rapid advance of commercial iron and steam shipbuilding to provide evidence to suggest that their construction was a mistake.

This book will challenge such views by presenting a balanced study of the evolution and active service of the wooden steam battleship, underlining its essential contribution to the development of naval technology and the factors that caused its sudden demise. In pursuing this aim it has been necessary to break with the tradition that places the study of warship design in a separate category from that of mainstream naval history. These areas are integrated around a central theme, the role of the Surveyor of the Navy from 1847 to 1861, Captain Sir Baldwin Walker, in the creation of the new steam battlefleet. To this core have been added all the issues that affected naval policy. In consequence it is hoped that a balance has been struck between the political and administrative decisions that determined the size of the fleet, the detailed design work that developed with the ships, and the gradual improvements effected in their overall performance.

It must be emphasized that in designing the wooden steam battleships both Dupuy de Lôme in France and the Surveyor's Office in Britain were making a clean break with sailing ship practice: de Lôme's *Le Napoléon* was intended to gain the greatest benefit from her machinery and sacrificed her sailing qualities accordingly; the British ships were designed to balance the tactical value of steam with the strategic requirement for long-distance cruising under sail. But both countries demonstrated a realisation that the battles of the next war would be fought under steam. When that war came in 1854, it was not the war that had been anticipated – an Anglo-French naval war – but one in which the long-time rivals were allied against Russia. The wooden steam battleship was to play a major role in that war, demonstrating that it was the most powerful instrument of seapower. The tactical value of steam was immediately apparent when the allied fleets assumed absolute control of the Baltic and the Black Sea without opposition from the large, but entirely sail-driven, Russian battlefleets. This advantage determined the strategy of the war, allowing the allies to undertake the amphibious descent on the Crimea secure in the knowledge that the Russian fleet could not threaten their vital sea communications.

Considerable attention has already been devoted to the early history of steam propulsion, while almost none has been given to the 1850s, and the steam battleship in particular. Therefore the basic theme of this book is the transition of the battlefleet from sail to steam. An admirable survey of the early advances of steam in the Royal Navy can be found in C J Bartlett's *Great Britain and Seapower, 1815–1853*. However this book will challenge his conclusions as to the significance of the wooden steam battleship.

Similarly the rise of the ironclad will be examined only insofar as it touches upon the demise of the wooden ship. J P Baxter's book *The Introduction of the Ironclad Warship* remains the classic account. At this stage it should be emphasized that Baxter's work, for all its qualities when dealing with the ironclads is both inaccurate and misleading when dealing with the wooden battleship. The opinions voiced in Baxter's book have been taken up by more recent authors and are primarily responsible for the low regard in which the wooden steam battleship has been held.

Finally Brian Lavery's book *The Ship of the Line* provides an excellent survey of the development of the ship of the line up to the 1830s. Consequently it has been possible to restrict this work to examining the later history of the sailing battleship as it affected the development of the wooden steam battleship and the naval policy of the era.

This being a subject not graced by any previous study it is necessary to establish certain terms of reference before starting. These are, in the main, concerned with the classification of ship types. Some are self-explanatory and have only been included for the sake of completeness, but others are new and important to the theme of this book.

Ship of the line: a sailing warship with two or three covered gundecks, in this period carrying between 70 and 120 guns.

Frigate: a sailing warship with a single covered gundeck, carrying between 32 and 60 guns. Used for scouting and commerce protection.

Paddle frigate: a large paddle wheel driven steam warship with a battery of very heavy guns.

Screw frigate: a frigate with steam screw propulsion.

Blockship: a British conversion of a small ship of the line, originally of 74 guns. Intended for harbour defence and coastal operations.

Wooden steam battleship: any ship of the line that was built for, or fitted with, screw steam propulsion. Two or three covered gundecks, 60 to 131 guns.

Converted ship: a ship originally commenced as a sailing ship of the line, but converted, either on the stocks or after completion into a wooden steam battleship.

New construction: a ship designed from the outset as a wooden steam battleship.

Floating battery: a French-designed armoured vessel of limited seagoing ability, intended for the bombardment of coastal fortifications.

Ironclad: a seagoing ship with armour plate, descended from the floating battery.

Nominal horse power: a rating of large steam engines computed from the dimensions of the cylinders. Not an accurate assessment of an engine's potential after 1845.

Indicated horse power: determined by a mechanical indicator fitted to the engine; a rather more reliable expression of performance.

Tonnage: the old method of determining the size of a ship, approximately one-third too small in terms of actual displacement.

Displacement: the modern method of determining the size of a ship, came into widespread use in Britain at the end of the 1850s, but was not used by the Navy for another decade.

Andrew Lambert,
Norfolk, 1984

1. The Sailing Battlefleet, 1815-1847

The paddle frigate *Valorous* of 1851, the last ship of this type built for the Royal Navy.
National Maritime Museum

For the first three decades of peace the construction of ships of the line was not attended by any great urgency. At no stage prior to the introduction of the wooden steam battleship was the Royal Navy in any real danger from even the most powerful combination of potential foes. However the size and material condition of the ships that composed the British line of battle were a constant source of concern.

The large reserves of war-built ships placed a low priority on new construction, emphasizing repairs and modifications. It was in this atmosphere that Sir Robert Seppings, a Surveyor of the Navy between 1813 and 1832 carried out his innovatory reform of the structure of the wooden warship.[1] Seppings had perfected a system of diagonal framing which replaced the old rectangular plan with a much stronger triangulated layout. He also increased the

use of iron knee pieces and introduced iron straps. He had developed a round bow and after the war he also devised a circular stern of more solid construction to replace the flimsy structures hitherto used – the weakness of the extremities as traditionally constructed had become exacerbated after Nelson and his contemporaries adopted breaking-the-line tactics which involved exposing the bow and stern far more than the old rigid line of battle.

Seppings' reforms were the first major breakthrough in the construction of warships since the introduction of carvel planking. Their total effect was to make practicable ships fully 25 per cent

The engines of the paddle frigate *Devastation* of 1841. The height of these engines and their exposure to gunfire is evident. *Science Museum*

bigger, and yet far stronger than their predecessors. Without Seppings it would have been impossible to construct the large two-decked 90-gun steam battle-ships that were the standard type of the 1850s. Three-deckers had always been built longer because of the additional strength inherent in the extra deck, and this practice was to continue into the steam era. Seppings' final contribution to the advance of wooden battleship design was the *Rodney* of 1827, the first British 90-gun two-decker. Built in direct response to American and French ships of the same type she was generally similar to the *Caledonia* class 120-gun three-deckers, without the extra deck. As a result the *Rodney* was the first British battleship to have the displacement and stability to carry a full battery of 32-pounder guns, dispensing entirely with carronades. The 90-gun two-decker offered the best balance of sailing and fighting qualities.

The 200-strong battlefleet of 1815 was unnecessary in peacetime, and the opportunity was taken to dispose of one hundred of the old or inefficient ships. The construction policy of the first decade saw a shift away from the Third Rate 74-gun ship, hitherto the standard type; none were ordered after the end of the war. Instead the smallest ships built for the line of battle were the 80- or 84-gun Second Rates. All the new ships of this period were based on well-known models, the *Caledonia*, the *Victory* and the 84-gun *Canopus* and *Christian VII*. During the late 1820s it became apparent that these ships were no longer adequate to face the latest American and French designs, both of which carried far heavier broadsides. The Navy Board ordered the building or reconstruction of ten 120-gun First Rates to mount an increased battery.[2] Despite being given additional beam the *Caledonia* type were quite unable to carry a full battery of 32-pounders. This failure demonstrated the folly of the construction policy of the preceding ten years when the Navy Board had attempted to standardise ship design by repeating old designs. The ships they constructed were consequently too small for any major rearmament. After 1826 the Navy Board, under Admiral Sir Thomas Byam Martin, the Comptrol-

ler, began to shift away from small ships, the first sign of this being the order for the *Rodney* in 1827.

The Tory Government that had ruled Britain for almost three decades fell in 1830. Earl Grey's Whig Reform Ministry placed Sir James Graham as First Lord of the Admiralty (1830–34). Graham, one of the leading reformers, abolished the Tory-dominated Navy Board in 1832 as part of a sweepng reconstruction of the Admiralty. At the same time he dismissed Seppings. This left the new Surveyor, Captain Sir William Symonds with an unheard of latitude in the design of the Royal Navy's ships. Symonds was essentially an amateur shipbuilder who had risen to prominence by his success in competitive sailing trials between small warships.[3] His selection implied a criticism of the dockyard-trained architects of the preceding 200 years, and therefore technical writers have tended to condemn his ships.

Symonds' ships were built on enlarged and radical lines. He used a triangular hull-form, broad-beamed with steeply rising floors, a marked contrast to the round-bilged and flat-floored form of all previous sail of the line. Symonds intended that these ships should require no ballast, stability being provided by the increased beam, although his primary concern was with sailing qualities. His battleships, the three-decker 116-gun *Queen*, the 90-gun two-decker *Albion* and the 80-gun *Vanguard* and *Superb* proved to be fast and weatherly, but they had a marked tendency to roll in adverse conditions. This affected their performance as gun platforms and gave rise to a torrent of criticism from the service.

That Symonds should have been concerned with sailing qualities above military efficiency demonstrated a typical peacetime malaise of the Royal Navy – the over-estimation of non-military functions. The period was dominated by the competitive sailing trials, and Symonds' success in these was his only recommendation for the job of Surveyor. However the Royal Navy had established the first Gunnery Training school, HMS *Excellent*, in 1832, and the results of this scientific and practical training were demonstrated at the bombardment of Acre on 3 November 1840. The fire of the British fleet was outstanding, both for its rapidity and its precision; Acre represents the high point of combat efficiency with wooden sailing war-ships armed with muzzle-loading smooth bore

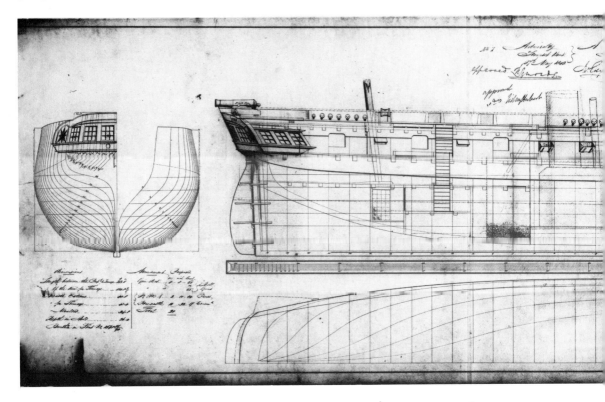

artillery. No other service could match the Royal Navy in this, or perhaps any, matter relating to the professional conduct of war at sea during the last years of sail or the steam battleship era.

Lord Minto (First Lord 1835–41) attempted to lay down a fixed ratio of battleships to be available at any one time. His memorandum of 1841 prompted by the Syrian Crisis of 1840, returned to the emotive figure of 100 ships: 80 were to be ready for service (70 in the water and 10 completed but still on the slip); a further 10 should be under construction, taking advantage of the improved longevity that could be achieved by slow and deliberate assembly; the final 10 ships were to be prepared in frame but held in readiness to replace the 10 advanced ships when they were launched. When Minto prepared his plan there were 73 ships afloat, 14 building and 5 in frame. Unfortunately the position was not as bright as the figures suggest. The bulk of the ships afloat were approaching the end of their economic lives, generally reckoned at thirty years. Furthermore 31 were old 74s, 9 of which were little more than floating lumber piles. These figures reveal the legacy of the 1830s when new construction failed to keep pace with the block

obsolescence of the war-built fleet.

Symonds' ships were not well regarded by the Tory Admiralty of 1841–46, especially as they were constantly criticised in Parliament. As a result co-operation between the Board of Admiralty and the Surveyor was reduced to an absolute minimum, which further restricted construction. Admiral Sir George Cockburn, the First Naval Lord who dominated the Admiralty during this period eventually suspended all work on Symonds' First and Second Rate ships on 9 December 1844. The Construction Board he assembled to justify his actions then declared: 'there is not at present any fixed principle by which the construction of our ships is regulated.'[4] In fact Symonds had a principle, and the real problem lay in his refusal to alter it in deference to any criticism, however well intentioned. When Captain Lord John Hay's Committee of Reference on Shipbuilding of 1846 recommended a modified hull-form, and when the Admiralty pressed Symonds to adopt it he resigned, ostensibly on grounds of ill health. As Sir Charles Napier observed, the overall effect of the debate on the merits of Symonds and his ships was to reduce the number of battleships built.[5] Only 14

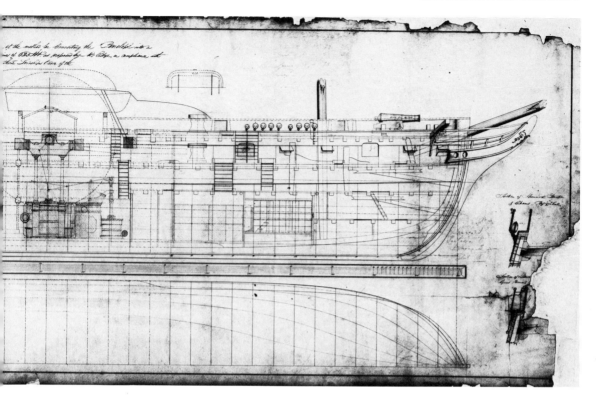

Symondite battleships were launched as sail of the line, 6 more being completed as steamships.

After 1815 the battlefleet became smaller and older. While individual units were both large and modern the bulk of the fleet was composed of old-fashioned ships that required an increasing amount of repair work. This reduced the already small labour force available for new construction.

In 1848 the First Lord, Lord Auckland (1846–49), called for a battlefleet of 80 First and Second Rate ships, 50 afloat, 15 building and 15 in frame (Third Rates were no longer considered fit to lie in the line of battle). Just before his untimely death Auckland adopted a programme of work to maintain the fleet at this level, having first satisfied himself that the new designs would justify such a step.[6] Four years later his successor, Sir Francis Baring (1849–52), reported that the fleet comprised 70 ships afloat, 18 First Rates, 6 large Second Rates, 19 small Second Rates and 27 Third Rates; 6 First and 8 large Second Rates were building. By this stage the steam battleship was considered a practical proposition and the steam battlefleet lay less than a year in the future.

The debate on the Symondite hull-form had

Inboard profile of the paddle frigate *Penelope*, 1843. Originally a *Leda* class sailing frigate she was cut in half and lengthened in order to fit in the machinery and the paddle wheels. This unsatisfactory ship indicated many of the problems that must have occurred in any attempt to create a paddle wheel battleship.
National Maritime Museum

reduced the number of modern ships built or building. In consequence there were few ships that were suitable to be converted into steamers, the greater part of the battlefleet comprising small 80- and 84-gun ships that were hard pressed to stow all their provisions with peacetime complements. The problem of below-deck space would become critical when engines and coal had to be added, and in this respect even Symonds' largest ships were decidedly lacking – the First Rate *Queen* had 1300 cubic feet less space below the orlop than the slightly smaller *Trafalgar*.[7] While the *Caledonia* and *Nelson* class three-deckers had the space to fit machinery they lacked the stability to carry a full battery of 32-pounder guns. One, the *Prince Regent*, had been so deficient in this respect that she had to be cut down into a 90-gun two-decker; the *St Vincent* merely lost her poop and forecastle, but both ships were much improved by reducing their upperworks.

While steam power had become an accepted part of the Navy from 1830, its impact on the battlefleet was restricted to the use of paddle steamers as tugs – there was no thought of putting paddle wheels on a battleship. The paddle wheel was open to many objections as the propulsion system for a warship;

this was especially so in the case of a line of battleship that was intended to fight in regular formation and at close range. Not only were the paddles themselves completely exposed to gunfire and must be damaged in any serious engagement, but the paddle shaft and much of the machinery were above the waterline, and therefore also vulnerable to gunfire. Furthermore the wheels took

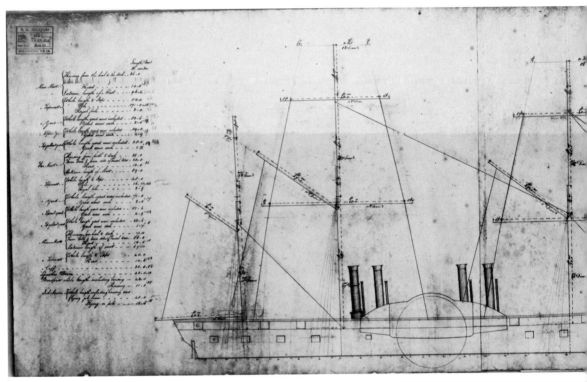

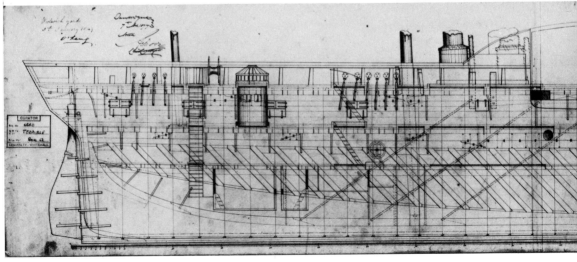

up a large part of the broadside of the ships to which they were fitted, reducing the number of gunports and rendering them greatly inferior in firepower to a sailing ship of the same size. This led to the adoption of very heavy guns on the later paddle frigates such as the *Terrible*. Finally the paddle wheel ruined performance under sail, making it difficult for mixed squadrons to operate in concert. These

factors ensured that no seagoing battleship was ever built with paddles, the reduction in broadside firepower alone rendering the concept impossible.

The screw propeller offered a solution to the problem of masking the broadside, but the pace of development was hesitant. As a result five years elapsed between the order for the first screw warship and the decision to build the first screw Fourth Rate, the *Arrogant*. Even then such developments took place with the express disapproval of the Surveyor. At the same time the Tory Admiralty ordered several large iron-hulled screw frigates, and four screw blockships (ex-74s) for harbour defence. The *Arrogant*, the blockships and the engines of the iron frigates were all destined to play a significant part in the development of the steam battleship. The iron frigates were converted by the following Whig Admiralty into transports after trials at Woolwich had indicated that the thin shell plating was no substitute for a wooden hull when it came to protection. The conversion entailed replacing their engines with smaller sets. This provided the next Surveyor with several sets of engines which were fitted to steam battleships. Those fitted to the *James*

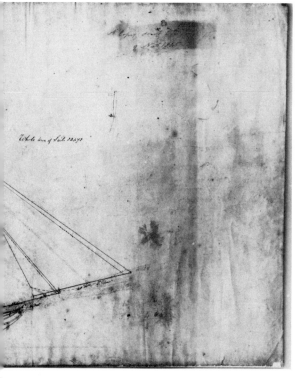

Sail plan of the *Terrible*.
National Maritime Museum

Inboard profile of the paddle frigate *Terrible* (1845), the largest and most powerful ship of this type ever built. Larger than the last 74-gun ships, nevertheless she mounted only 19 guns.
National Maritime Museum

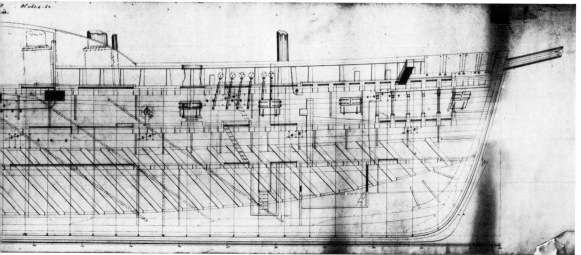

The paddle frigate *Gladiator* of 1841.
National Maritime Museum

Watt and the *Algiers* were both unreliable and of mediocre performance.

When Lord Auckland became First Lord in 1846 he found the design of sailing ships uncertain and the future of the steamer undecided. He resolved to use the best opinion in the service to answer these questions, both by reference to expert constructors and to practised seamen. Auckland began by consulting Admiral Sir William Parker, commanding the Channel Squadron, then almost permanently based in the Tagus. When Parker was moved to the Mediterranean, Auckland replaced him with the brilliant but controversial Rear-Admiral Sir Charles Napier. Napier's strongly-worded criticism of Symonds' sailing ships and steamers on the floor of the House of Commons led many to think him partisan, but nothing could have been further from the truth. His comments were prompted by a genuine concern for the state of the Navy, and Auckland realised this, as did Cockburn, for many years the target of his attacks.

The Channel Squadron (or Western Squadron) under Auckland's administration was a curious hybrid. It was second only to the Mediterranean Fleet in force of ships and like all stations combined a considerable amount of diplomatic activity with the more routine duties. However Auckland was determined to use the limited nature and kinder waters of the station for experimental and evolutionary squadrons. Napier was the ideal officer for the command: he was relatively young at 60, had a reputation for energy and was interested in the design problems that faced Auckland.

Initially Napier was concerned to press the claims of the paddle frigate *Sidon*, which he had designed. Fortunately she turned out well, and even Auckland had to admit her merits, ordering the *Leopard* – the last such vessel to be built – to follow her design. Auckland's view of steam development had already progressed beyond the paddle wheel, being influenced by the early cruises of the screw corvette *Rattler* off Ushant in the summer of 1846. Therefore Napier was given the converted screw frigate *Amphion* and later the blockship *Blenheim*. Both ships were imperfect, but demonstrated the practical

The iron screw frigate *Megaera* after her conversion into a troopship. Her original engines were used in the steam battleship *Algiers*.
National Maritime Museum

advantages of the screw. The *Amphion* was so over-crowded by her machinery that she could stow few provisions, but the *Blenheim*'s relative success convinced Auckland that the future of naval architecture lay in effecting the best combination of the auxiliary screw propeller with superior sailing qualities.[8] Before deciding what form of hull lines would produce the required qualities, he awaited the trials of the second blockship, the *Ajax*, which had not had its stern modified. If she equalled the sea-going performance of the lengthened *Blenheim* then all the theoretical and practical evidence of the need for a fine run aft would be controverted.

Auckland had reached these conclusions ahead of his naval advisors and his death on 1 January 1849 delayed the full appreciation of the success of the screw for almost two years. His successor, Baring, still looked for further trials of the paddle steamer,[9] despite the fact that the first steam battleship had

already been ordered; indeed some naval architects were still working on paddle frigate designs in the early 1850s, James Peake proposing ships of similar dimensions to the last steam battleships.[10]

Auckland's panel of expert constructors, the Committee of Reference on Shipbuilding under Captain Lord John Hay, was instrumental in forcing Symonds to resign in June 1847. Until a successor was appointed in February 1848 the Surveyor's Department was run by John Edye, the Assistant Surveyor and principal draughtsman. Edye had joined the service in 1803, being indentured to Joseph Tucker, who was later a Surveyor of the Navy. After working at Plymouth and Pembroke Edye went to India in 1818 to report on its shipbuilding resources. He had been appointed Assistant Surveyor at the same time as Symonds, but was to remain in office until 1857.[11] Edye was responsible for all the detailed drawing done during Symonds' term, the Surveyor himself being an amateur and no draughtsman. His major contributions to the service were his improvements of Seppings' timbering plan, particularly the use of iron rather than wooden diagonal riders, and the inspired design of the *James Watt* that formed the basis for the British new construction throughout the steam battleship era. While Edye had supported Symonds in opposing the premature advance of steam he was prepared to work with the new element when it became inevitable, as the success of the *Agamemnon* demonstrated. For all that, he remained a cautious and conservative man in the old style of dockyard-trained men, a factor that precluded him from the highest office of his profession. During Edye's period in control the large Symondite ships suspended by Cockburn were modified: four *Queen* class three-deckers and one *Albion* class 90-gun ship not yet laid down were lengthened by 5 feet overall and had their midsection modified.

Using the authority of the Committee of Reference, Hay began to impose his views on the Surveyor's Office. Typically he caused a letter to be sent to Edye, via the Board of Admiralty, in the form of a memorandum from the Committee, expressing the most trenchant criticism of the detailed carpentry arrangements Edye proposed for the Committee-designed 90-gun ship *Caesar*. Edye's mistake had been to follow the Symondite timbering plan that the Committee had decided to abandon in favour of a return to that of Seppings.[12]

Hay, the Third Naval Lord, was a proponent of steam and made it his concern to ensure that the resources of the steam department were fully employed. To this end he advanced a plan to apply steam power to ships of the line. However he did not consider that the qualities of a sailing ship could be combined with screw steam propulsion, and in this opinion Hay was abreast of the majority of his contemporaries. He envisaged a sailing battlefleet with short-range steam blockships for harbour defence and operations in narrow seas, especially the Channel and the Straits of Gibraltar.

Hay was familiar with the four old 74s then converting into blockships. They were intended to have a limited seagoing capability under sail, with masts and yards on a reduced scale.[13] However this project of the preceding Tory Admiralty held little appeal for Hay and he anticipated failure: 'I am disposed to think, that on the coast of England a line of battleship would be a better man-of-war without the screw than with it.'[14] Yet at the same time he proposed that the two sisters of Seppings' masterpiece, the *Rodney* (the *Nile* and *London*), be altered into steam blockships, using the 700 nominal horse power machinery removed from the iron frigates *Vulcan* and *Simoom* on their conversion into troopships; neither of the ships had been commissioned, although they had been afloat for ten years. Hay considered their form 'objectionable', and fancied they would be slow sailers. When examined he admitted, 'I only propose putting engines in those ships because we had them [the engines]. I would not build ships for the purpose.' He saw no other means of 'getting rid' of the machinery. Hay thought that the better method of applying steam to the battle line lay in the provision of tugs,[15] which was a method already being

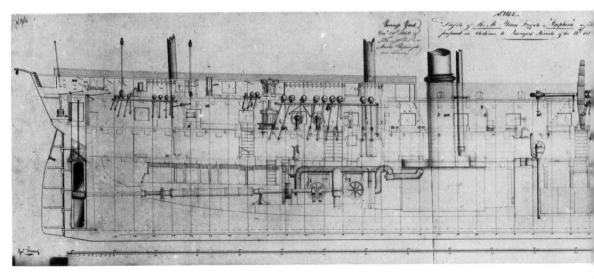

The engines of the highly successful screw frigate *Arrogant*, 1846, built by Penn.
Science Museum

employed by Sir William Parker in the Mediterranean and Sir Charles Napier in the Channel.[16]

It was fortunate that a new Surveyor was appointed before Hay could press through his schemes for the *Nile* and *London*. Captain Sir Baldwin Wake Walker had yet to take over his new office when the Select Committee heard evidence, but he displayed a more reasoned approach to the current problems of naval architecture than Hay. He did not consider it 'prudent' to alter such valuable ships in view of the current lack of knowledge regarding the effect of screw propulsion on large warships, and preferred to await the results of the first trials with the blockships.[17]

Hay had taken control of construction policy after the departure of Symonds. His ideas on the future of steam were no more advanced than those of many other officers and in some areas he was dangerously misguided, so it was fortunate that the Select Committee met at the perfect time to expose

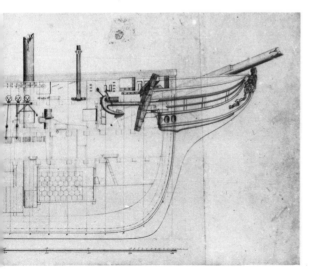

Inboard profile of the pioneer screw frigate conversion *Amphion* of 1846. She was a much more successful ship than the paddle wheel *Penelope*.
National Maritime Museum

the poverty of his intellect. The deliberations of the Committee also assisted Lord Auckland and his Board to re-define the duties of the Surveyor, a process that Hay had attempted to delay and divert; it is not clear whether Hay sought the office of Surveyor, or merely wished to give full vent to his views on the subject, maintaining a position of influence without responsibility.

To have altered the *Nile* and *London* along the lines that Hay proposed would have been an act of vandalism. They would have been grossly over-crowded by the bulky, old-fashioned iron frigate engines to very little advantage. The blockship was a false step in the evolution of the steam battleship, and although the first four ships were a valuable experiment, to have followed them with larger and more powerful conversions before the originals had been tried at sea would have ruined two modern Second Rates. Not only were such ships scarce but the waste of time and money would have been considerable. In the selection of a new Surveyor the Admiralty looked for an officer of 'sound, practical knowledge', to prevent just that type of error Hay had been about to commit.[18]

The hull of the *Powerful* class 84 *Ganges* being broken up at Plymouth in 1929. This view demonstrates the final development of Sir Robert Seppings' diagonal construction. The wooden diagonals were replaced by iron in the modified arrangement adopted by John Edye, the Assistant Surveyor 1832–57.
Royal Naval Museum

2. Captain Sir Baldwin Walker and the Steam Battlefleet

Born in 1802 Walker entered the Navy in 1820 and during his early years he earned a reputation as an outstanding seaman.[1] The Royal Navy was at peace, but he saw service in a voluntary capacity in the minor operations of the Greek War of Independence, notably the taking of the Morea Castle. On reaching the rank of Captain, in 1838, he was permitted to accept the post of Commander-in-Chief of the Ottoman Navy, and in this capacity he took part in the bombardment of Acre in 1840, being the first foreigner to command a Turkish fleet in action. For his conduct at Acre he was publicly commended by Admiral Sir Robert Stopford and awarded the Commandership of the Bath. Walker also performed notable feats in attempting to reorganise the administration of the Turkish service. Returning to the Royal Navy in 1845 he commanded the Symondite First Rate

The *Princess Royal*, 1853, as flagship of the East Indies and China Station at Plymouth, 1864 or 1867.
Imperial War Museum

Queen in Admiral Sir John West's evolutionary squadron; in the following year he took the frigate *Constance* to the Pacific Station. Returning in late 1847 he was selected for the post of Surveyor, taking part in the 1847 Committee on Naval and Military Estimates before being confirmed in office on 5 February 1848.

Walker's term at the Surveyor's Office has been largely ignored, yet his contribution to the perfection of the steam battleship, the successful conclusion of the Russian War and the introduction of the ironclad should each justify his elevation to the first rank of naval administrators. One reason why this most important part of Walker's career remains

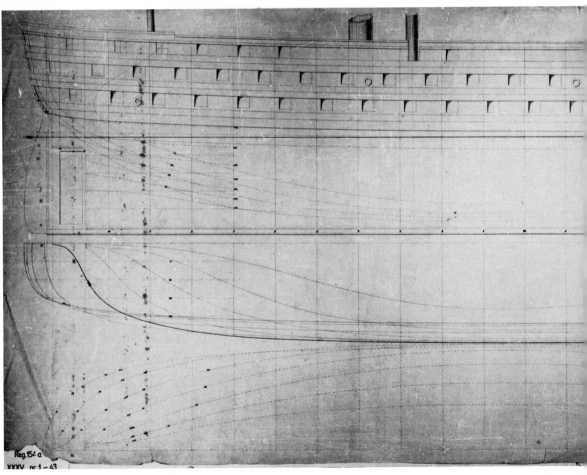

Le Napoléon in 1858.
Musée de la Marine

Sheer draught of the French steam battleship *Le Napoléon*, 1850.
Musée de la Marine

unknown is that the entry in the *Dictionary of National Biography* passes over it in a single, brief sentence:[2] Sir John Laughton virtually copied out the entry on Walker from O'Byrne's *Naval Biographical Dictionary* of 1848,[3] adding very little on his later career. However, before considering Walker's term of office it would be well to reflect on the problems that must have arisen if Hay, or an officer of similar merits, had been selected.

Bearing in mind their experience with Symonds, and the performance of Lord John Hay on the 1847 Committee the Admiralty determined that the new Surveyor should not be a designer of ships. Walker's instructions were commendably precise and marked a shift both in the duties of the Surveyor, and in the qualities expected of him. Walker was selected on his proven abilities as a seaman and as an administrator.[4] He was directed to search for general principles to govern construction and fitting out, always guarding against 'rash experiments'. He was to oversee the dockyards, the *matériel* of the Navy and prepare a programme of works for each year. In all this he was to rely on his own talents, leaving the detailed design work to his two assistants, John Edye and Isaac Watts, the latter of whom was appointed at the same time as the new Surveyor.[5] In essence Walker was to liaise between the designers and the Admiralty, adopting the position of an experienced sea officer who might have to use the ships that were built. In this manner the Admiralty hoped to avoid the type of blunder that had characterised the early years of the decade.

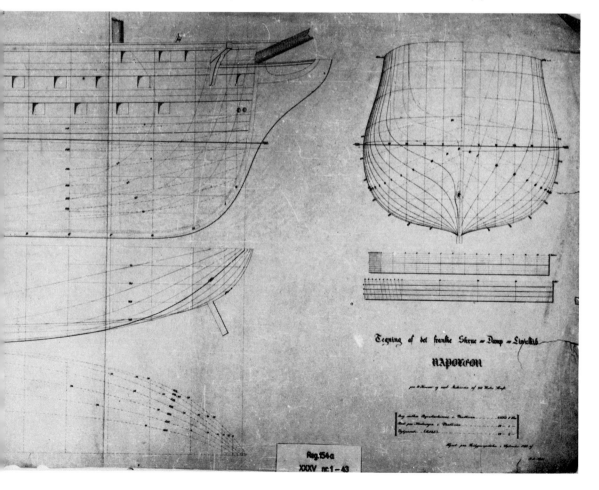

The *Sans Pareil*, 70 at Plymouth on her return from China, 6 June 1863. To the right is the *Edgar*, 90 carrying the flag of Rear-Admiral Dacres.
National Maritime Museum

The complete lack of co-operation between Sir George Cockburn's Board of Admiralty and Symonds had allowed the progressive civilian Lords of the Admiralty to force through the programme of iron-hulled frigates that were to be considered such failures.[6] However the same civilian Lords had also pushed the Admiralty to adopt the screw propeller, again with the express dissapproval of the Surveyor.[7] After his retirement Symonds sent a trenchant critique of the whole policy of adopting steam screw propulsion to the Admiralty. His basic argument was that the new power would ruin performance under sail. It was highly significant that the Symondite ships converted to screw steamers were generally acknowledged to have been adversely affected by the work to a far greater degree than the old-fashioned heavily ballasted ships. Having dedicated his professional life to improving the performance of sailing ships it was not surprising that Symonds adopted the most hostile attitude toward steam.

The requirement that Walker should seek general principles to govern construction and fitting out was a reference to detailed carpentry arrangements, and not to a new design principle to replace that of Symonds. The main difficulty with Symonds had been the excessive rigidity with which he applied his design concepts, and it was hardly likely that the Admiralty wanted Walker to fix on some similarly inflexible principle.

When Walker took office the great debate on the ship of the line had reached its final stages. There was a variety of designs at various stages of construction: several were Symondites, some of which had been altered by the 1846 Committee of Reference, and others were ships designed by the same body; furthermore Cockburn had ordered ships from Oliver Lang, Master Shipwright at Woolwich and from members of the old School of Naval Architecture. Subsequently the three 80-gun ships of the *Orion* class had been ordered as late as March 1848, but they were the last sail of the line commenced in Britain. The situation was complex and admitted of no easy solution; and there were so many ships already started that no major programme could be prepared for several years. In early 1848 the future of the sailing battleship was uncertain. The slow advance of steam had made the steam battleship a possibility that could no longer be ignored, but it was not until September that Lord Auckland declared: 'I am satisfied that the whole theory of shipbuilding will be diverted from the old notion of sailing ships to the manner in which the screw auxiliary may be best combined with good sailing qualities.'[8]

In France Dupuy de Lôme's epochal *Le Napoléon* had been ordered as early as May 1847.[9] The British reply had been prepared by John Edye, but his appropriately named *James Watt* had not been commenced. The first cautious step came with an Admiralty order in June 1848 to consider the possibility of conversion to steam power when drawing up lines or converting timber.[10]

The direction of any future policy depended to a great extent upon the performance of the blockships and screw frigates then completing. In his evidence before the 1847 Committee Walker, not yet confirmed in office, gave opinion that the most satisfactory method of applying steam power to the line of battle lay in the use of tugs. Yet like many contemporary officers he was certain that no ship smaller than a Fourth Rate should be built without

The *Agamemnon* in 1857 taking onboard the Atlantic cable at Greenwich. The hut before the mainmast indicates that the cable was stowed in her empty forward hold.
National Maritime Museum

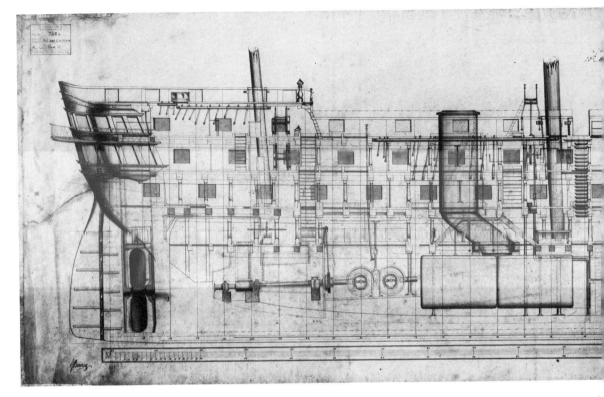

steam.[11] The Committee had met at a critical juncture. Auckland, Edye and Walker all emphasized the necessity of waiting for further trials of the first blockship, the *Blenheim* before taking any further steps. The *Blenheim* had already been at sea and was proving moderately successful. Her alterations reflected the increased knowledge of hydrodynamics imparted by the early experiments with screw propellers. Thomas Lloyd, Chief Engineer at Woolwich, had suggested that fine lines aft would be essential, a point he proved in the *Dwarf* experiments of 1846.[12] Following his advice the *Blenheim* had been lengthened 5 feet by the stern while the *Ajax* was merely fitted with a propeller in her original deadwood, an economy measure tried experimentally on the advice of John Fincham, Master Shipwright at Portsmouth. The other two blockships were adapted on the same plans, the *Hogue* following the *Blenheim* and the *Edinburgh* the *Ajax*. They had originally been conceived as steam batteries solely for harbour defence, but in September 1845 they were given a reduced rig, rather than none at all, to make them seagoing ships, following a suggestion of H T L Corry, the Political Secretary. As a result the original ships

chosen – worn out hulks – were replaced by the more seaworthy ships eventually converted.

The blockships were to be a cost-effective experiment of great value to Walker. However in his first year of office he began by taking stock of the situation and gathering a vast amount of information on the dockyards and the dockyard work-force. His first act was to cancel the conversion of four old frigates into screw blockships on the grounds that they lacked the internal volume to carry the necessary coal and stores for a sea passage.[13] Walker had already realised the critical importance of internal volume in designing a steam warship, but there would be further problems before a complete solution would be found. However on 2 October he produced a five-year plan outlining the force to be built which took into account the advance of steam and was adopted by Lord Auckland.[14]

Walker brought to the Surveyor's Office a passion for order and certainty that filled the role set out for him by the Admiralty without preventing progress. He preferred to make certain of every step, and there were no rash experiments because every development was directly related to previous experience. With this approach Walker was to be

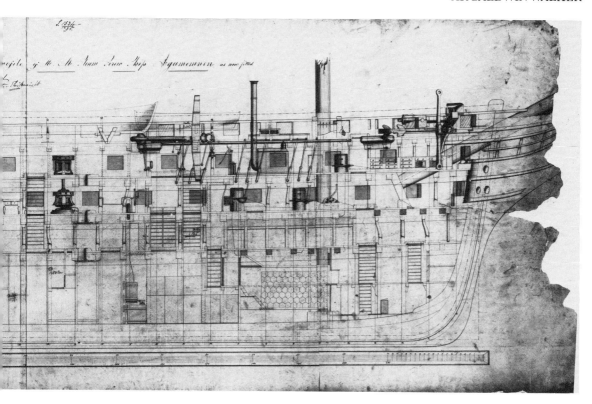

Inboard profile of the *Agamemnon*, 1852.
National Maritime Museum

the ideal Surveyor for such a vital period of evolution in warship design. His prime concern was with ships as fighting, rather than sailing, machines and he gave more attention to space on the battery deck than to an extra knot of trial speed that could not be equalled in service.

THE LISBON TRIALS OF 1850

Before forming a policy for the development of the steam warship Walker considered it necessary to assess the legacy of his predecessors. A squadron of frigates, including the 47-gun screw frigate *Arrogant* designed by John Fincham, was sent out to the Lisbon Station under Commodore William Fanshawe Martin in the *Prince Regent* (92 guns). The older screw frigate *Dauntless* and several small steamers accompanied the squadron.[15] It was the *Arrogant* that caused the greatest surprise: in all the trials of sailing she managed to get the better of at least one of the large sailing frigates. Even so Martin was critical of the position of her mainmast, which made her slow to answer the helm. He realised that the auxiliary screw steamer was the only practical solution to the current problems of naval architec-

ture. Full powered steamers, designed for high speed under steam alone, were inefficient cruising men-of-war, coal consumption being so high, given the low boiler pressures of the day, as to preclude long voyages. Furthermore Martin observed that after five days of steaming all the ships of the squadron were more or less defective in their machinery. This lack of reliability influenced Martin far more than the distant observers at the Admiralty. It so coloured his appreciation that he decided that the form of an auxiliary steamer should be optimised for performance under sail, having observed that the form required by the two types of propulsion were almost entirely different. Consequently he called for a speed under steam of 6 knots; such a vessel would be a sailing ship with machinery and coal replacing her ballast and would fight under steam power. The outstanding frigate throughout the trials had been the *Phaeton* which was heavily ballasted, unlike her Symondite competitors, and Martin, a High Tory of Cockburn's colour had no time for the products of the previous Surveyor. However Martin was too much a realist to think that he had found a universal panacea and he wisely concluded, 'These observations are not intended to apply to Block Ships or other vessels employed for peculiar or local purposes, nor is it to be inferred that our proceedings in this matter can be altogether irrespective of what is done in foreign Navies.'[16]

Martin's reports were well received at the Admiralty, their painstaking detail adding emphasis to his opinions. Rear-Admiral Sir Maurice Berkeley, the First Naval Lord, shared Martin's enthusiasm for the sailing ship with an auxiliary screw steam engine. Captain Alexander Milne, Fourth Naval Lord, took the practical view, urging that all future sailing ships be built with a double sternpost so as to reduce the cost of fitting screw machinery in the future.[17]

The performance of the *Arrogant* under the guidance of Martin was the last, and most significant, trial of the screw propeller for use in large warships. The results indicated that a ship could be built to combine the qualities of sail and steam without undue detriment to the requirements of the former. It was this ability to retain all the features of a sailing ship that ensured the success of the screw steamer, winning the grudging approval of such conservatives as Cockburn.[18] Without this ability the advent of the steam battleship would have been long delayed. By comparison the tugging exercises of the *Rattler* and *Alecto*, and the *Niger* and *Basilisk*

were merely a crude and over-dramatic indication that the screw was superior to the paddle wheel. They had no relevance to the steam battleship in which fighting qualities were always placed above those of mobility. The *Arrogant* demonstrated that the additional feature of steam power could be worked in without affecting the overall combat-worthiness of the sailing ship.

The success of the *Arrogant* was secured in spite of her machinery, the trials of the steamers highlighting the considerable demands that a warship could make on the low-powered engines of the day. Problems with reliability, overheating, endurance and ventilation ensured that the use of steam was something to be avoided. Considerable progress would have to be made in this direction before the potential demonstrated by the *Arrogant* could be employed in an all-steam navy. Even the propeller shaft caused difficulties, its rotary motion having a tendency to work the stern and loosen the caulking. The *Arrogant* had been commendably free of that particular vice but Martin had recommended that special attention be given to the sterns of future ships. Locating the funnel to cause the minimum interference with the working of the sails admitted of no easy solution. There was simply no position in which it did not foul either main- or mizzenmasts. Walker found it necessary to refer the matter to the Captains of the large steamships already in service.[19] The blockships *Ajax* and *Edinburgh* had their funnels behind the mainmast, and this location

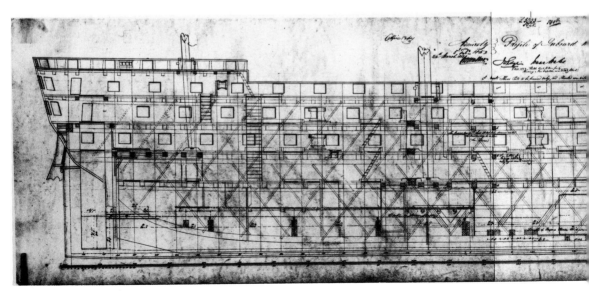

was followed for the first two steam battleships, the *Sans Pareil* and *Agamemnon*, but was thereafter abandoned. The Board had ordered these two steam battleships in 1849, clearly anticipating the

The *Duke of Wellington*, 131 guns, in dock at Keyham in March 1854. She bears the pennant of Commodore Sir Michael Seymour, shortly before proceeding to Portsmouth where she became the flagship of Vice-Admiral Sir Charles Napier. *National Maritime Museum*

Inboard profile of the *St Jean d'Acre*, 1851, the first ship that can be directly attributed to Sir Baldwin Walker's influence. An expansion of the *Agamemnon*, her superior qualities were developed in the succeeding *Conqueror* and *Duncan* classes of 101-gun ships. *National Maritime Museum*

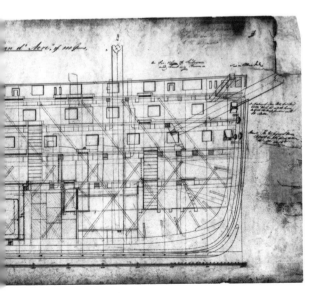

successful outcome of the Lisbon trials, and in this they were taking a step ahead of many screw enthusiasts. Captain E P Halstead, for example, called for further *Arrogant*s, but declared, 'it yet seems premature to bring in the line of battle-ships.'[20]

The first steam battleship to complete, the *Sans Pareil*, delighted only the denigrators of the screw. She was a poor seaboat and her engines were only remarkable for the frequency with which they broke down.[21] The *Sans Pareil* had been commenced as an 80-gun sailing ship based on the previous, ex-French, *Sans Pareil* ordered by Cockburn's Committee of 1845. At a late stage she been lengthened 15 feet at the stern and fitted with old-fashioned engines of 350 nominal horse power (nhp), constructed by Watt and originally intended for the blockship frigate *Horatio* which had been cancelled by Walker in 1848. This machinery proved both too large and too heavy, and 10 guns had to be sacrificed before she could proceed to sea. The combination of excess weight and unreliability proved so detrimental that the *Sans Pareil* was re-engined at

The *Irresistible* 1859, during her only commission, as Coastguard ship at Southampton – typical converted 80-gun Symondite. *Imperial War Museum*

the height of the Russian War[22]; even then she remained a third class ship.

By contrast the *Agamemnon*, 91, ordered on 25 August 1849, was a complete success. Her design was based on Edye's *James Watt*, which was not ordered until 14 January 1850, presumably having been delayed by the need to collect and season her timber. In order to complete the *Agamemnon* quickly it was decided to use materials that had been collecting at Woolwich since March 1842 for an 80-gun sailing ship of the same name. However these had no influence on the ship eventually built and the *Agamemnon* was the first British battleship designed from the outset as a steamship. She was fitted with new machinery of 600nhp built by Penn and capable of driving her at speeds in excess of 10 knots. These were the first large engines to produce a significantly higher figure for indicated horse power

than they were nominally rated for: where the blockships had developed double the nominal rating of their engines, the *Agamemnon* reached almost four times the nominal horse power of her machinery. While Penn's trunk engines were the most powerful of the steam battleship era they, like all the others, relied on increased boiler pressures. Those of the *Agamemnon* would have been worked by steam at 10–15 pounds per square inch (psi), figures that remained standard throughout the 1850s for large naval engines. In smaller naval and commercial installations over 20psi was often used, but such figures were only acheived at a considerable sacrifice in reliability. With the *Agamemnon*'s engines the large single expansion marine steam engine reached a level of efficiency that would not be exceeded for ten years; only their size and ultimate power increased.

The *Agamemnon*'s performance was equally due to her improved hull-form. Unlike the *Sans Pareil* she had been designed for steam machinery, and was therefore longer and finer than the preceding sailing ships of the same armament, the *Albion* class. Where the *Albion* was 205 feet by 60 feet, the *Agamemnon* was 230 feet by 55 feet, the altered form being entirely due to Edye's attempt to combine sail and steam. Many commentators have claimed that the wooden steam battleship was just a sailing ship with engines. This was not the case. All the steam battleships designed as such, and those subjected to a thorough conversion, were treated in the same manner as the *Agamemnon*. They were given a finer bow and a rounded and elongated stern. The bluff form of the sailing ship of the line was completely unsuited to screw propulsion: it quickly piled up a huge bow wave, while the propeller cavitated in the air pockets of the broken water created by the square stern. It must be emphasized that the simplest conversion, putting in a screw without altering the stern, created ships like the *Ajax* which could neither sail nor steam efficiently; the *Agamemnon* by contrast could do both extremely well. Her success was emphasized by the fact that her basic design was still being used ten years after it was drawn up (for the *Defiance*). The French new construction was dominated by the requirements of the screw to an even greater degree. Where the British ships struck a balance between steam and sail, the form of the French ships made sail an auxiliary to steam.

The steam battleships shared one feature, namely uniform-calibre battery decks. The introduction of the shell-firing gun had upset the classic arrangement of the previous centuries when each deck had carried one calibre of artillery. Through the 1830s and 1840s ships of the line had been equipped with a small, but growing number of shell guns on each deck. Commodore Martin reported that the efficiency of heavy ships would be improved by a return to uniform-calibre decks. Walker shared this view and the reintroduction of the single-calibre deck was a feature of his administration. On new 90-gun ships the gun deck was armed with 65cwt 8-inch shell guns, the main deck with 56cwt 32-pounder 6-inch solid shot guns and the upper deck with 42cwt 32-pounders. The new steam battleships had a 95cwt 68-pounder solid shot gun on the forecastle bearing over the bows on a pivot mounting. The pivot gun, a feature taken from the paddle frigates, was a useful addition to the armament of the steam battleship for their increasingly fine bows prevented the effective use of the old bow batteries installed by Sir Robert Seppings in the bluff ships of his era.

By early 1851 reasonably accurate information had been obtained about the performance of *Le Napoléon*, a 90-gun ship with engines of 940nhp. While the *Agamemnon* would be quite adequate to face the French ship Walker wanted to create a more powerful response. The result was the 101-gun two-decker *St Jean d'Acre*, ordered on 15 February 1851, using materials collected at Devonport for an *Albion* class 90-gun ship. Walker's assistants designed the ship to use the 650nhp engines removed from the iron frigate *Simoom*, already proposed for the *London* in 1847.[23] Later new 600nhp machinery by Penn, identical to that fitted to the *Agamemnon*, was substituted. The *St Jean d'Acre* was the first ship designed at the Surveyor's Office that could be directly attributed to Walker's influence. She demonstrated his ideal solution to the problems inherent in applying steam power to the battle line. For a ship equipped with steam to carry the same armament as a sailing ship her dimensions had to be enlarged. There was a need for greater internal volume to find the space for machinery and coal, as well as the stores and water carried by a sailing ship. In the blockships the problem had been so acute that even for coastal operations they had been forced to surrender 14 guns, and when Martin tried the *Hogue* in 1851 he proposed sacrificing 20 more in order to increase her stowage and accommodate the crew. As a 40-gun ship she would still only stow five weeks' provisions and thirty days' water.[24] The introduction of Grant's cooking and distilling galley in place of the old fire hearth effected a vital improvement in the endurance of steamships, hitherto reliant on their tanks for boiler feed water.[25] One week's supply could now be distilled from seawater in a day. Steam machinery raised the internal temperature of ships, especially below the waterline, which necessitated improved magazine arrangements, most significantly the adoption of metal-lined powder cases. Therefore Dell's cases

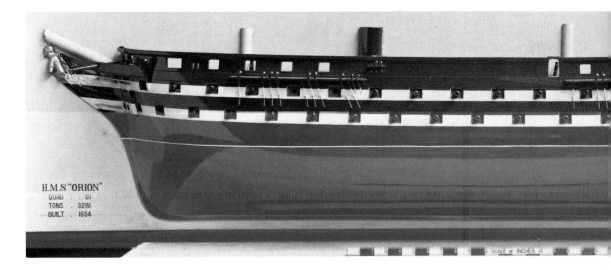

H.M.S "ORION"
GUNS . 81
TONS . 3281
BUILT . 1854

A half model of the *Orion*, 1854, showing her hull form.
Science Museum

were specified for the magazines of all steam warships.[26] The coal bunkers were also lined with sheet iron to cut down the risk of fire.[27]

In early 1852 Baring revealed the construction policy he had adopted. Lord Auckland had called for 50 First and Second Rates afloat, but all work on sailing ships had been stopped in 1849 in view of the progress of steam. However Baring did not favour any long-term programme of steam construction – following Walker's advice he declared that any steamships built at the present time would be rapidly rendered inefficient by subsequent developments. Therefore he proposed the construction of only sufficient ships to match the French, relying on Britain's superior shipbuilding and marine engineering resources to provide a capacity to accelerate whenever necessary.[28]

Walker's next step was to prepare a screw First Rate with the least delay. He had a high regard for the fighting power of the the three-decker, considering that its concentrated broadside at close range would remain a decisive factor in naval combats. Therefore in December 1851 he despatched Isaac Watts and John Abthell to inspect the 120-gun *Windsor Castle* then awaiting launch at Pembroke.[29] Following a favourable report from his assistants, Walker recommended altering the ship into a steamer of 131 guns, using the engines of 700nhp from the iron frigate *Simoom*.[30] The conversion entailed cutting the ship apart in two places,

adding 23 feet amidships and 7 feet at the stern to make her 240 feet between perpendiculars.[31] The ship was launched on 14 September, the day of the Duke of Wellington's death, and her name was later changed to honour his memory.[32] The alteration of Oliver Lang's 120-gun *Royal Albert* was not attended by such urgency and was therefore submitted to a committee of shipwrights and engineers. They reported in favour of a complete remodelling of the stern and the use of new 400nhp machinery, rather than that of 700nhp removed from the *Euphrates*.[33]

During the year Walker took stock of the ships approaching completion. In August he recommended that the 90-gun sailing ships *Algiers* and *Hannibal* be adapted for the screw. Both were modified Symondites: the *Algiers* had been made 5 feet longer by Edye while the *Hannibal* had 2 feet less beam and a fuller midship section by courtesy of the 1847 Committee of Reference. Walker selected them as the least advanced of the 90-gun two-deckers, and therefore the best suited to be altered. Experience with the *Sans Pareil* and *Agamemnon* already indicated that the larger ships would prove better suited to steam. In consequence Walker delayed making any decision on the Symondite 80-gun ship.

36

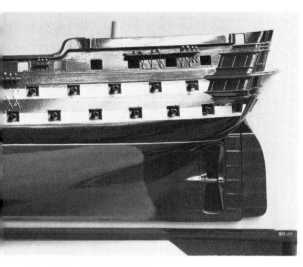

The *Algiers* at Malta in 1861.
National Maritime Museum

THE STEAM BATTLEFLEET

The defeat of the Whigs on 20 February 1852, on Russell's Militia Bill, brought a change in Government. Lord Derby's Tory party took a precarious hold on the reins of power that only required a consensus between the Whigs and the Peelites to ensure its defeat. At the same time the growing power of Louis Napoleon in France produced another invasion scare. As the winter of 1852 approached, the crisis – more of confidence than reality – deepened. Only the performance of *Le Napoléon*, which was claimed to have exceeded 13 knots under steam, could in any way justify the nation's concern. Even then intelligence from abroad suggested that all was not well, vibration at full speed being so intense as to make the ship uninhabitable.[34] However there were signs that the French Navy was preparing for a concerted effort to

match Britain in screw ships of the line; stocks of timber were high and engine building facilities were being enlarged.

Walker's appreciation of the naval situation led him to recommend the adoption of a new policy. He realised that converting existing unfinished sailing ships would not produce the best results. To match *Le Napoléon* it would be necessary to build purpose-designed ships such as the *Agamemnon* and *St Jean d'Acre*. Yet the sudden progress of the French required an immediate response, as much to allay public concern as to satisfy the Navy.

This double need, both for first class ships and for a quick response, placed Walker on the horns of a dilemma. A new wooden battleship needed at least four years on the stocks if it was to be properly seasoned throughout the construction process. The terrible lessons of the war-built ships of the Napoleonic period were remembered and he had no intention of rush building first class ships. His response was to formulate a programme combining new construction and conversion in an attempt to balance the conflicting requirements of the fleet. He declared that the period of experiment was at an end, but noted that the nation could not afford an all-new battlefleet. He ordered three new ships, the *Edgar* and *Repulse*, 91s and the *Conqueror*, 101; they were based on the *Agamemnon*, *James Watt* and *St Jean d'Acre* respectively. The conversions included the 120-gun *Marlborough*, a sister of the *Duke of Wellington*, as yet only in frame; the *Orion*, an 80-gun ship in the same state; and the 1847 Committee designed *Caesar*, 90.[35] The growing sense of urgency saw him add the almost complete 90-gun ships *Princess Royal* and *Exmouth*, and the old 120-gun *Royal George*, then docked for repairs, before the end of the month.[36] After initial hesitancy,[37] the Duke of Northumberland's Board agreed to the Surveyor's submissions, but did not provide the necessary money for the machinery. By early November Walker was badgering the Board with hectoring and mildly alarmist letters, suggesting that if the money were not forthcoming the purchase of engines must be delayed. Dark allusions to the 'progress of foreign powers', served to emphasize his contention.[38] Once the programme had been confirmed Walker lost no time before ordering the conversion of all necessary stern-frame timbers so as to allow all possible time for them to season before

being planked over.[39] He also ordered four pairs of engines from both Penn and Maudslay.[40]

In pressing the Admiralty to make £100,000 available, which they did in December, Walker had instituted the first major construction programme for forty years. It marked the decision to build a steam battlefleet, rather than a sailing fleet with a leavening of steamers. By the end of the year Walker had added further ships to the list of conversions: the *Nile*, 90 and the *Cressy* and *Majestic*, 80s, largely in order to gain experience. All three were to be fitted for the screw with the least possible alteration of the stern. The latter pair were small ships and Walker considered that they could never be so efficient as larger vessels. However having started to create a steam fleet it was necessary to keep abreast of foreign developments. Only this need to build a fleet quickly and economically prevented him cutting them down into double-banked frigates or leaving them as sail of the line.[41] He realised that although their steaming and sailing powers were limited and their stowage small they did offer a significant force for operations in home waters at a fraction of the cost of a new ship.

During the brief life of the first Derby Administration Walker had cause to tender his resignation. Sir Augustus Stafford, Political Secretary to the Admiralty, complained of Walker's choice of dockyard officers and tried to place all such appointments within the control of the Board. A decision of Parliament in 1847 had established that all promotions in the dockyards should be on merit alone. However the Tories had been out of office for many years and their adherents looked to have a reward for their loyalty. Stafford considered that the Admiralty would make an excellent electioneering machine, and acted swiftly. Walker, lacking political acumen, treated Stafford's strictures as a criticism of the professional merits of his appointees and defended himself accordingly.[42] The affair reached a select Committee of the Commons, dominated by Stafford's opponents, and his career was ruined.[43] Disraeli considered that Walker had acted with a political motive, treating his obvious naivety as a sham, and it was to be a grudge he would maintain throughout the second Derby administration.[44] For all Disraeli's complaints, Walker was not a political man, as befits a permanent servant of the state. If he had any bias it

The screw frigate *Euryalus*, 1853, a conversion based on the incomplete hull of a 60-gun sailing frigate.
Royal Naval Museum

was towards the Whigs, but this was only a reflection of the politics of his naval patrons anf friends; indeed it was the two Derby ministries that gave him the greatest support.

The policy advocated by Walker and adopted by the Tory Admiralty to build a steam battlefleet greeted the next First Lord, the Peelite Sir James Graham, when he took office in December 1852. Graham, the most influential First Lord of the nineteenth century, was a cold and distant man who inspired little personal regard, yet he raised the political weight of the Admiralty both by his ability and by the free hand given him by the Prime Minister, Lord Aberdeen.[45] Renowned for his pessimism, Graham had placed the worst possible construction on the new administration in France, especially with regard to the personal qualities of the Emperor. Consequently he raised no objection to Walker's programme. When he left the Admiralty two years later he recommended the Surveyor to his successor as a man well versed in the problems of the Admiralty.[46] This was all the more remarkable in view of Graham's parsimony with Admiralty funds. He had realised that the steam battlefleet was essential, and accepted the need for a long-term effort to provide the finest ships – indeed he maintained this anti-French programme throughout the Russian War to a far greater degree than contemporary commentators realised. The programme of October 1852 had taken up all the

available dockyard capacity and when the darkening eastern horizon forced Graham to fit out reinforcements for the Mediterranean Fleet there was added cause for urgency. Similarly the Home squadrons, which were nearly non-existent, had to be built up against the slight possibility of a Russian movement from the Baltic. In June 1853 Graham collected 10 sail of the line and 10 war steamers at Spithead, but later sent the *Agamemnon*, *Sans Pareil* and the sailing ships *Queen*, 116 and *London*, 92 to the Mediterranean. The *Duke of Wellington*, 131 and the screw frigate *Imperieuse*, 51 went to Cork with the Western Squadron, where they were joined by the *St Jean d'Acre*. The three latter ships were all highly successful, reinforcing Walker's desire to create an all-steam battlefleet. Graham concurred, especially after the veteran Admiral Sir Thomas Byam Martin advised him to use only steam battleships in a possible Baltic Campaign.[47] As a result several ships nearing completion were repeatedly expedited while new construction on which little work had been done was ignored. This created a shortage of new ships by early 1858, while the rapid completion of several converted ships caused the altered stern frames to be planked over before they had been allowed enough time to season fully. In view of the short effective lives of the steam battleships it would be difficult to assess the results of this work on the longevity of the ships, although some had decayed within five years. Walker had made a sharp distinction between new ships and conversions. The only new ship accelerated was the *James Watt* which was already fully seasoned in her frame and largely planked over. While a new ship could be finished within a year if the seasoning limitations were ignored, Walker realised that this would produce poor ships. Therefore none of his new ships were completed within 40 months. The decision to expedite the converted ships must have been made simpler by the nature of the Russian fleets. There were no steam battleships in either the Baltic or the Black Sea, and Russia could not be expected to build efficient ships, given her lack of modern engine works. Therefore second class, converted ships would be sufficient to keep the Russians in check. At the same time the new ships could be

prepared to meet the long-term threat from France that had been pushed into the background by all except Walker and Graham. When the war ended the converted ships would be available for second-line duties. In France the same policy of converting older ships was adopted while new construction was pressed at a faster pace, reflecting a different set of requirements.

Walker's service as Commander-in-Chief of the Turkish Fleet was called on by Graham in May 1853. The pro-war party within the Aberdeen Coalition, led by Palmerston, were advocating sending the Mediterranean Fleet up the Dardanelles to occupy the Bosphorus. Walker considered this position to be potentially very dangerous, since the Russian Army would be able to seize both Constantinople and the Dardanelles, trapping the fleet.[10] Throughout the first year of the War Graham referred to Walker on all matters of strategy.

3. The Russian War, 1854-1856

The *Royal Albert*, 1854, during her service as flagship of the Channel Fleet.
Imperial War Museum

The international crisis that developed into the Russian War concerned the fate of the European possessions of the Turkish Empire. It necessitated a rapid increase in the commissioned strength of the Royal Navy to cover Russian fleets in the Baltic and the Black Sea. Rear-Admiral Sir Edmund Lyons, appointed second-in-command of the Mediterranean Fleet, insisted on flying his flag in a steam battleship and selected the *Agamemnon*.[1] Graham was placed on the horns of a dilemma by the crisis, for despite the repeated acceleration of those ships converting to steam there would not be enough of them for one fleet, let alone the two that were required. The only solution he could adopt was a compromise. The Mediterranean Fleet was restricted to two steam battleships, the *Agamemnon* and the *Sans Pareil*, despite the fact that the French

fleet had three, the *Montebello*, 120, the *Charlemagne*, 80 and *Le Napoléon*. The British steamers were concentrated in the Baltic Fleet. Vice-Admiral Sir Charles Napier flew his flag in the 131-gun *Duke of Wellington*, and took with him the *Royal George*, 120, the *St Jean d'Acre*, 101, the *Princess Royal*, *Caesar*, *James Watt* and *Nile*, 91s, the *Cressy* and *Majestic*, 80s, and the four blockships. Graham did not consider this force adequate to deal with up to 30 Russian sail of the line so he also sent 6 sailing battleships. However Napier wisely kept them to the rear with the inferior steamers under his nervous second Rear-Admiral Corry. He was later joined by 9

French battleships, only one of which, the *Austerlitz* was a steamer, and he was thereafter forced to employ a mixed squadron.

In both theatres the Russian fleets remained secure behind the stone walls of Sebastopol, Sveaborg and Cronstadt. Consequently the allied steam battleships had no opportunity to demonstrate their worth in a fleet action. However all that was in the future when Walker decided that the only method of creating further ships for war service lay in converting existing tonnage on the simple plan applied to the *Majestic*. Not wishing to modify First or large Second Rate ships in this fashion he turned to the Symondite 80s that were either complete or in an advanced state of construction. On 17 January 1854 he ordered the conversion of the *Colossus* and followed this with the *Centurion* and *Mars* and the incomplete *Brunswick* and *Irresistible*.[2] These conversions were not part of Walker's long-term plan for the development of a steam battlefleet. He had a low regard for the 80-gun ships and preferred to meet the sailing fleets of Russia with hurried adaptations of these second class ships while continuing work on new and converted First and Second Rates to counter the growing threat from France. Walker and Graham shared a conviction that after the war France would resume her role as Britain's principal rival at sea, and both men considered that only a long-term programme of new construction could provide a suitable fleet. Therefore Walker ordered the conversion of the *Royal Sovereign*, an incomplete sister of the *Duke of Wellington*, and the new *Donegal*, an improved *St Jean d'Acre*.[3] Early in 1855 he obtained the sanction of the Admiralty to commence two new steam three-deckers, the *Victoria* and *Howe* of 120 guns; and also the 91-gun *Revenge*.[4] The former pair, like all the new construction of the Russian War, bore no relation to the requirements of the moment, being a direct response to the new French steam three-decker *Bretagne*, 130. However, unlike the *Bretagne*, the British ships took over five years to build, reflecting Walker's concern over the quality of materials used on new ships. When Graham left the Admiralty on 22 February Walker lost his strongest ally. The new First Lord, Sir Charles

The stern galleries of the *Duke of Wellington* during her service as a Receiving Ship at Portsmouth.
Conway Picture Library

Wood (1855–58), did not share Graham's understanding of naval matters, nor did he possess the same political influence. Consequently no new work was put in hand to follow the ships then building; all thoughts were turned to the war effort, and in particular to the Crimea. However Walker had considerable freedom to run his department, the more so as Wood was advised by Graham to refer administrative problems to him.[5] Furthermore Walker was free to issue orders directly to the dockyards for the duration of the war.[6] By cutting out the need to refer to the Admiralty the Surveyor's office was able to cope with the vast increase in paperwork occasioned by the war.

Graham had always held out against any unnecessary wartime expenditure in much the same manner as Gladstone, the Chancellor of the Exchequer. When Napier called for gunboats and mortar vessels to carry the Baltic campaign to the Russians he had been advised to hire Swedish steamers. The Admiralty also fitted out some old steam packets as makeshift gunboats – until one of them blew up.[7] The sums expended on new steam battleships during the same period were considerable, but Graham did not object to this, for unlike gunboats, battleships would be needed for the French war he considered inevitable. However the need of both fleets for small craft became so glaring that he was forced to act. The first half dozen gun vessels were unsatisfactory and completed too late for the Baltic operations of 1854. The requirements of the northern theatre, for craft to bombard Sveaborg and Cronstadt, led to the programme of October 1854. Graham, having realised the strategic value of the Baltic, prepared a force to carry the fight to the Russians. A combination of 5 floating batteries, 5 more blockships, a score each of gunboats and mortar vessels, and a similar French force, promised to give the allied fleet the equipment it needed. Yet Graham still found it necessary to sweeten the £650,000 pill for Gladstone by observing that all the types built would also answer for coast defence after the war.[8] While some commentators have considered the October programme deficient of any strategic rationale,[9] it must be observed that the tactical ability to overcome major sea-forts and threaten the Russian capital was a priceless asset for allied statesmen in late 1855.

Walker realised that this huge programme would

hamper the steam battlefleet. Therefore he placed all the work, save the blockships, out to private tender, leaving the Royal yards to finish and equip the vessels. At the same time the imminent return of the Baltic Fleet threatened to swamp the royal yards with repair work. Before the ships came home Walker prepared a list of home ports for every ship, stating that no alterations would be permitted and that the ships' own artificers were to carry out all possible repair work.[10] Only the crank *Royal George* was altered to any great degree, losing her forecastle and quarterdeck. This policy allowed the dockyards to concentrate on new work, both steam battleships and the October programme, and was repeated in the following year.

Over the winter of 1854–55 Walker had to prepare two all-steam battlefleets for the new season. Lyons, now Commander-in-Chief in the

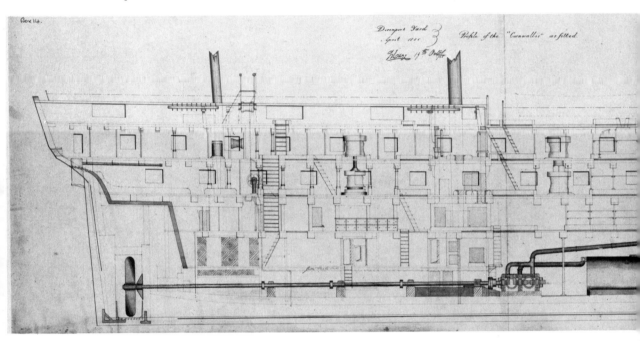

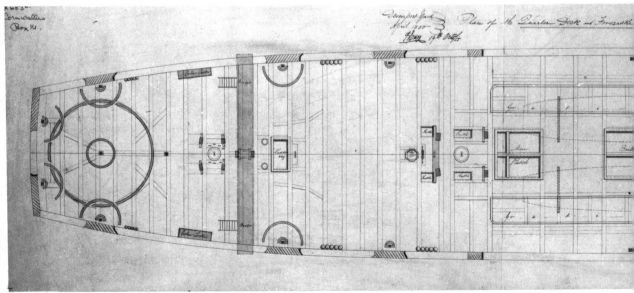

Inboard profile of the 60-gun blockship *Cornwallis*, 1855. A teak-built 74 she was adapted for coastal bombardment by the simple installation of 200nhp engines. There was no provision for a hoisting propeller.
National Maritime Museum

The quarterdeck and forecastle plan of the *Cornwallis* showing the pivots for her heavy upper deck battery of 2–68pdr/95cwt and 4–10in/85cwt. All six guns would be fought on the same broadside.
National Maritime Museum

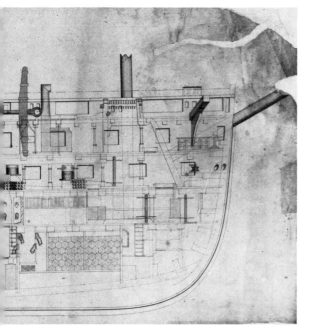

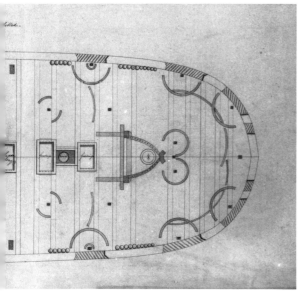

Black Sea, called for an all-steam fleet despite the completely disabled condition of the Russian ships inside Sebastopol harbour. The support of Graham ensured that he had some of the most efficient ships: the *Royal Albert*, 120, the *St Jean d'Acre, Princess Royal, Hannibal* and *Agamemnon*; only the *Algiers* was unsatisfactory.[11] By contrast the Baltic Fleet was left with only four first class ships: the *Duke of Wellington, Caesar, James Watt* and the new 91-gun *Orion*; the other ships, the *Royal George* (now with 102 guns), the *Exmouth* and *Nile*, 90s, the *Cressy, Majestic* and *Colossus*, 80s, and 9 blockships were all slow, while some were weakly armed and others poor seaboats. Sending such ships to a theatre where the Russians maintained a large battlefleet reflected the low level of interest shown by the Palmerston Administration in the Baltic after the departure of Graham. It had been decided to send no troops and merely keep the Baltic open as a diversion.[12]

THE BOMBARDMENT OF SHORE POSITIONS

During the Russian War the allied battlefleets took part in three major bombardments of Russian shore fortifications; they also prepared at great length for another such operation. Shore bombardments had always been the most severe test of wooden ships and such engagements were considered hazardous in the extreme by the majority of naval officers. However the refusal of the Russians to try conclusions at sea made some sort of combat between ships and forts almost inevitable.

In the Black Sea the allied fleets, having carried the armies to the Crimea and guaranteed their supply lines were expected to assist the first assault on Sebastopol. Lord Raglan, the military Commander, considered that a combined attack was most likely to be successful.[13] However Vice-Admiral Sir James Dundas, the naval commander, was extremely reluctant to engage his ships with the impressive casemate batteries guarding the seaward approaches to the city.[14] He believed that such a contest would be unequal, and that if his ships were badly damaged the Russians might make a dash at the transports. Even a temporary loss of command of the sea would be fatal for the whole expedition.

On 15 October Dundas, in consultation with the French Commander, Vice-Admiral Hamelin, agreed to join the attack whenever the Generals thought their contribution would be most useful: either when the bombardment on shore began, or when an assault was launched. The Generals hungrily requested a diversion for both events. The Admirals agreed, and resolved to bombard while underway, to prevent the Russian gunners having a fixed mark. This method did not appear to the French military commander, General Canrobert, to offer sufficient threat of decisive action. Therefore he ordered Hamelin to engage at anchor. This decision reached Hamelin late in the evening of 16 October, only hours before the attack. Hamelin conveyed this news to Dundas, and the two Admirals then changed their plans accordingly. The French being short of ammunition it was also decided to delay going into action until late in the morning.

The sailing ships that made up the bulk of the bombarding squadrons were to be towed into and out of action by a steamer lashed alongside. The British would engage the forts to the north of the harbour entrance, the French those to the south. During the night preceding the attack a party under the Fleet Surveying Officer, Captain Spratt, had sounded a channel within 800 yards of Fort Constantine and it was decided that Rear-Admiral Lyons would take his advance squadron to exploit this feature. Dundas was not happy with any aspect of the plan, as he told Spratt on the morning of the attack: 'look at my position. . . I shall be exposed to the fire of the batteries which can reach me, and my guns will be all out of range save the lower deck guns.'[15] In a General Memorandum issued on the morning of the attack Dundas did state that: 'the object of the attack. . . is to destroy the batteries of the enemy on the North side of Sevastopol and by that means assist the attack of our troops.' However he was really far more concerned with the safety of the fleet, and this dominated his memorandum.

Keeping our ships in an efficient state is a very great point, as the Army depends so much on our assistance; I therefore wish every Captain to consider his own position after he gets into action, and if he finds he is in very particular danger of being dismasted, getting on shore, or otherwise, to haul off without delay.

It will be impossible in the smoke for the Vice-Admiral to see the different ships and he is well aware that the responsibility on this point cannot be better placed than in the hands of the Captains of the ships under his command.[16]

The land bombardment commenced at 06.30,

but a large French magazine exploded and the firing from their lines ceased soon after 10.30. This was the effective end of the land attack. Dundas did not weigh anchor until 10.50, so there had been time enough to cancel what was now an entirely futile operation. No-one had expected the naval bombardment to produce any results of itself: it had always been part of a combined assault and had no raison d'être after 10.30. The French ships opened fire soon after 12.30 at ranges varying between 2000 and 1500 yards. Lyons' division, the *Agamemnon* and *Sans Pareil* with the sailing ships *Albion* and *London* and the sailing frigate *Arethusa*, occupied the channel surveyed by Spratt, anchoring at about 14.00. The *Britannia* leading the *Trafalgar*, *Queen*, *Rodney*, *Vengeance* and *Bellerophon* opened fire at 14.20 at a range of 2000 yards. Writing the following day *The Times* correspondent observed: 'The firing was terrific. At a distance the sound was like a locomotive at full speed, but infinitely grander.'[17]

The steamers not required for towing operated inshore, kept underway. The *Terrible* used her heavy guns to considerable effect, disabling the barbette guns of Fort Constantine. The battle centred around Lyons' flagship the *Agamemnon*, which maintained her position throughout the day, although her seconds were forced to withdraw. The *Albion* was set on fire twice by red-hot shot and hit by four shells inside 90 minutes. She left the line having suffered 11 killed and 17 wounded. The frigate *Arethusa* was forced to leave after an unequal struggle with the Wasp battery which saw her waterline planking blown in. The *Sans Pareil* and *London* then departed having fired off their ammunition allowance of 70 rounds per gun. Three more ships came to Lyons' aid: the *Bellerophon* temporarily silenced the Wasp battery, but the *Queen* was set on fire three times and had to withdraw; the *Rodney* went so close to the shoal that she grounded by the stern. The *Agamemnon* slipped her mooring at 17.15 and was followed by the *Rodney*. The recall went out at 18.30, and by 19.00 the action had finished.

Although the allied fleet fought at anchor they were able to retire from the action as and when they chose because of steam. This was a priceless advantage and helped to limit the casualties and damage. The British lost 44 killed and 266 wounded; the *Albion* and *Arethusa* had to visit Malta for repairs. The *Agamemnon* had been hit 214 times, but she had only 27 casualties (4 fatal), because of her favourable situation under the guns of Fort Constantine.

The Russian casualties were light – 11 killed and 31 wounded. However Fort Constantine had only 5 out of 27 guns serviceable at the end of the day. As a result the Russians concluded that the earthwork Wasp and Telegraph batteries were far more dangerous to the ships, despite having only 8 guns each.

After the capture of Fort Bomarsund in the Baltic during August, Captain Sir Henry Chads, the Navy's leading gunnery expert, conducted experiments against the Russian casemates. He concluded that the maximum effective range for ships to have any chance of breaching such works was 500 yards. Dundas had been aware of this, but noted that weakened, unsupported and undefended works are a very different proposition to an efficiently served battery.[18]

The whole operation of bombarding Sebastopol had been a 'false' one in Dundas's opinion, and he lost no time in letting Raglan know of his displeasure.[19] The fleet had been placed in danger when there had been no real hope of success; the more so as the land bombardment had failed even before he weighed anchor. Dundas had not considered it possible for the ships to overcome the forts, and he was not prepared to risk the fleet to test the correctness of this view. There can be no doubt that his primary concern had been the safety of the fleet. Dundas overrated the danger posed by the Russian Fleet, already disarmed, and allowed it to exercise a morbid control over his counsels. However his plan to bombard underway would have been equally useful as a diversion; and only the interference of Canrobert caused the allied fleet to take risks commensurate with an attempt to overcome the forts.

The opinion of the leading expert on smooth bore naval gunnery, General Sir Howard Douglas, on the subject of bombarding shore positions and with special reference to the action at Sebastopol is instructive. He stated that:

When the object is to crush buildings, bomb shells, fired at considerable elevation should be used, in order that the momentum acquired in their descent may be sufficient to penetrate magazines or casemates down to the foundations and there exploding, set fire to the buildings and create havoc and disorder among the troops.

The *Conqueror*, 1855. Although the negative of this photograph is damaged it remains the best view available of this ship, which was lost in 1862.
Imperial War Museum

For this purpose the finest weapon was the mortar; Douglas observed that the lack of such weapons caused

...the inability of fleets to contend with fortresses and other powerful land batteries unless the ships be very close to them.

This was because

approaching ships should be properly cannonaded, as soon as they come within reach of powerful and well served long-range guns. This not having been done at Algiers and Acre..., the daring and success of the operations against those places have tended to create the erroneous notion that land service batteries cannot under any circumstance withstand the concentrated fire of ships of the line.

The element of proximity was essential, because only at short range would the superior number of guns carried by battleships be able to outweigh the greater accuracy of land-based pieces. At close range, even if the land-based guns were not disabled, the volume of fire would keep the gunners from serving them effectively. At Sebastopol the steady Russian artillerymen were not impressed by the long-range cannonade, and it was not possible to get closer than 750 yards. By blocking the fairway of Sebastopol harbour the Russians had prevented any attempt to force a passage into the heart of the arsenal. No other type of assault could be anything more than a diversion.

Writing with reference to the attack Douglas considered:

The disappointment which the nation felt at the result of this action was heightened in consequence of an erroneous opinion having been formed that ships possessed necessarily, battering powers in proportion to their magnitude.

As to the value of the operation he declared:

The co-operation of the fleet could only be useful as a diversion in favour of a land attack when the army should be prepared to assault the enemy's positions at the same time; but under the then existing circumstances it could produce no such effect... The effects produced... were far from justifying an opinion that the fleet could have attacked the place with any prospect of reducing it.[20]

Like Admiral Dundas, Douglas would have preferred to support the final assault. The operation had been requested by the generals, and when they feared that it might not create the effect they desired they pressed the admirals to change their plan. Canrobert, in overall command of all the French

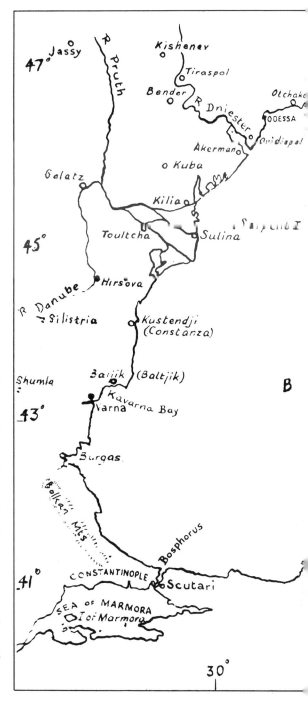

forces ordered Hamelin to act, relying on Dundas's honour to complete the triumph of the generals.

In the Baltic theatre Vice-Admiral Napier, as he had anticipated, found his fleet equally unsuitable for tackling the Russian fortresses of Sveaborg and

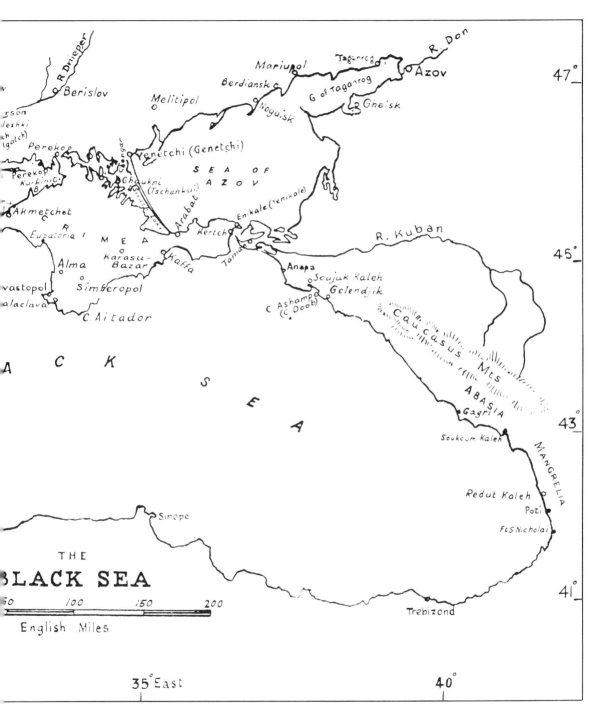

The Black Sea at the time of the Russian War.
By courtesy of the Navy Records Society

Cronstadt. His only major operation was a combined attack on Fort Bomarsund in the Åland
Islands during August. His call for mortar vessels
and gunboats was only answered after Sir James
Graham had decided to remove him from the com-

The Baltic at the time of the Russian War.
By courtesy of the Navy Records Society

mand, because he would not undertake a potentially ruinous bombardment of Sveaborg with his battlefleet.

The force Graham ordered, the October programme, went into action as Sveaborg between 9 and 11 August 1855; only the floating batteries were not present. Under the skilful direction of the Fleet Surveyor, Captain Bartholomew Sulivan, the mortars and gunboats ruined large parts of the Russian dockyard and arsenal. As a diversion two of

the new blockships, the *Cornwallis* and *Hastings*, with the pioneer screw frigate *Amphion*, under the command of Captain Wellesley of the *Cornwallis*, attacked a battery at Sandhamn, six miles to the west of the main operation. The action lasted 3½ hours, during which the ships were repeatedly hit. Although only 14 non-fatal casualties were suffered

Sulivan condemned the action as futile.[21]

Once again wooden ships had the worst of a fight with batteries because they were only acting as a diversion. At a range of 800 yards the blockships, with only 32 guns on the broadside were quite unable to overcome 14 well-served guns behind earthworks, only one gun being temporarily dismounted. Had they closed to less than half that distance there would have been every prospect of success, but – as at Sebastopol – such a coup would have produced no advantage commensurate with the loss in lives and ships. It is worth noting that these blockships had been prepared for just such a task. Walker had even instructed the dockyards to use secondhand materials wherever possible, even down to their ground tackle (designed for mooring head and stern with springs on the cables).[22]

On 17 October 1855 the greater part of the allied naval force in the Black Sea, including three French floating batteries, attacked the fortress of Kinburn at the mouth of the Dnieper River. The batteries aided by six mortar vessels, opened fire at 09.00 from 1000 yards, at which range their heavier calibre artillery remained effective. They were joined by gunboats and frigates. At noon the *Royal Albert*, *Princess Royal*, *Agamemnon*, *Algiers*, *Montebello*, *Jean Bart*, *Ulm* and *Wagram* approached the fort in line abreast, an arrangement dictated by the nature of the coast, and swung into positions only 1½ cables apart previously buoyed by Spratt. Even though they had but two feet under their keels the ships were still almost 1600 yards off. The *St Jean d'Acre* and *Hannibal* engaged other batteries on the river front. This new and more rapid battering from two directions soon caused the Russians to cease fire, their defences having been partially wrecked by the precision fire of the floating batteries and mortar vessels.[23]

Kinburn has always been considered the proving ground of the armoured warship. However it was of more significance to contemporary observers, along with Sveaborg, as a demonstration that a well handled combination of vessels could overcome major fortifications. This realisation played a major role in determining the new strategic policy for 1856 after the fall of Sebastopol had failed to end the war. Allied strategy shifted to the Baltic and prepared for an assault on St Petersburg by land and by sea via Cronstadt.[24]

THE GREAT ARMAMENT

After the success of Rear-Admiral Sir Richard Dundas at Sveaborg the Admiralty began to order gunboats and mortar vessels in large quantities. Eventually more than 200 of the former and 100 of the latter were prepared for the 1856 campaign. This placed great strain on the Thames-side private yards where the majority were built, and on the engine-builders Penn and Maudslay who provided all the machinery for the gunboats. Four more floating batteries were also ordered.

As with the October programme of 1854 Walker placed the greatest part of the construction work out to private tender, leaving the royal yards to finish off the ships and fit them out. Walker had several steam battleships and frigates coming forward which could be ready for the 1856 campaign: the *Conqueror*, 101, the *Brunswick* and *Centurion*, 80s, and the *Chesapeake*, 51. All the royal yards had their slipways taken up with the construction or conversions of steam battleships, in line with the Graham/Walker policy to counter post-war French naval ambitions. This work dominated the construction policy of the Admiralty during the Russian War to a far greater extent than has been realised.

The organisation of the Baltic gunboats in 1855, employing them as tenders to the larger ships, was not a success. With the great increase in numbers planned for 1856 a new system was required. The plan adopted was for the gunboats to be formed into divisions, with a partly armed steam battleship as a support vessel. Each division would comprise 2 large and 4 small gun-vessels with 40 gunboats.[25] There would be three divisions, under Captain Codrington in the *Algiers*, Captain Keppel in the *Colossus*, and Captain Hastings Yelverton in the *Brunswick*. A further inshore squadron of 2 gun-vessels and 20 gunboats was formed under Captain Cooper-Key in the *Sans Pareil*.[26] The selection of these steam battleships reflected their unsatisfactory seagoing performance.

The mortar vessels and rafts were given a similar organisation, again in response to the increased number. The 90-gun sailing ships *Rodney* and *London* were selected as depot ships because both had been in commission in 1855 and they were modern ships with the benefit of Sir Robert Seppings' diagonal construction. They retained their lower masts, to hoist out the 13-inch mortars, but were otherwise rigged as second class frigates. Beside powder and shell they carried 110 spare mortars and workshop stores to repair the barrels of mortars damaged in action.

The completion date specified for the great armament had always been 1 March, but its ambitious nature ensured that the whole project was not ready in time. On 19 February Walker directed that all work not intended for the Baltic be abandoned and called for the mortars.[27] The journals of Rear-Admiral Sir Richard Dundas give a minutely detailed account of the formation of this great armament at Spithead. The only part of the fleet to reach the Baltic in 1856 was the Flying Squadron of frigates and the battleships *Caesar* and *Majestic*.[28] Before the main body of the fleet or the bombarding division could be completed political developments had rendered their departure irrelevant. The threat to St Petersburg contained in the Baltic Fleet of 1856, together with a diplomatic offensive in Sweden and Denmark, proved decisive in bringing the Czar to accept peace terms. The Baltic Fleet was only used for a Grand Steam Review on St George's Day to celebrate the peace, and then disbanded.[29] Within weeks all thoughts turned to the French fleet and the need to build more steam battleships and large frigates.[30]

While the steam battleship had taken a minor role in the actions of the Russian War its significance was felt in the strategic decisions of both sides. The Russians, with no steam battleships, felt unable to contest the command of the Black Sea or the Baltic and withdrew their naval forces into the fortified arsenals of Sebastopol, Sveaborg and Cronstadt. With no opposition even the hesitant councils of the joint allied naval commanders-in-chief could not fail to blockade the Russian positions and make menacing demonstrations. In the Baltic Sir Charles Napier prepared plans to attack the Russian arsenals, anticipating using his battle line for a final close-range bombardment. The complete allied command of the Black Sea was the principal factor in making the invasion of the Crimea possible. Similarly in the Baltic the isolated fortress of Bomarsund was taken because the Russians could not reinforce or relieve it.

In 1855 the Russians concentrated their Baltic naval forces at Cronstadt, allowing the British to institute a close blockade. As a result the steam battleships were used for subsidiary functions, such as harrassing coastal batteries and supervising cruiser squadrons. In the Black Sea the absence of any naval threat allowed Rear-Admiral Lyons to use his battleships as troop transports during the two expeditions to Kertch and the capture of Kinburn, where they also delivered the *coup de grâce* to fortifications already damaged by mortars and the French floating batteries.

From the outset it was clear that the British and French would be forced to adopt a maritime strategy against Russia. The value of the steam battleship lay in the complete command of the sea that it conferred on the allies. Never had a war between naval powers given rise to so little activity at sea by the weaker power.

Walker's control of the nation's shipbuilding resources grew in stature as the war progressed. By late 1855 he had brought the full economic and technical strength of Britain to bear on the war effort; this factor alone was responsible for the great size and latent power of the Great Armament of 1856. The work of Walker during the Russian War was the first example of an industrial nation mobilising its new found power for warlike purposes and a direct precursor of the two World Wars of the twentieth century. For the first time a war had been decided by the greater industrial base of one belligerent, rather than mere financial reserves or population.

4. The Post-War Situation

The *Gibraltar*, 1859, at Devonport about 1867 – the ultimate development of the two-decked wooden fighting ship. The ship over her bows is probably the *Queen*.
Imperial War Museum

One of the facts that had been emphasized by the Russian War was the relative uselessness of sailing ships as companions or opponents for steamers. Consequently both Britain and France officially stated that sail of the line were no longer considered suitable for use in wartime.[1] However that did not prevent the Admiralty continuing to employ sailing ships on the distant stations until 1861, in order to mass the steamers at home.

The wartime acceleration of those ships most quickly completed gave rise to a shortage of ships in the immediate post-war years. This was especially noticeable in the new ships which had been all but suspended in favour of conversions. With the peacetime run-down of the dockyards and the considerable amount of repair work left over from the war, the dockyards were quite unable to carry out the programmes set out by Walker. Not one steam battleship was launched or completed converting from a sailing ship during 1856. At the same time there was a need for a large programme of frigate construction and conversion, the French having taken a numerical lead in that class of ship. This work involved similar amounts of timber, dockyard labour and sets of steam machinery. Indeed the huge frigates *Mersey* and *Orlando* were at least as expensive as any steam battleship.

While the dockyard at Cherbourg was expanding

The *Renown*, 1857, at Malta.
National Maritime Museum

rapidly,[2] the steam battlefleet of France was not, at this stage, sufficiently large to be a cause for concern. Therefore Walker was content to return to the careful and considered methods of peacetime construction. The size and variety of the steam battlefleet employed during the Russian War provided a considerable body of information on the problems of designing large military steamers. The first issue to be considered was the ideal type to be reproduced. The general consensus favoured the large two-decker with 91 or 101 guns. Walker in particular had no time for the 80-gun ships: the addition of steam engines had exacerbated the already overcrowded stowage and gun decks of these ships, while their performance under steam or sail was mediocre. Walker also maintained a high opinion of the three-decker, although the majority of service opinion was against him. The draught of water and target area of the First Rates made them appear hostage to the increasing power of individual artillery pieces. Only their concentration of fire at close quarters, which Walker considered to be a vital factor in future naval battles, could justify

their retention.[3] In this matter the Surveyor illustrated his view that long-range fire was not a decisive factor. He was later to oppose the use of heavier artillery in battleships on the grounds that the resultant decrease in close-range rapid fire was unacceptable. In financial terms the difference in cost between the 120-gun three-decker *Victoria* and the 101-gun two-decker *Duncan* was no more than that between the *Duncan* and the 91-gun *Renown*. That the First Rate was no longer a uniquely expensive ship to build reflected the great size of all steam battleships. As a type they were far larger than it was economically possible to build in wood. Even so the *Victoria* and *Howe* were the last three-deckers to be started, and with the *Bretagne* the only steam three-deckers designed as such.

The two-decked ships were developed and enlarged. The 101-gun type were redesigned with an extra 400 tons and engines of 800nhp. The 91s were given similar engines, while their smaller increase in size was largely taken up with an additional 15 feet overall for a finer length-to-beam ratio and improved lines.[4] In the 1859 programme the two types were merged to produce a 91-gun ship on the dimensions of the 101-gun type. Two ships built on this plan – the *Bulwark* and *Robust*, the latter having been commenced as a 101-gun ship – were preserved on the stocks until 1872, the remaining seven being converted into *Caledonia* class ironclads.[5] These last two-deckers were 252 feet overall, while the *Victoria*, being a three-decker, was 260 feet. However this was not the limit of wooden construction: Walker ordered the *Mersey* class frigates to be 330 feet overall. That they displayed all the classic symptoms of weak construction, such as leaky seams, demonstrated that wood was no longer suitable for the construction of the largest classes of warship.

THE STERN AND THE RUDDER POST

During the war several ships had been disabled by injury to the rudder, notably the *Royal Albert*, *Agamemnon*, *Algiers* and *Cressy*.[6] At the same time almost all steam battleships suffered from leaks around the stern, requiring recaulking after the first steam trials.[7] The former problem arose because the sailing ship rudders fitted were not suitable to work behind a screw where they were under pressure if any helm was used. The latter difficulty demonstrated the combined effects of engine vibration and extreme length. It appeared that the longer and finer the ship the greater the motion of the stern,[8] the only solution to both problems being to work in large amounts of ironwork to strap up the weak wooden structure. In the late two-deckers this was carried right round the stern, linking the rudder post to the main frame timbers.[9] The need for iron reinforcement arose from the weakness of any wooden structure when stretched beyond the limits imposed by the size of the individual pieces from which it was built. The powerful motion of the propeller shaft quickly exposed this defect,[10] and wore out the screw aperture. This latter problem almost caused the loss of the *Royal Albert* in 1856, but with the introduction of lignum vitae bearings the danger passed.[11]

MACHINERY

The failure of Boulton and Watt's machinery for the *Sans Pareil* and the contrasting excellence of Penn's installation for the *Agamemnon* convinced the Admiralty that heavy steam plant should be pro-

The *Orlando*, 1858, the sister ship of the *Mersey*.
National Maritime Museum

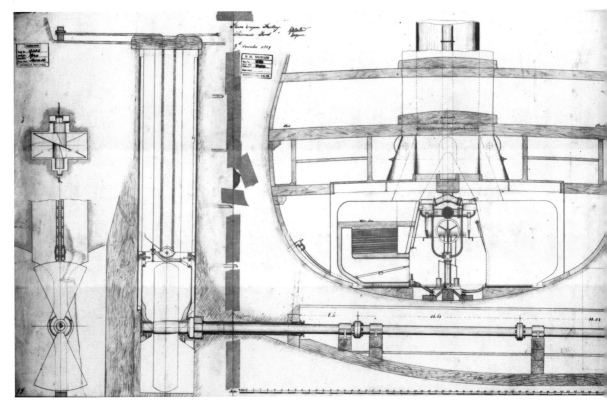

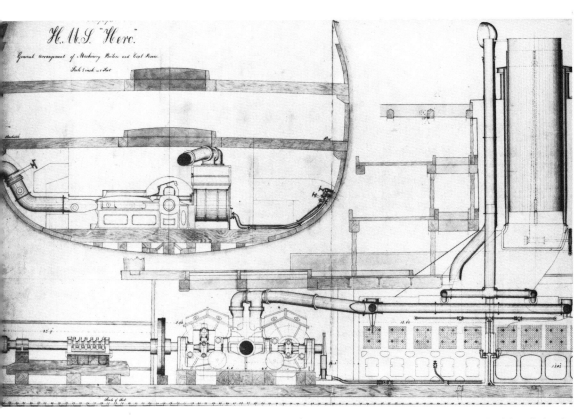

Machinery drawings of the *Hero*, a standard installation by Maudslay. The hoisting propeller and telescopic funnel are typical of the British battleships.
National Maritime Museum

The *Marlborough* and *Phoebe* at Malta, emphasizing the similar dimensions of the larger wooden steamships of the period.
Royal Naval Museum

cured with care. Penn and Maudslay, the two largest marine engine builders in the world, were the only firms invited to tender for new engines until 1855. The failure of Watt's rebuilt engine from the iron frigate *Vulcan* in the *James Watt*, and Fairbairn's ex-*Megaera* engine in the *Algiers*, confirmed the wisdom of this policy. The former had to be reworked in late 1854, while the latter was scrapped in 1856 as utterly useless.[12]

During the war the pressure of work on the two favoured concerns forced the Admiralty to consider other firms. Miller and Ravenhill supplied three sets of high-pressure machinery for the floating batteries *Glatton*, *Thunder* and *Trusty*[13] and the success of these installations induced the Admiralty to give Miller the contract for the *Brunswick*'s engines in late 1855.[14] In the previous year Watt had suffered the indignity of having a set of 400nhp engines already built turned down.[15] However the Admiralty preference for Penn and Maudslay remained in effect until the ironclad era. The Committee on Marine Engines of 1859 reported that Penn's trunk engines were, at that date, the best type for very high power. Maudslay's double piston rod design was considered superior to all similar installations on account of its simplicity and reliability.[16] Humphrey & Tennant, Watt, Napier and Miller all built engines of 400–500nhp for converted sailing ships, but the prime contracts for new ships all went to Penn and Maudslay, who eventually engined 24 ships each. All the new post-war ships used 800nhp machinery, except the 1000nhp *Victoria* and *Howe*, the contracts being shared. The three-deckers were also unique in having two funnels, one on either side of the mainmast. In all the new ships the Surveyor's

department was able to fulfill the hopes expressed by Commodore W F Martin during the Lisbon Trials of 1850 by replacing ballast with machinery. The 101-gun *Conqueror* required no additional ballast whatsoever.[17]

The fine lines of the post-war ships allowed them to exceed 12 knots under steam in the light condition. Further advances were prevented by the great increase in weight that would have been required to improve the lines and increase the machinery. Even the huge *Mersey* could not exceed 14 knots on trials with 1000nhp. Similarly the large American *Merrimack* class frigates that had inspired the *Mersey* failed to make their design speed. In the light of the *Mersey*'s performance the unprecedented

The *Donegal* at Portsmouth in 1872. She is very light forward. *Imperial War Museum*

speed attributed to *Le Napoléon* must be treated with considerable scepticism. Not only was she 100 feet shorter than the *Mersey*, but her engines were a long way behind those of the British frigate in terms of design and performance.

One major difference between the British and French steam battleships lay in the attitude their designers took to the use of steam. The French ships were designed to make the best possible use of steam, with auxiliary sails, while the British ships always paid great attention to the ability to sail. This reflected the world-wide commitments of the Royal Navy and the short distance objectives of the French Marine. It was considered that the propeller must hamper performance under sail so the British designs used a hoisting propeller. All British battleships and large frigates were fitted with a double stern post. The propeller was then mounted in a banjo frame between the two posts and fitted with a coupling. When the ship wished to sail she would uncouple the propeller and haul it up into the ship. The ironclad *Warrior* still displays this feature.

The *Phoebe*, 1860, a more typical 51-gun frigate of the period than the huge *Mersey* type.
National Maritime Museum

ARMAMENT

The armament of the new steam battleships continued after the pattern of the *Agamemnon*; succeeding decks of 8-inch 65cwt shell guns, 32-pounder 56cwt and 42cwt solid shot guns and one 68-pounder solid shot gun for a bowchaser. This was standardised in 1854.[18] For broadside action up to 1000 yards and solid shot practice up to 1600 yards this arrangement was the most effective that could be devised. However the range and power of new pieces, notably the 11-inch Dahlgren carried by the American corvette *Niagara*, led many commentators both amateur and professional to suggest that the time had come for a radical shift in the armament of battleships.[19] Walker had been prepared to mount a very heavy battery of 68-pounders and 10-inch shell guns in the frigates built in reply to the American designs, but he was not

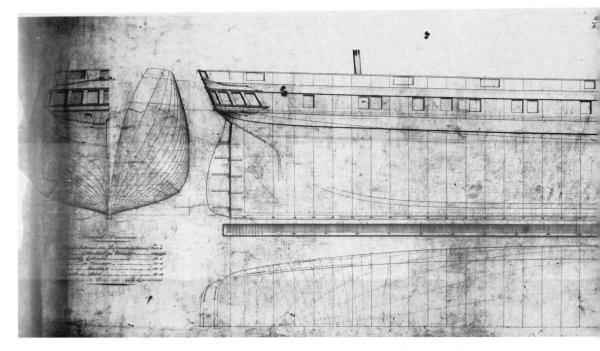

happy at the idea of using such pieces on the crowded gun decks of a battleship. He considered that the guns would be more difficult to handle and therefore slower firing. To mount them in existing ships would reduce the number of guns carried and require gunports so large as to weaken the structure of the vessel. Furthermore ships already part built would require costly and time-consuming alterations, while new vessels must be built on enlarged dimensions, at greatly increased cost. Walker thought that a more economic solution lay in the use of the new Armstrong breech-loading guns should they come up to expectations.[20] These weapons were later mounted on the upper decks of the converted old three-deckers and *Powerful* class 84s;[21] they were also rushed out to the ships of the North American and West Indies Squadron in the aftermath of the '*Trent* Crisis'. Captain Hewlett of the gunnery training ship *Excellent* favoured an upper deck battery of 68-pounders to stop large frigates with long-range guns 'harrassing and perhaps driving into port' a battleship[22] but Walker's reply was that the upper works of existing ships were unequal to such artillery, and that the weight needed to make new ships sufficiently strong would have a detrimental effect on stability. He also viewed with horror the possibility that the close-range rapid fire

of a battleship might be sacrificed – the idea that a frigate might encounter a battleship struck him as ridiculous. Battleships were designed for the line of battle and not for independent cruising, therefore he saw only folly in reducing their number of guns,

and thereby seriously affecting their power and efficiency as line of battle ships, unless we should be obliged to do so in consequence of foreign ships of the line adopting this description of armament.[23]

Walker's opinion was justified as the French battleships were never rearmed in this fashion. Walker's upper deck batteries were repeatedly criticized by admirals and captains as being overcrowded and thus having a tendency to set fire to the lower rigging. Consequently they were reduced after Walker had left office, a process hastened by the fitting of Armstrong breech-loaders in their place.[24] Below decks Walker's ships were extremely well laid out, so this over-gunning of the upperworks must have been a minor aberration arising out of his desire to keep a large number of the faster firing short guns for close action.

The development of the armament of the British steam battleships emphasizes Walker's strong preference for evolution rather than revolution. He would take no major step that was not forced on

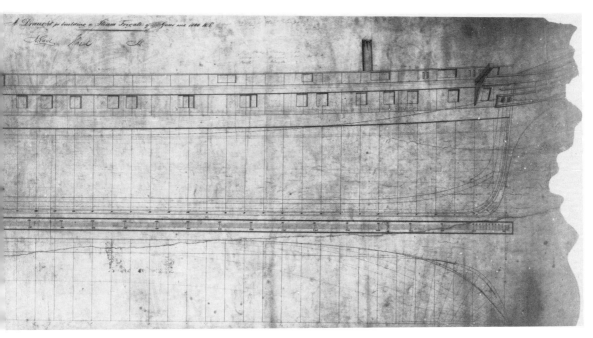

Inboard profile of the *Mersey*, 1858, one of the huge frigates built in response to the United States *Merrimack*.
National Maritime Museum

him, rather looking to improve existing types. When Britain's rivals attempted to get ahead he was always ready to react in the most comprehensive fashion:[25] the American steam frigates were outmatched by the *Mersey* and *La Gloire* by the *Warrior*.

MASTS

The steam era brought no new developments in masts and rigging, only a gradual increase in scale. The early steam battleships were fitted on the same establishment as their sailing predecessors, following the lines laid down by Sir William Symonds. However there were problems stepping the mainmast. The majority of steamers had their engines placed before the mainmast, so the propeller shaft had to pass along the line of the keel, just where the mast should be stepped. The only solutions were either to carry the mast on one side of the propeller shaft with an iron leg, or to step it on the orlop deck. In the converted ships this decision was largely made by the machinery, the former solution being adopted in the Maudslay-engined *Majestic*, the latter in the Penn-engined *Orion*,[26] and the Miller-equipped *Brunswick*.[27]

All the new two-deckers were fitted on the scale of the *Albion*, but converted ships often had to use a smaller mainmast, the *Princess Royal* using one from

a *Powerful* class 84 because it proved impossible to step the larger item.[28]

The finer hulls of the steam battleships enabled them to improve on the speed of the sailing ships with the same rig, but only in a strong breeze. They also benefitted from the improved rigging adopted by Symonds, enabling them to sail closer to the wind than older ships. In the Baltic fleet of 1854 Napier had problems with station-keeping, largely due to the inequality of masting. His flagship, the *Duke of Wellington* 'sailed like a witch',[29] but the old *Royal George*, her next astern, was crank and unable to sail half as close to the wind as the flagship. As a result her Captain, Henry Codrington, came in for a good deal of abuse.

COAL

During the early movements of the Baltic fleet of 1854 Napier came to realise that steam was a mixed blessing. Napier had not been on board a steam battleship before, and this was the first occasion on which so large a collection of steamers had been gathered for warlike operations. Whenever the fleet raised steam an immense pall of smoke hung over the area. Not only would this tell-tale betray it to the enemy, but it would also prevent ships from reading signal hoists either on leaving harbour, or on going into battle.[30] The Admiralty had chosen on grounds of economy to provide the fleet with North Country coal, famous for the volume and density of the smoke it produced; only the *Duke of Wellington* had been supplied with the superior Welsh steam coal, which burned more cleanly. The Board suggested that the two types should be mixed 'in proper proportion' to reduce the nuisance.[31] Part of the rationale behind Napier's standing order on the use of steam in battle was to reduce the need for signals: he even supplied an outline table of gun charges, information hitherto communicated to the fleet from the flagship immediately before a battle.[32]

Graham had been made aware of the problem of

coal supply by Sir Thomas Byam Martin, and therefore Milne, as Fourth Naval Lord, was directed to pay special attention to the requirements of the fleet. Lacking any guidance from Napier he reached an initial estimate of 5000 tons per month.[33] However, Napier was aware of the problem and instructed his Captains that they were to 'consider their ships as sailing ships while cruising'.[34] This was a necessary reminder, as many of them saw steam as an excuse for poor seamanship. Consequently the only problem experienced with coal in the campaigns of 1854 and 1855 was where to store the surplus that quickly built up. The final arrangement adopted was for the colliers to cross the North Sea from Newcastle and rendezvous in Faro

The *Revenge*, 1859.
Imperial War Museum

Sound.[35] In this manner the Admiralty was able to keep a tally of the total available in the Baltic and regulate the supply to meet the requirements of the fleet. The colliers were called up to Baro Sound (or during the Bomarsund operation Ledsound) as and when necessary. They were then emptied, ballasted and sent directly home. Occasionally a special requirement would call for a different disposition, notably in early June when Milne sent a collier to Danzig to supply the weekly steamer from the fleet that called there for the mails and despatches.[36]

Milne's handling of the coaling demands of the Baltic fleet was a triumph, and through his careful management the Admirals commanding were never embarrassed by a lack of coal. The same can be said of the fleet in the Black Sea, where greater distance from home and a smaller demand were easily overcome. In the Baltic both Napier and Dundas complained of the quality of the coal. Milne also realised that North Country coal was inferior to Welsh, but the issue was not simply one of cost. The transport of coals between Newcastle and London was an old and well organised trade with an ample reserve capacity to meet the demands of the Baltic fleet. At a time when the transport requirements of the Black Sea theatre were making great demands on the Mercantile Marines of Britain and France it would have been unwise to ignore the Newcastle trade's advantages and to attempt to organise a new supply from South Wales. This would have called for larger colliers and longer journeys, both of which would have been expensive, while the latter might have led to delays in covering the needs of the fleet. After the war Milne noted that the supply of Welsh coal, which in 1855 was little larger than that of North Country, had become three times greater in 1856–57. Also the total supply had increased from 100,000 tons in 1853 to 240,000 in 1856.[37] This realisation that the high quality Welsh coal was essential to the efficient conduct of naval warfare under steam was a product of the two Baltic campaigns. At the end of the 1854 campaign Sulivan, the Fleet Surveying Officer, emphasized the dangers of North Country coal, both in action and manoeuvres, and in damaging the sails, masts and yards.[38] However it was not until the 1856 Steam Review that Welsh coal was specified for the fleet,[39] and then only to prevent the smoke from obscuring the Queen's view.

Milne continued to study the logistic aspects of the coal question after the war. By 1858 he had decided that wartime consumption would average one ton of coal per tenth of each nominal horse power per day.[40] In the following year he prepared a paper outlining the necessary coaling stations and the reserve tonnage required in the event of a war against France.[41]

SEAGOING PERFORMANCE

The early steam battleships, such as the 230-foot *Agamemnon*, combined a measure of speed under sail or steam with similar manoeuvring powers to the sailing ships. This persuaded Walker to try even longer hulls, the *Renown* being drawn out to 244 feet 9 inches and the *Bulwark* to 252 feet.[42] While these post-war ships, from their greater length and finer lines, reached higher speeds they did so at the expense of the facility and precision of their response to the helm. New ships such as the *Donegal*, 101 and *Renown*, 91 were considered slow in their stays. This lack of handiness was emphasized by operating in company with older ships such as the *St Jean d'Acre*, 101 and *James Watt*, 91 which lacked speed, but tacked and wore far more easily. Lord Auckland had anticipated this problem in 1847.[43]

The majority of the converted ships, especially the Symondites, were considered poor. The Captain of the Fleet in the 1860 Channel Fleet, George Elliot, reported that they rolled even more than they had done as sail of the line. The three Symondites in the fleet, the *Aboukir*, 90, the *Queen*, 86 and the *Mars*, 80 were so bad that Elliot recommended that they be used only in an emergency.[44] The *Neptune*, 86, one of the 1858 emergency programme conversions, was very crank, yet the similar *London* was outstanding;[45] but the *Neptune* had been regarded as the finest sailing three-decker in the service.[46] Geoffrey Phipps Hornby did his best with the old ship, but she remained a 'dummy', in sharp contrast to his next command, the superb *Edgar*.[47]

The new ships were very fast under all plain sail with the wind strong and favourable but they were often embarrassed by the older and converted types in light airs. This was because of their increased surface area and the greater frictional drag it created. The science of hydrodynamics, pioneered by William Froude and John Scott-Russell, was in

The stern of the *Defiance* during her service as the Torpedo Schoolship at Devonport.
Conway Picture Library

its infancy, and it was not until Edward Reed designed the ironclad *Bellerophon* in 1863 that the conflicting requirements of speed and manoeuvrability were combined in one hull. This tendency to build very long ships reached a climax with the early ironclads of the *Warrior* and *Minotaur* classes. Walker's opinion was that:

Speed is of the utmost importance in all ships of war, and absolutely essential in seagoing ships cased with iron; both for their own safety and for attack, it becomes necessary to build them of extraordinary length and in order to obtain the necessary strength they must be constructed of iron.[48]

The immense length of the ironclads built to this precept made them even more unreliable wearing or staying than the wooden battleships.[49]

The different appearance of the French ships, especially at the stern is clearly evident in this detail from the Roux portrait of *Le Napoléon* (see also the front endpaper).

DECAY

The major reason behind Walker's decision to keep the construction of new and converted steamships separate lay in the problem of decay. Experience in the Napoleonic Wars had taught the Navy that only ships built over a long period with the finest materials would last. Therefore Walker refused to rush work on new ships, filling the resulting gap with conversions. Even so the new factors introduced into the wooden structure by the steam engine, heat, damp and vibration, were well calculated to point up any weakness and accelerate the process of decay.

When the *Princess Royal*, 91, was docked at Portsmouth in 1858 her after part was found to be greatly defective. The only explanation that the shipwrights could offer, unless the caulking had been neglected, was that the conversion had been so rapid that the surfaces of the adapted and additional frame timbers had been given insufficient time to season before being planked over.[50] It is probable that a combination of these two factors lay at the root of the decay. The entire steam battle-fleet was afflicted by working of the stern, with the attendant strain on the seams. The combination of unseasoned timber and damp would provide the perfect environment for the progress of rot. The *Royal Albert* was defective in the same areas as the *Princess Royal*, indicating that the problem was at least partly due to the acceleration of 1853–54.[51] Even the new *Victor Emmanuel*, 91 of 1855 displayed similar defects (although not confined to the stern) that could only be attributed to the use of timber not fully seasoned.[52] This demonstrated the most significant problem caused by the Russian War, the shortage of seasoned timber, and illustrated exactly how the careful plans of Walker had been upset.

By 1860 the problem of finding sufficient timber became almost the dominant concern of the Surveyor's Department,[53] emphasizing the timely nature of the move to iron ships – in 1860 the Admiralty spent £460,000 on timber.[54] If Walker was correct in his opinion that the French were

Inboard profile of the *Hero*, a modified *James Watt* completed in 1859, showing the large percentage of the hull given over to engines and boilers.
National Maritime Museum

using unseasoned timber their problems in this respect must have been far greater than those of the Royal Navy.

TIMBER

The actual amounts of timber required to build a battleship increased dramatically with the adoption of steam. Sir William Symonds' modifications had caused a 19 per cent increase in the number of loads, and a 30 per cent increase in the number of man-hours. However the figures that separated the Symondites from Walker's steam battleships were 56 per cent and 47 per cent respectively.[55] The relative advance in cost was, if anything, even larger. Many technical explanations could be advanced to account for the use of more timber. The principal one must have been the need to build the ship up more akin to a solid structure to withstand the great strains set up by the machinery. The steamships were also longer and fitted with stronger gun decks, but even these were unable to withstand the shattering effect of the new heavy guns.[56] The increased amount of timber required helped to make the iron-hulled ship cheaper to build as well as cheaper to maintain and finally seal the fate of the wooden warship.

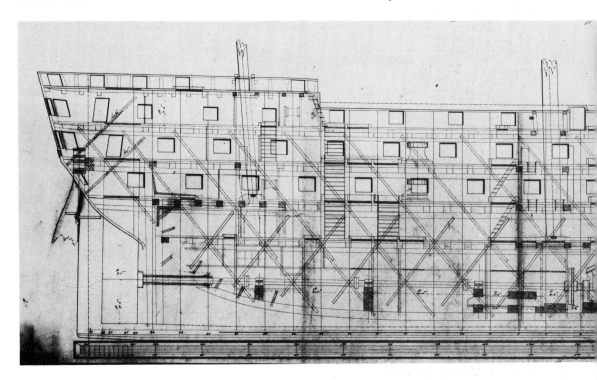

AESTHETICS

Sir Robert Seppings' modifications to the bow and stern of the wooden warship gave them enhanced strength, but left them far from pleasing to the eye of many naval officers; Napier was notably caustic in his opinion of the round stern. Symonds' models were far better received on these grounds, his elliptical stern being particularly commended for its beauty and practicality. It was both stronger and provided a better battery than Seppings' round stern. In general Symonds' ships were noteworthy for their regular upperworks, the waist being built up so as to present an unbroken sheer line from the bow to the quarterdeck. The latter feature was lengthened to give a very distinctive appearance.[57] While Walker modified Symonds' hull-form he was quite content to follow his predecessor's pattern for the upperworks. The greater length and finer form of the new steam battleships emphasized the refined elegance of Symonds' upperworks. The post-1815 trend towards a wall-sided hull had provided more spacious gun decks while cutting down on the need for expensive curved timber. This effect was most noticeable in the two-deckers, the three-deckers still requiring considerable 'tumblehome' to preserve stability.

The total effect of the various developments can best be observed in large two-deckers such as the 101-gun *Duncan* and *Gibraltar*. They presented a very different appearance from the Baroque splendour of the early eighteenth century, with their regular outline bereft of almost all embellishment beyond the elliptical stern galley and the figurehead and painted in the severe black and white bands of the era. These were the most striking and intimidating of all the wooden warships, replacing elegance with majesty. As such they were fitting precursors for the industrial architecture of the ironclads.

The French steam battleships were even more severely modern in outline that the British ships, their lower and main deck batteries being carried round an entirely unadorned stern; only the upper deck was graced by a light stern walk. Further points of contrast can be found with the upper works, the French quarterdeck being so slight as to pass unnoticed, while the bulwarks were pierced for a full battery of guns on the upper deck. How the French proposed to fight this waist battery when the less heavily armed upper deck of the British ships was found to be grossly overcrowded remains uncertain.

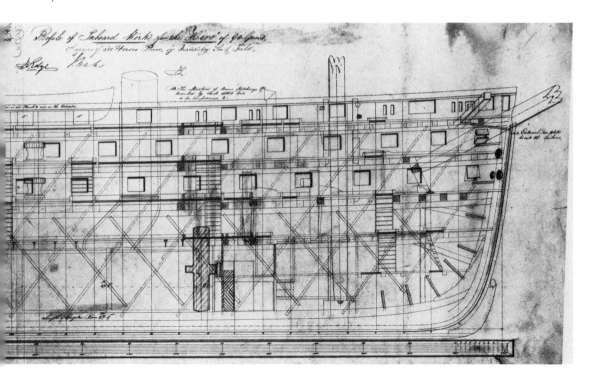

Symonds' elliptical stern for all its strength facilitated the preservation of the quarter galleries, which British ships carried on every deck above the gun deck. Thus the stern was the area of greatest contrast between the ships of the two nations, although it would be difficult to mistake the nationality of a steam battleship from any angle.

The machinery of the *Waterloo* (later *Conqueror*), by Ravenhill & Salkeld.
Science Museum

5. Alarms and Emergencies, 1858-1861

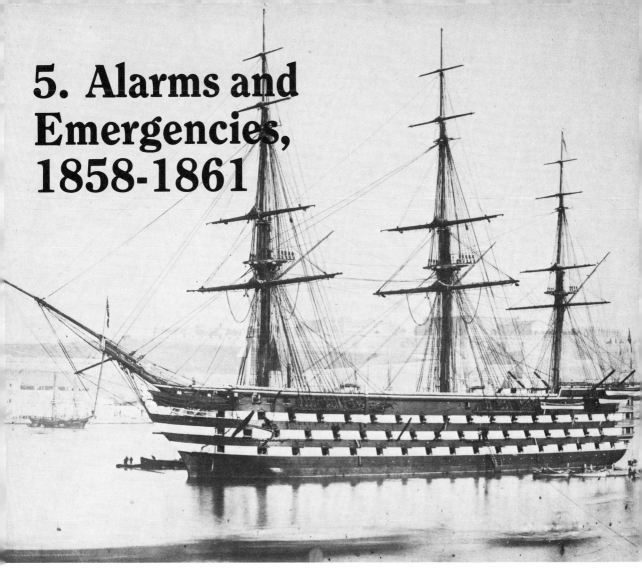

The *Victoria* at Malta.
National Maritime Museum

In March 1858 the Palmerston administration was defeated on the Conspiracy to Murder Bill.

Palmerston's conduct in this affair, arising from Orsini's attempt to assassinate Louis Napoleon with a bomb manufactured in Birmingham, convinced many of his erstwhile supporters that he was giving way to the bombastic demands of the French. This was very far from the truth, but his views on the value of French co-operation were rather more involved than those of his Parliamentary and public adherents.

The Second Administration of Lord Derby took office in February 1858; once again it was a minority government relying on the divisions among its opponents to keep it in office. Sir John Pakington, later Lord Hampton became First Lord of the Admiralty, the Duke of Northumberland having

refused his old office.[1] Rear-Admiral William Fanshawe Martin was the First Naval Lord. Before the new Board had settled in, the question of the naval balance was brought to the forefront by Walker. Even Derby, under pressure from the Queen,[2] had to admit the validity of the Surveyor's policy, despite his advocacy of peace abroad and retrenchment at home. Both Derby and Disraeli maintained a grudge against Walker that dated back to the Stafford affair of 1852 and Disraeli needed to be convinced that the Surveyor was genuine.[3] However Derby was certain that both ironclads and more steam battleships were vital, declaring:

We *must* have a naval preponderence over France, however inconvenient the outlay might be, and however unreasonable the system on her part which forces on us corresponding efforts.[4]

The first reliable indication that France was close to achieving parity with Britain in the number of steam battleships came in early 1858 and was coupled with signs of a *rapprochement* between France and Russia. Walker seized on the most sensational aspects of the news and, observing the current shortfall in all construction programmes, pressed the Admiralty to increase the resources of the dockyards and convert several ships in order to maintain bare equality with France. Despite his preference for new ships Walker was still not prepared to force the pace of new construction beyond the time required to season the structure as it was built. Some ships, notably the *Victoria*, *Howe*, *Prince of Wales* and *Duncan*, were expedited, but all four were already well seasoned.[5] However the remainder of the ships affected by the emergency programme were old sailing ships. The most suitable group of vessels were the 120-gun three-deckers of the *Caledonia* and *Nelson* classes. The exact nature of the work needed to turn these old ships into effective steam battleships was already known from the unfortunate

experience with the *Royal George*, which had to be cut down twice before she could be trusted in a gale, and the success of the *London*.[6] Following the *London* the ships would be cut down into two-deckers and lengthened 15 feet by the stern for engines of 500nhp; the cost would be approximately £25,000 per ship, compared with £105,000 for a new 91.[7] Walker had hoped to keep the *Queen* as a three-decker, but was overruled, wisely in the event as she rolled badly enough as a two-decker.[8] That these old ships (the *Royal William*, *Waterloo*, *St George*, *Neptune*, *Trafalgar* and *Queen*) were still in good condition after up to thirty years afloat was a tribute to the improved construction methods and measures to preserve ships adopted after 1815. This work was given the highest priority: initially workers were taken off small ships and moved between the yards to assist their completion,[9] later work on new steam battleships was also curtailed.[10]

At the root of the shortage of ships lay the problems of the dockyards. Walker was certain that the Russian War had interfered with the construction of new ships, since seasoned timber set aside for battleships had been used for other work and skilled labour diverted to more pressing projects. Post-war

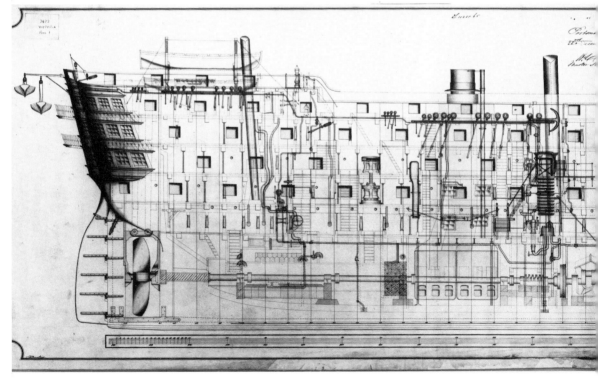

retrenchment and a larger frigate programme had further exacerbated the problem. As a result the programmes prepared by Walker had been found to be beyond the capacity of the dockyards. Some ships ordered to convert two years previously – in 1856 – had yet to be started. Consequently the only solution lay in expanding the dockyard labour-force without delay.[11] The French ironclads added another dimension to the problem, for although Walker considered that they would fail they still increased the French battle line.[12]

As the situation stood in mid 1858 both navies had 30 steam battleships, excluding the 9 British blockships. At the end of 1859 Walker calculated that Britain would have 36 and France 40, without counting *La Gloire* and her ironclad sisters. The 6 additional conversions he proposed would cover this shortage, but only just.[13] In the event the French only ever completed 38 steam battleships, 5 of the most formidable in 1860.

The 1859 programme included the conversion of the *Nelson*, a 120-gun ship built in 1814, the *Rodney*, and the *Royal Frederick*, a sister of the *Queen* that remained on the stocks. They were to be adapted according to the plans used for the *London* (first two)

and *Queen* respectively. All had the advantage of large dimensions and so could mount 86 guns with room to spare. In Walker's opinion such ships would be satisfactory fighting machines, despite their problems as seaboats.

The French programmes had benefitted from the progress made in 1855, while Britain was concentrating on the Baltic armament for 1856. It was during the immediate post-war years that they moved into a position approaching parity. However the situation was never quite as grim as Walker painted it. The French ships were built with far less care in the selection of timber, and soon began to suffer the ravages of dry rot. Furthermore they were considerably lighter on a measure of tons burthen per gun and must have been weak, bearing in mind the structural stresses set up by steam machinery, even if their design did accept considerable limitations on stowage.[14]

In 1858 the Queen, having been alarmed by her visit to Cherbourg, asked the Admiralty if the Navy

Inboard profile of the *Victoria*, 1859. The two sets of four boilers on either side of the mainmast and the two funnels were unique to this class.
National Maritime Museum

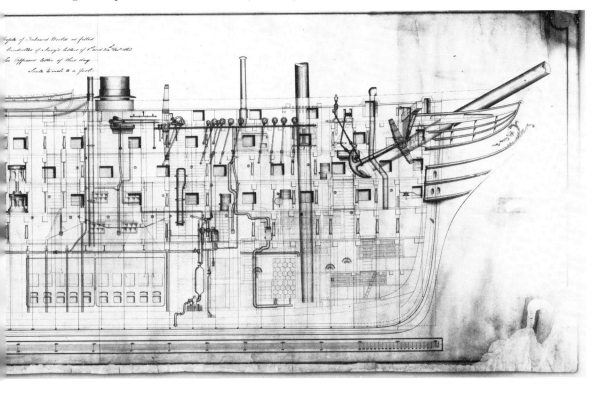

was adequate for the tasks it might have to perform in wartime. The task of answering this enquiry fell to Milne, the Third Naval Lord, and his appreciation of the duties of the Navy placed the numbers of steam battleships and frigates required far above the existing figures.[15]

	Steam Battleships	Frigates
Channel Fleet	10	12
North Sea Squadron	3	7
Irish Sea and Bristol Channel	4	8
Blockade of Cherbourg and Brest	10	12
Reinforce the Channel Islands	—	—
Reinforce the Mediterranean	8	8
Reserve	10	10
Reinforce and secure the Colonies	30	70
Total (active ships)	65	117

Walker also called for a battlefleet of between 60 and 80 steam battleships.

THE DERBY COMMITTEE

By late 1858 Lord Derby had taken sufficient notice of the widespread public alarm over the relative sizes of the British and French navies to set up a Parliamentary Committee to consider the major issues involved. The terms of reference were wide; it was to investigate the increase in naval estimates between 1852 (the last Tory Administration) and 1858; and consider the strength of the Navy with reference to other powers, especially France.[16] The members of the Committee were George Hamilton, Secretary to the Treasury; Henry Corry, Secretary to the Admiralty and later First Lord; Sir Richard Bromley, the Accountant General of the Navy and W G Anderson, Chief Clerk of the Treasury. They were directed to pay special attention to the opinions of Walker, an instruction that they took very much to heart.

The increase in the estimates was easily explained on the logical ground that the application of steam had forced up the cost, both of the ships and of their manning and maintenance. Even the docks had been enlarged as the overall length of the longest ships had expanded from 205 to 330 feet. Over the preceding six years steam machinery had accounted for an average of £570,503 per annum. The size of the Navy came in for a more detailed appraisal, the figures for battleships and frigates giving rise to some concern, although the smaller classes were

perfectly adequate. Walker revealed that after 15 years a heavy ship needed a complete repair, while their effective lives could not be estimated beyond thirty years. The dockyard labour-force, 4000 shipwrights and apprentices with slightly over 6000 ancillary workers was only just sufficient to produce 3 battleships, 3 frigates and 6 sloops in a year, while undertaking all necessary repairs. Walker therefore called for an extra 1500 shipwrights, with other

The *London* in 1875 showing the typical bow of the steam battleships; however her glazed-in gunports and extra 'heads' amidships are not warship fittings.
Conway Picture Library

trades in proportion at a cost of £500,000 per annum for two years in order to effect a solution.[17]

The Committee observed that Walker proposed to use this enlarged dockyard force to convert the remaining 16 effective sail of the line into steam battleships or frigates. The latter would be adapted from the six *Powerful* class 84s, the Symondite 80s *Vanguard* and *Collingwood* and the 70-gun *Boscawen* and *Cumberland*. Observing that the timber in stock was suitable they favoured a remedy for the most glaring shortage, that of steam frigates. The Committee was unaware of the great difference in fighting power between the French paddle frigates whose numbers inflated the real danger posed by

The *London* in 1875 while on her way to Zanzibar to become the depot ship of the anti-slavery patrol. The enlarged gunport on the lower deck amidships and the cluttered upperworks betray her non-military function.
Conway Picture Library

France, and the British screw frigates. Walker was careful not to enlighten them on this issue.

In their recommendations the Committee whole-heartedly endorsed Walker's views on the need for a short-term solution to the deficiency of battleships and frigates, quite aside from the ironclad issue. They compared the costs of a new two-decker (£105,000) with those of converting an old three-decker (£25,000), noted that the latter task only required ⅝ths of the labour, and noted the saving in materials. In conclusion the Report stated:

The process of conversion, on the other hand, is speedy, as compared with that of building. The present seems a state of transition, as regards naval architecture, inducing the French Government to suspend the laying down of new ships of the line altogether, and it is more especially so with regard to artillery.

The late invention of 'Armstrong's gun', it has been stated to us, may supersede the use of ordinary ships' guns, and possibly affect even the size and structure of ships of war. We therefore venture to suggest, for your Lordship's consideration, whether, if the force in the dockyards were to be used next year in the conversion of ships of the line and frigates, as far as available dock accommodation will admit, the most useful results might not be attained at a comparatively small expenditure.[18]

Through the medium of the Derby Committee Walker was able to keep his views to the forefront and ensure the vital continuity of British construction policy. The ships converted following the report were the *Prince Regent* (an old *Caledonia* class ship that had already been cut down), the *Albion*, the *Collingwood*, and the *Powerful* class 84, *Bombay*. The *Powerful*s were Seppings' modification of the French *Canopus* captured at the Nile, and were noted for outsailing even their illustrious model. The *Powerful* was originally selected for conversion, but when she was taken in hand it was found that she was in an advanced state of decay[19]; the *Bombay* was then selected as a replacement. Throughout this period of alarm, when Walker was complaining of the shortage of men in the dockyards he never put any work out to private tender. At least one yard, Pitcher's at Northfleet, approached him offering to undertake such work, but all battleship construction and conversion remained in the royal yards.[20] By contrast the first ironclads were all contract-built.

Sir John Pakington earned the respect of the Navy by his application of funds to several areas of apparent difficulty, most of which had arisen out of the neglect of the previous administration. Even Napier, an inveterate critic of all naval administrations, praised Pakington for his intelligent handling of the estimates. Guided by Pakington the Derby Administration was content to trust in the Navy for the ultimate defence of the nation. As a result no effort was spared to ensure that it remained adequate for that task. Even the uncertainty as to the future of naval armaments observed by the Derby Committee did not shake Pakington's faith in the Navy. In this respect it is worth noting that one member of the Government, Lord Stanley, later

15th Earl of Derby, considered that Pakington played up to the naval officers to gain popularity with big estimates.[21] Whatever the truth of this, Pakington's policy was far more effective and consistent than that of his successor.

THE LAST OF THE WOODEN WALLS

Palmerston's second administration took office in June 1859 at a time when the recommendations of the Derby Committee were being put into effect. The emergency conversions were being pressed on while several new *Bulwark* class two-deckers were ordered. These measures promised to ensure Britain's parity with France, a matter of no small consequence when many feared that the Navy might have to meet the combined strength of France and Russia in the near future. In order to achieve a 'two-power' standard in steam battleships – because

The *Aboukir*, another poor conversion effected on a Symondite hull.
National Maritime Museum

they must remain the common currency of sea-power for some years to come – Palmerston was determined to continue work on the wooden battle-fleet.[22] The new First Lord of the Admiralty, the Duke of Somerset, added weight to the Prime Minister's argument by observing that the Whitworth rifled artillery should be able to send shells through the 4½-inch belt of the early iron-clads.[23] However Somerset was later to claim that he had not laid down any wooden battleships, only completing sufficient to regain parity with France and Russia.[24] This was a lie: five 91-gun Second Rates were laid down in 1860, at least six months after Somerset took office.[25] But this policy does explain why the large *Bulwark* class ships were retained on the stocks while the smaller *Defiance* was launched in 1861 – the larger ships were better suited for conversion into ironclads and were held in reserve for that purpose.

Somerset has been considered a more astute administrator than Pakington; Colin Baxter rated him the best First Lord of the nineteenth century.[26] Much of this praise stems from his having had the benefit of Sir James Graham's long experience of Admiralty administration, their children having

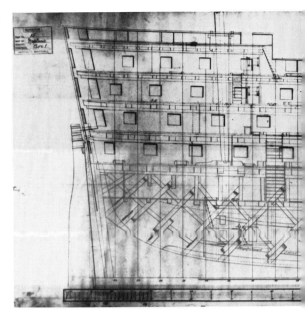

married. The first consequence of this was that Somerset was saddled with a Board drawn up by Graham and including several of his protégés: Vice-

The *St George* at Devonport.
Imperial War Museum

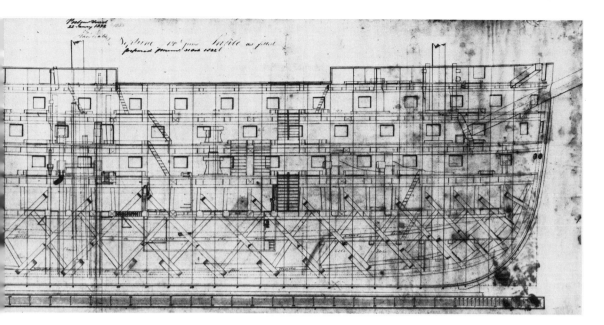

Admiral Sir Richard Dundas as First Naval Lord and Captain Lord Clarence Paget as Parliamentary Secretary.[27] Under Somerset Walker lost his dominant voice in the determination of construction policy, although the long-term programme he had set in motion provided both the last wooden battleships and first ironclads. He had been uncertain of the value of ironclads, even being ready to convert them into troopships should they prove as vulnerable to improved artillery as the 1845 iron frigates. Therefore he suggested regaining parity in wooden ships and keeping pace with French ironclad construction. The new type he observed must initially be treated as a supplement to the old, and not a replacement:

Although I have frequently stated it is not in the interest of Great Britain, possessing as she does so large a navy, to adopt any important change in the construction of ships of war which might have the effect of rendering necessary the introduction of a new class of very costly vessels until such a course is forced upon her by the adoption by Foreign Powers of formidable ships of a novel character requiring similar ships to cope with them, yet it then becomes a matter not only of expediency but of absolute necessity.[28]

The naval inadequacy that had led to the Derby Committee in 1858 was replaced in 1859 by a more general fear of invasion, stimulated in part by the imminent completion of the first French ironclad. At the root of this new scare lay the new technology – it was a fear of the unknown. However the conduct of the Government was hardly calculated to instil confidence. Looking to score political points, soon after taking office, Somerset declared that the fleet was not adequate to defend the coast,[29] while Sidney Herbert, the Secretary for War, was quite happy to point out the apparently defenceless state of the dockyards, describing them as 'inviting targets' that shackled the fleet to their defence.[30]

Herbert considered that the French fleet would be able to slip past the Channel fleet and stage a grand raid on one of the major dockyards. This naive conception of naval strategy implied that the fleet might be elsewhere when needed, merely because steam allowed ships to travel in any direction. Palmerston was of the opinion that because the blockade must be carried out under sail a steam force could sortie past it at any time. Therefore the age-old strategy of covering the French ports was rendered futile.[31] Somerset should have advanced a better appreciation of the role of the Navy, but he had no deeper insight than Herbert. The type of defences that were needed were those that could counter a minor raid by an individual cruiser, not an entire battlefleet.

At Herbert's prompting, on 20 August 1859

The *Victor Emmanuel* as the depot ship for the Ashanti campaign of 1873-74, for which she was granted a battle honour.
Conway Picture Library

The *Bombay* completing her conversion in dock at Chatham in 1861. A *Powerful* class 84 she was the last such ship to be completed. Destroyed by fire off Montevideo, 22 December 1864.

Palmerston appointed a Royal Commission to consider the defences of Great Britain. The Chairman was a Royal Engineer, General Sir Harry Jones, and he was assisted by Major General D A Cameron, Rear-Admiral George Elliot, Major-General Sir Frederick Hallet, Captain Astley Cooper-Key, Lieutenant-Colonel J H Lefroy and James Ferguson of the Treasury. The composition of this body was not such as to give rise to any confidence in the impartiality of its findings. It was hardly likely that Jones, or his Engineer colleagues would claim that forts were unnecessary, or even advocate a limited programme. The declaration that, 'the nation cannot be secured against invasion if depending for its defence upon the fleet alone', displayed a considerable ignorance of history, geography and logistics. Indeed much of their argument was based on a comprehensive misunderstanding of the lessons of the siege of Sebastopol, where Jones had been the Engineer in charge of the 1855 operations. He thought that a fortress like Sebastopol could hold up an invasion, forgetting that the only object of the allies in landing in the Crimea had been to capture Sebastopol itself.

Gladstone, the Chancellor of the Exchequer, perhaps alone among the Cabinet, had a realistic conception of the needs of Britain's defence. He regarded the danger of invasion as altogether 'visionary',[32] yet he favoured a strong navy and tried to ensure that the Navy estimates were expended on the most useful vessels. Having decided that ironclads must be the ships of the future he consistently opposed spending money on wooden ships, calling for the transfer of monies voted for timber to the construction of ironclads.[33] In this he clashed with Palmerston who considered it necessary to match the French in both types of battleship.[34] In his advocacy of naval rather than military defences, Gladstone was joined by all the leading naval figures in the Commons, with Sir Charles Napier at the forefront.[35] Unfortunately there was no stopping 'Palmerston's follies', as they were subsequently christened. The public called for them, and Parliament was prepared to pay for them. In the event developments in artillery rapidly outmoded stone fortification, and Herbert's long-term investment[36] turned out to be rather less useful

than a moderate programme of naval reinforcement. Indeed one of the major lessons of the Russian War had been the complete superiority of open earthwork batteries over the type of stone casemates that were built. Yet the Royal Commission recommended stone casemates that were as much hostage to improved artillery as the *Warrior*'s $4\frac{1}{2}$-inch iron belt.

During the first two years of his second administration Palmerston gave considerable attention to naval matters. The forts issue aside, he proved to be far better attuned to the naval service than Somerset. It was Palmerston who noted that Admiral Dundas was 'a heavy sailer and not quite alive to the necessity of keeping up with other people'.[37] Occasionally the Prime Minister fell prey to the type of lurid alarmism that had brought on the 1859 invasion scare, seeing French designs for a major war behind improved coal stocks in the West Indies and the issue of revolvers.[38] Somerset, on the other hand, was assisted in his deliberations by several influential 'experts' on naval matters; in consequence his decisions were less clear cut. He continued work on wooden battleships after the majority had decided that they were obsolete, largely to satisfy Palmerston. He built small, inferior ironclads in response to Lord Clarence Paget's brusque advocacy, despite the opinion of Walker against such misguided economies. Paget was also responsible for the damning condemnation of Walker on the floor of the House of Commons, which caused the Surveyor to tender his resignation. Finally Somerset concurred in the building of large-scale fortifications that took money away from the Navy and damaged its prestige. Dividing the cake so many times indicated at the very least a lack of will-power and can hardly be graced with the description of a policy. Only Walker had a long-term policy, largely because he was content to follow the frenetic efforts of the French, rather than taking the lead in any area of naval technology. In a period of such uncertainty his rational approach

Sail plan and general arrangement of the French ironclad frigate
La Gloire, the first seagoing armoured warship.
From Admiral Paris' 'Souvenirs de Marine'

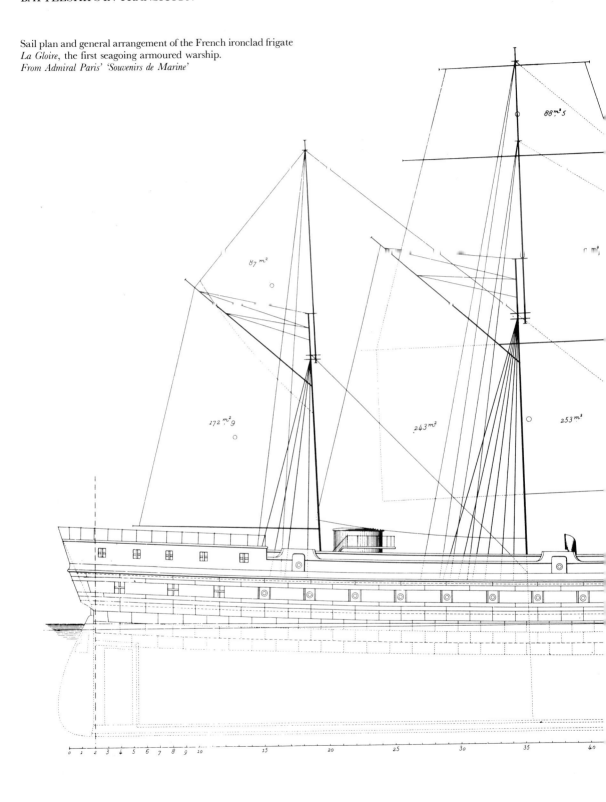

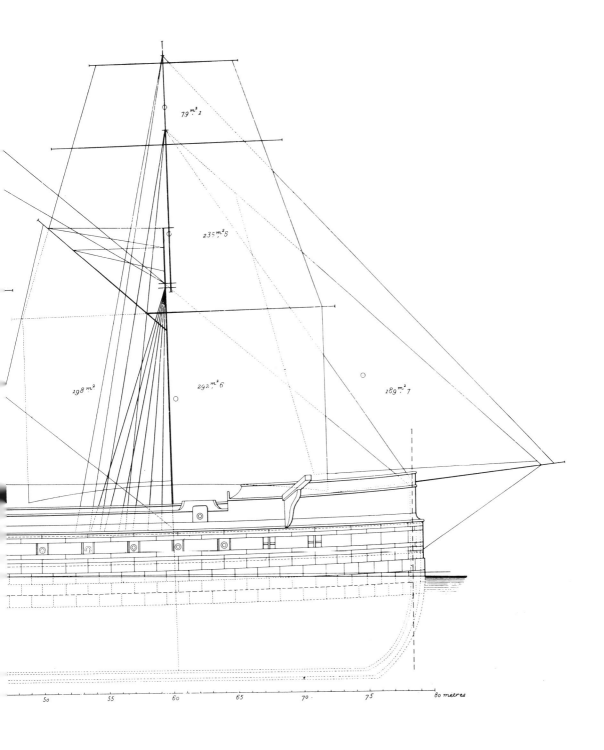

$79\,{}^{m^2}\!.1$

$235\,{}^{m^2}\!.8$

$198\,m^2$

$292\,{}^{m^2}\!.6$

$189\,{}^{m^2}\!.7$

50   55   60   65   70   75   80 metres

was the only one that offered both safety and relative economy. On 7 February 1861 Walker resigned from his office, which had been renamed that of Controller in the preceeding year. He was replaced by Rear-Admiral Sir Robert Spencer Robinson. By this stage Palmerston was advocating cutting down and armouring the last sailing battleships, rather than reducing the number of steam battleships.[39] In April the Commons vote on Lindsay's motion calling for an end to the construction of wooden capital ships marked the end of the steam battleship.[40]

Having reached parity with France in wooden battleships Somerset, on the advice of the Controller, favoured completing the *Bulwark* class ships as ironclads.[41] Seven ships of this class were eventually converted, the two most advanced, the *Bulwark* and *Robust*, being retained on the stocks until August 1872,[42] by which time they were of no value even if converted into ironclads. Three more ships of this class that had not been laid down, the *Blake*, *Kent* and *Pitt*, were finally abandoned in 1863.[43] The *Royal Sovereign*, 120, was cut down to the main deck and fitted with four of Cowper-Coles' turrets to test their suitability for use on wooden ships. However the desire of Palmerston to keep a powerful second fleet of wooden ships prevented any widespread programme to convert existing ships. John

Henwood prepared a scheme to convert the *Duncan*, 101, into a fully rigged ship with two turrets, but this was categorically rejected by the Controller's Department.[44] Robinson did have plans prepared for the *Bulwark* to be converted into a twin turret breastwork monitor but they were never used. As Edward Reed pointed out this was a wise policy as they would have been inferior to, and yet more costly than, iron-hulled ships built from scratch.[45] Robinson did not share Reed's views and misguidedly favoured wooden-hulled ironclads on grounds of strength and economy.[46]

By the end of 1864 Spencer Robinson, while advocating further ironclad construction, considered that the number of wooden battleships required for the reserve was only eight, the number already used for Coastguard duties. In this role they served as depots for reserves of seamen and as readily available warships. He also advocated recalling all those on foreign stations and replacing them with a new type of ironclad frigate[47] but the consistent failure of attempts to create a useful small armoured ship ensured that the wooden steam

Bermuda harbour in late 1862. The ship in the right foreground is the station flagship *Nile*, to her left is the *Aboukir*, and to the right the second flagship *Edgar* and the ill-fated *Conqueror*. *National Maritime Museum*

The *Prince Consort* (ex-*Triumph*), a *Bulwark* class ship completed as a broadside ironclad.
Conway Picture Library

battleship served for another half decade on the distant stations.

One year later the Board approved a proposal to spend an average of £22,000 each on the repair of six wooden ships: the *Hero*, *Agamemnon*, *James Watt*, *Victor Emmanuel*, *Renown* and *St Jean d'Acre* would then be available as an effective reserve.[48] This work was not carried out, so that two years later only the ten Coastguard ships were considered available for war service inside three months: *Duncan*, *St George*, *Royal George*, *Frederick William*, *Donegal*, *Revenge*, *Irresistible*, *Lion*, *Pembroke* and *Trafalgar*.[49] Even so the First Lord, Henry Corry, declared that wooden ships were still worth including in any fleet action. To support his contention he advanced the opinions of the American Admiral Farragut and the lessons of the Battle of Lissa.[50] The ships he had in mind were the best of the two-deckers: *Anson*, *Atlas*, *Defiance*, *Renown*, *Revenge*, *Donegal*, *Duncan* and *Gibraltar*; with the frigates *Undaunted*, *Newcastle*, *Doris*, *Orlando*, *Mersey*, *Ariadne*, *Galatea*, *Liffey*, *Phoebe*, *Forte* and *Glasgow*.

In the event no significant work was carried out on any of these ships, even those on Coastguard duty being allowed to rot away. Lindsay's motion had brought an end to all major work on wooden battleships. Their last public appearances came at the 1867 Spithead Review, which included the *Victoria*, *Donegal*, *Duncan*, *Revenge*, *Irresistible*, *Lion*, *St George*, and *Royal George*[51]; and the cruise of the Reserve Fleet in 1869, in which the *Donegal*, *Duncan*, *Royal George*, *St George* and *Trafalgar* took part.

THE IRONCLAD ERA

The first ironclads were massed in the Channel, reflecting the invasion scare that had brought about their construction. Even there however, the flagship was still the wooden two-decker *Edgar*, a fact that served to emphasize the poor manoeuvrability of the ironclads. In the Mediterranean the first British ironclads were the *Caledonia* class converted two-deckers that arrived in 1865. The Commander-in-Chief on this station between 1860 and 1863 was Vice-Admiral Sir William Fanshawe Martin. Martin's pre-eminence as a fleet Admiral – he was almost alone in having considered the tactical impact of steam – ensured that he spent much of his time in ship-handling exercises. During his three-year term he developed the basic principles of steam ship handling that were to remain in use until the

end of the Victorian Navy. Only his diplomatic duties, notably those arising out of the unification of Italy, interrupted this work. However his tactics were reliant upon a precision of movement that could not have been achieved in action. At the same time Martin advocated reducing the upper deck armament of the ships, adding ventilators and improving the pumping arrangements.[52] It was largely at Martin's insistence that the upper deck batteries of those wooden ships that remained in commission were improved by replacing the two 68-pounders and six 32-pounders with a pair of 110-pounder and a pair of 40-pounder Armstrong breech-loading rifles.[53] The only ship to use them in action, the *Conqueror* (ex-*Waterloo*) at Shimonoseki in 1862, found them more of a danger than a benefit.

The delicate breech mechanism of the Armstrong did not take kindly to the type of maintenance normally given to muzzle-loading smooth bores. Many were ruined after firing only a few shots.

The other major fleet of the early 1860s, the North American and West Indies squadron under Rear-Admiral Sir Alexander Milne, actually came close to war. Relations between Britain and the Northern States during the American Civil War were strained close to breaking point by the '*Trent* affair'. Immediately afterwards Milne was heavily reinforced. In the event of war it was realised that Canada could not be defended, so it would be necessary to put pressure on the Northern states by blockade. By early 1862 Milne had 9 battleships and 7 frigates, including the *Mersey* and *Orlando*. A year

While Milne watched the Northern forces he also had to be aware of the French expedition to Mexico. Having placed the Austrian Archduke Maximilian on the throne, Louis Napoleon was obliged to send a large army out to support him. This was transported in a fleet of 17 disarmed steam battleships escorted by the ironclad *Normandie*. Milne sent the *St George* to observe the French activity at Veracruz, while the *Sans Pareil* brought out a party of Marines to guard British interests at that port. The only notable naval event of this embarrassing fiasco for the French was a severe outbreak of Yellow Fever on the *Normandie* which killed at least 200 men.[54]

The real end of the wooden steam battleship came with the rapid decline of the French challenge after 1865, a trend reinforced by the temporary halt in French construction after the Franco-Prussian War of 1870–71. The block obsolecence of her wooden-hulled ironclads left the Royal Navy pre-eminent. In consequence Britain had no need for the large number of wooden ships that remained, the more so as they would cost a small fortune to maintain. The last steam battleship in full commission was the *Rodney* on the China Station, which returned home in 1871. Thereafter the steam battleships performed a variety of subsidiary functions – the *Victor Emmanuel* even won a battle honour for her part in the 1875 Ashanti War, despite being used as a troopship. The *London* became the depot for the anti-slavery patrol based at Zanzibar, while others filled a variety of harbour roles, notably as training ships.

In the 1860s two steam battleships were lost. The new 101-gun two-decker *Conqueror* was wrecked on Rhum Key, to the west of Jamaica, on 29 December 1861 through an error of navigation. The old *Waterloo* was given her name, both to hide the embarrassment of her loss and to avoid the name Waterloo causing offence to the French. The last of the converted ships, the *Bombay*, caught fire and blew up off Montevideo on 22 December 1864 apparently from an accident in the spirit room.[55]

later the crisis had passed and he retained only his flagship, the *Nile*, and 5 smaller frigates. Throughout the period of crisis Milne had kept his battlefleet at Bermuda, for despite its small harbour it proved to be the ideal base for observing the Northern blockade of the South. However Milne remained uncertain what he could do with the battleships, even if war did break out. He found them unequal to the weather off the American coast in winter, too deep for blockading and quite useless against modern coastal batteries. Once he felt secure Milne called for them to be replaced with frigates and corvettes. Somerset then stationed the first four ironclads at Lisbon, so that they would be available for service in the Channel or the West Indies if it proved necessary.

Model of the *Howe*.
Science Museum

The *Rodney*, the last wooden steam battleship to remain in full commission – as flagship of the China station until 1870.
Royal Naval Museum

6. Tactics and Technology

THE DEVELOPMENT OF STEAM TACTICS

The Baltic Fleet of 1854 was the first squadron with more than four steam battleships, and the first with a steam flagship. Within and without the fleet there was a considerable difference of opinion as to the tactical impact of steam assistance. At the Admiralty Alexander Milne, hardly a reactionary, prepared a standing order to the effect that steam was not to be used in action, from the danger of damage to the boilers or the screw being fouled by broken rigging.[1] Napier, who had attempted to use steam in battle in 1833 and had often practised using steam frigates to tow sail of the line, would have nothing to do with Milne's appreciation. Realising that coal smoke would add to the great pall of gun smoke that obscured every major

The ironclad *Royal Oak* shows the general appearance of the converted *Bulwark* class ships. She was the first to be completed (in 1863) and is shown here with canvas ventilators rigged, sometime before 1866.
Conway Picture Library

engagement, he instructed his captains to look for opportunities to rake the enemy. He was well aware that any system of tactics must break down once battle was joined.[2] Napier's captains realised the value of steam but their suggestions reflected the tight discipline of the peacetime evolutionary squadron rather than fleet action. Henry Codrington of the *Royal George* proposed a very complex tactic whereby the steam fleet would run from the Russians and then suddenly double on them.[3] As Napier well knew, his ill-trained fleet would have found such a plan impossible to execute,

87

since maintaining cruising order was difficult enough. This dichotomy between Napier and Codrington underlay the hesitant development of steam tactics during the period of the wooden steam battlefleet.

The two schools held radically different ideas on the contribution that steam would make to tactical problems. Napier had no time for formal systems, and his views reflected the application of a genius for war and long experience. He was committed to the doctrine of close-range action as the only method of securing complete victory, and this dominated his perception of steam tactics. He wanted to use the new-found independence of steam to simplify the tactical niceties of forcing close action on an unwilling foe. Other commentators lacked Napier's talent and this was made glaringly obvious by the formalised tactics that they proposed. Their complex evolutions were excellent training in seamanship with the new motive power and helped officers to come to terms with its possibilities, but as plans to win a sea battle they were little short of farcical.

William Fanshawe Martin, credited with the invention of serious steam tactics by Geoffrey Hornby, spent the Russian War as Captain of Portsmouth Dockyard. He did not go to sea again until he took command of the Mediterranean Fleet in 1860.[4] Hornby noted that his plans were too complex for the heterogeneous fleet of steam battleships with varying levels of performance. His captains could not adjust their speed to maintain station under steam with the facility of earlier, sailing, days and Martin spent much of his time attending to the basic control of steam warships in close order.[5] Elements of his plan had been evolved while serving as Senior Naval Lord during the second Derby administration and reflected labour at a desk, rather than on the quarterdeck. Considering his important role in the evolution of the steam battleship this lapse into paper schemes was curious. Sir Howard Douglas realised the advantages of a gunnery platform that was independent of the wind and called for an *en echelon* battle order.[6] While this looked excellent on paper, especially with diagrams to show the broadside arcs of fire that could be exploited, it could never have been used at sea. George Biddlecombe, Master of the Baltic Fleet in 1854, had proposed a similar tactic even before the

These and following pages: the ironclad *Caledonia* in dock at Malta. Laid down as a *Bulwark* class steam battleship she was cut down and lengthened into an ironclad frigate.
Conway Picture Library

general adoption of steam.[7]

The only officer who actually prepared to take a fleet of steam battleships into action was Napier. His instructions to the captains of the steam battleships ignored any formal system of tactics. He realised that no plan prepared before an action could hope to meet all eventualities, and that the captains would be better served by a set of general instruc-

tions that covered the gun charges to be used and the principles by which their actions should be governed. Basically the steam ships should use their advantage over the Russian sailing ships to secure positions from which they could rake. As Napier realised, fleet actions soon degenerated into a confused mêlée, and his instructions reminded his captains how to make the best of such a situation. His tactics were based on two themes, simplicity and speed. He relied on the superior gunnery of the Royal Navy to provide the decisive edge in battle. Without the acid test of combat it is impossible to judge the efficacy of the rival systems, but the history of the ironclad era points to the conspicuous success of simple, practical tactics outlined before the battle, notably those of Tegettoff at Lissa.[8] The rival systems of detailed evolution smelt too much of the lamp and were many years in advance of naval technology. The steam battleship destroyed the relative uniformity of movement that had been possessed by the sailing fleets, perhaps forever, and rendered the fleet far more difficult to control. This was no time for making tactics more complex, rather it was time for Napier's wise appreciation of the independent movement given by steam. With a general direction that relied on the fighting spirit and ability of the captains for its implementation, it would be possible to achieve great results.

At no time during the career of the wooden steam battleship did the Royal Navy ever employ a squadron of ships that were in any way uniform in performance under sail or steam. All the fleets combined new and converted ships. While this served to emphasize the varying levels of performance within the battlefleet it also precluded any system of tactics that was not based on the performance of the weakest ship – usually a Symondite 80. Only a fleet of ships with similar steaming power could make the best use of steam and only a fleet of new ships could demonstrate the full advantages of the steam battleship. As a result the only formation that was considered for combat in this period was the line of battle. It was not until the pace of naval technological advance had slowed down and squadrons of almost equal ships could be assembled that any significant tactical advances could be made.

Therefore, beyond providing an ability to operate independently of the wind, steam did not advance tactical development during the brief life of the wooden steam battleship. While Admiral Sir William Martin was drilling the last great wooden battlefleet into something approaching the precision of the sailing manoeuvres he had used for the 1850 frigate trials off Lisbon, the ironclads in the Channel were demonstrating that the days of evolutions under sail were over.

THE WOODEN STEAM BATTLESHIP AND THE EVOLUTION OF NAVAL ARMAMENTS

Many commentators have dismissed the wooden steam battleship as an anachronistic hiatus between the final development of the sailing ship and the coming of the ironclad. However, this view is misguided. During the period 1847 to 1860 there were several developments that made the ironclad possible and the wooden ship unsuitable: firstly, this period witnessed a great leap forward in the design of large marine steam engines, primarily due to the demands made by the very large steam-powered warship; secondly, the wooden battleship was far stronger than has been supposed. Relying on a letter from Lord Auckland to Napier, Bartlett declares,

these vast wooden ships had something of the dinosaur about them. They bore immense armaments, but until the introduction of the ironclad there was no balance between their offensive and defensive qualities. Well handled ships of the line could destroy each other in almost as many minutes as their predecessors had taken hours at Trafalgar.[9]

The offensive power to which Bartlett referred was that of the shell-firing gun. J P Baxter, basing his argument on the Battle of Hampton Roads, in which two becalmed wooden frigates were overwhelmed by the close-range fire of the *Merrimac*, declared that this was the end of the wooden fighting ship. He ignored the performance of the Austrian steam battleship *Kaiser* at the Battle of Lissa in 1866, when this supposedly useless ship ranged across the confused battlefield, ramming an Italian ironclad and taking several 300-pounder shells at point blank range.[10] While she lost her bowsprit and foremast, and was set on fire she was ready for action the following day. Similarly when the allied fleet bombarded Sebastopol on 17 October 1854, it was exposed to a heavy fire of shells and red-hot shot for several hours. Although all the

heavy ships were hit – some over two hundred times – only one, the *Albion* required the assistance of a dockyard.

It must be emphasized that for all the startling results of shell *practice* the effects of shell-fire in combat were unimpressive. At Sinope, six Russian sail of the line, three of them 120-gun ships, took several hours to destroy a similar number of frigates and corvettes at close range: with tolerable gunnery equal results would have been expected from solid shot practice. The friction of warfare ensured that the perfect conditions of Vincennes and Shoeburyness were not reproduced at sea. Therefore the shell guns of the 1840s and 1850s did not revolutionize naval warfare. A combination of inaccurate artillery and poor fuses ensured that they never lived up to the expectations of the French artillerist Paixhans. He had brought them to the fore in the early 1820s as a method of humbling the naval might of Britain.

Similarly the move towards extremely heavy artillery in the late 1850s did not provide as great an advance in *effective* fighting power as the performance of the guns would have suggested. This development was lead by the Americans, who had always favoured heavier calibres. They had adopted the solid shot 42-pounder for the lower decks of their ships of the line just as the Royal Navy was abandoning it. They considered that its superior performance outweighed the disadvantages of excessive weight and a reduced rate of fire that had influenced the British decision. When they abandoned the ship of the line the Americans adopted heavy shell guns as the principal armament of their strikingly large frigates and corvettes of the 1840s. This was a major shift in ship design, relying on a smaller number of guns with increased range and striking power. It reached a climax with the huge steam corvette *Niagara* which carried only 12 guns, although each was of 11-inch calibre. Such an armament would have proved disastrous in a battle on the high seas, but the American Civil war was fought almost entirely in coastal waters that did not expose the handling difficulties caused by attempting to use very heavy guns on board small wooden ships.

The greater experience of the British and French was reflected in their refusal to follow the American lead. Neither navy ever mounted very heavy guns on their wooden battleships, save as pivot guns in the Royal Navy. The opinion of Walker on this point (see Appendix II) repays study. Even so the decks of the British ships required continual re-planking in consequence of the destruction wrought by the recoil of their artillery. New guns with reduced windage shot further and recoiled harder, and the use of heavier guns in the first decade of the ironclad era exposed the folly of the American practice. At Lissa the artillery of the Italian ironclad fleet was generally so large and cumbersome that the ill-trained crews were unable to hit any targets that were not almost touching their ship. By contrast the smaller, but more numerous batteries of the Austrian ships scored many hits, one proving fatal to the *Palestro* while the others helped to confuse and paralyse the Italians. The success of Tegetthoff's ramming tactics demonstrated the folly of monster artillery. It would be another twenty years before the full potential of very heavy guns could be exploited. Before that they were a folly that should never have survived the searching examination of Lissa.

Walker did concede that a gun deck battery of 95cwt guns would be an advantage, but the 58cwt 32-pounder was also a very powerful gun and unless the ships were built far bigger there would have to be an unacceptable reduction in the number carried. When added to the reduced rate of fire, this would have adversely affected the combat-worthiness of the ship. The only criticism that can be levelled at the armament policy established by Walker, Rear-Admiral Berkeley and Captain Sir Thomas Maitland (Captain of the *Excellent*) in 1854 lay in the number of shell guns called for. On the upper deck Walker crammed as many 45cwt 32-pounders as he could, without placing them on the gangways around the waist. They proved to be dangerous and inefficient, so the number was later reduced. On the gun deck his desire to keep the considerable advantages of a single calibre battery caused him to fit 8-inch shell guns throughout. Sir

The *Marlborough*, 1855, flagship of Sir William Fanshawe Martin during her long career as a receiving ship at Portsmouth. *Conway Picture Library*

The Austrian steam battleship *Kaiser* on the day after the Battle of Lissa, 21 July 1866.
Conway Picture Library

Howard Douglas was not the only artillerist who would have preferred to see more 32-pounders in the place of almost all the shell guns. Once it had been established that the 32-pounder was safe for use with red-hot shot there was no requirement for more than half a dozen shell guns. Red-hot shot was far more dangerous to wooden ships and in fitting so many shell guns Walker followed his opinion that the Royal Navy would continue to seek close action, as it had done for the preceding two hundred years. In view of the outstanding gunnery displayed at Acre in 1840, a direct result of the training given on board the *Excellent*, it would have been better to have relied on the greater precision of British guns and gunners to disable enemy ships before accepting the levelling risks of close action. French armament policy was, in this respect, better balanced, since they never fitted complete decks of shell guns.

Throughout the brief life of the wooden steam battleship the greatest danger that such ships were exposed to was that of fire and the most effective method of setting fire to a wooden ship was to use red-hot shot. The only European battleship destroyed in action between 1815 and 1860 was the Danish *Christian VIII*, at the Battle of the Eckern-fjorde in 1849. J P Baxter claims that she was blown up by shell fire,[11] but the eye-witness account of Colonel Stevens states that red-hot shot were the fatal missiles.[12] The use of red-hot shot from warships is not reliably documented before the Greek War of Independence, but the history of these projectiles is rather longer. The general principle was simple. A solid shot would be heated in a furnace until it reached a dull red heat. It would then be quickly loaded into the gun on top of an extra, soaked, wad. The gun would then be fired as quickly as possible, to prevent a spontaneous combustion and before the shot cooled. The intention was that the shot should lodge in the timbers of an enemy warship, causing a fire that could only be extinguished by removing the shot. However, there were problems with this type of projectile. The shot had to be clean otherwise it might jam in the bore. It had to be removed from the furnace at the right moment, or it would lose its shape. Also the gun had to be of the strongest construction, since the heated shot was larger which increased the breech pressure.

The use of red-hot shot at the siege of Gibraltar, 1780–82, was only resorted to when the situation became grave. In 1826 Captain Abney Hastings of the Greek steamer *Karteria* used them to the consternation of the Turks and Egyptians. At the Battle of Eckernfjorde four 18-pounder guns firing hot shot set fire to the *Christian VIII*. Two factors ensured that red-hot shot would come to prominence during the Russian War: firstly modern artillery was capable of enduring this hitherto dangerous practice; secondly the widespread use of steam gave many ships a suitable furnace. On 28 February 1854 all steamships in the Royal Navy were equipped with a pair of red-hot shot bearers. This was the first official recognition of the practice in British service. Some time later precise instructions were issued, and only solid shot 32-pounders were considered safe.[13]

During the Russian War, 1854–56, the Royal Navy had few opportunities to fire red-hot shot, but the Russians made widespread use of them, from their fortresses on the Black Sea and Baltic. At the bombardment of Odessa on 22 April 1854 the French steamer *Vauban* was set on fire by this method, and she was forced to retire and find assistance to remove the shot. Before Sebastopol on 17 October 1854 the inshore squadron under Rear-Admiral Lyons was badly mauled by hot shot; the *Albion* was set afire twice and the *Queen* three times. In the Baltic several small craft were hit, notably the *Penelope* at Bomarsund on 10 August, but being of light scantling the shot passed through her side and caused no more damage than unheated rounds.

The Russian War gave an immeasurable impetus to the development of naval science. This was most noticeable in the areas of offence and defence, which was a direct consequence of the ships-against-forts nature of the naval war. One of the most unusual ideas was a refinement of the red-hot shot. A Mr Martin developed a hollow shell lined with hair that could be filled with molten iron. Despite the dangers inherent in the preparation of such projectiles, notably the need for a furnace, this weapon was taken up by the Board of Ordnance and issued for service. Trials at Shoeburyness on 4 April 1857

illustrated the great improvement that the molten iron shell offered over the red-hot shot. The hot shot left a regular wound channel in a target representing the upper works of a ship of the line, the shell a jagged hole of considerable size.[14] A year later the Secretary at War, General Peel, suggested that means be set in hand to place a furnace on board a warship. Walker and Anderson, the Inspector of Machinery at the Royal Arsenal, were directed to confer on this issue.[15] Within the Navy news of the power of the molten iron shell spread rapidly. Alexander Milne, Third Naval Lord declared,

the new mode of firing molten iron, so vastly more destructive than either red-hot shot or shells, will prevent our present ships from attacking any fort which had the means of firing this terrific and fearful missile, which at once sets fire to wood or any other inflamable material.[16]

Captain Hewlett, of the gunnery training ship *Excellent*, had been involved with the molten iron shell from an early stage. He wrote to the Commander-in-Chief at Portsmouth calling for the adoption of the shells for shipboard service:

I cannot finish this letter without again expressing my opinion as to the immense importance of these shells when engaged in tolerable close action, for if they are so efficient in their incendiary qualities against empty ships, what must the effect be when the molten iron is scattered among stores and other combustible matter in ships prepared for sea.[17]

Hewlett realised that there would be problems using the shells at sea, but he considered that their advantages outweighed any difficulty. He recommended that they be used aboard line of battle ships, especially those prepared for coast defence, and the new 'iron-cased frigates'. The War Office was impressed by Hewlett's advocacy, but decided to restrict the application of furnaces to iron frigates and coast defence ships; the *Warrior* still carries her furnace.[18]

The bombardment of Sebastopol demonstrated that red-hot shot was a greater danger to wooden battleships than shell-fire, and the damage to the *Kaiser* at Lissa was not so marked as to refute that experience.[19] The effect of the molten iron shell, with the additional incendiary effect produced by the spread of liquid iron, would have proved more dangerous to a wooden ship than any explosive shell. On a crowded battery deck loose powder and ready-use charges must have taken fire and caused the violent destruction of the ship.

John Scott-Russell, the noted iron shipbuilder, considered that it was this missile that signalled 'the conclusive defeat of wooden walls, and the certain inauguration of iron'.[20] With the failure of the heaviest shells to destroy the *Kaiser* it must be concluded that the molten iron shell played a vital role in the rapid decline of the wooden warship. It offered iron warships a telling advantage over their wooden predecessors, since iron armour could defeat such shells, but a wooden hull was open to attack at any point.

For all its advantages the molten iron shell was never used in action. Indeed many regarded it as underhand and felt a moral revulsion at the idea of covering men with molten metal, but these fine feelings did not extend so far as to preclude blowing them to atoms with explosive shells. The non-appearance of the molten iron shell in combat led Henry Corry, the First Lord of the Admiralty in 1867, to suggest that the wooden battleship could still play a vital part in any future naval battle. However the Royal Navy had no need of wooden ships to maintain their superiority over the French after 1865 and so they were neither repaired nor re-armed. It was these two factors that denied them an effective career after 1865.

The *Queen*.
Royal Naval Museum

7. The Wooden Steam Battleship and Naval Policy

THE NAVAL POLICY OF FRANCE

After the humiliation of 1840, when her naval weakness had forced a backdown over Syria, naval policy became a major political issue in France. The law of 95 millions introduced by Thiers in 1846 laid down the basis for expansion, but the fall of the Orleans Monarchy in 1848 prevented this growth from taking place.

The principal fighting strength of the French battle line throughout the last thirty years of the wooden warship lay in a large number of large two-deckers of 90 or 100 guns. These vessels had been designed in the early 1820s by a Committee composed of Messrs Sané, Rolland, Laird, Tupinier and de Lamorienciere. Ships on these lines continued to be laid down until 1848, although the majority were commenced before 1830. By 1850 the design was

The *Ville de Nantes*, 1858, a typical French new construction two-decker of the *Algesiras* class.
Musée de la Marine

outdated, being too small to carry a full battery of long guns; they all mounted carronades on the upper deck.[1] Similarly their sailing properties were decidedly inferior to the older French ships, demonstrating the folly of laying down so many ships on untried lines.[2]

In France the policy of leaving ships on the stocks until they were required was taken to even greater lengths than in Britain. The majority of the large two-deckers were held in this state. Consequently by the end of the sailing era the majority of the 26 sail afloat were old ships, many dating back to the First Empire. In the dockyards the position was little better as all the ways were taken up with the old-

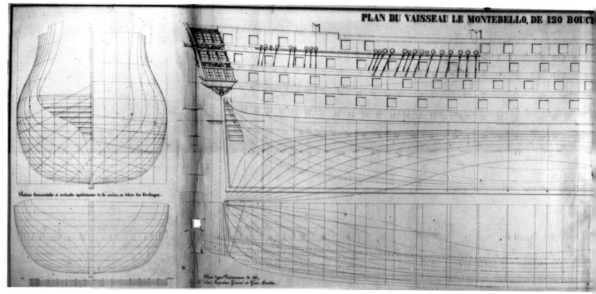

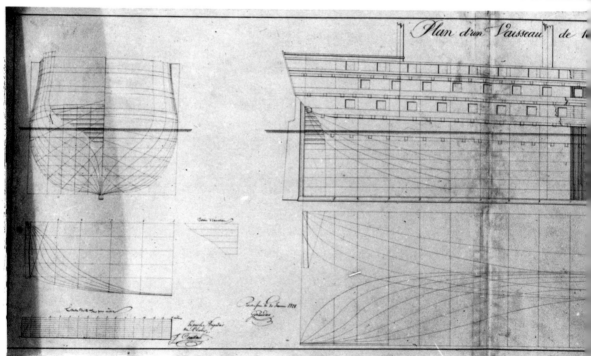

The *Turenne*, typical of the French two-deckers of the post-1815 period.
Musée de la Marine

style two-deckers and even older three-deckers. The obvious solution, given the inevitability of steam, lay in converting all suitable ships into steamers. The success of Dupuy de Lôme's *Le Napoléon* indicated that new ships would be decidedly

superior to such modifications, but it would be impossible to create a large fleet by any other method.

French efforts to pioneer steam-powered warships, for all the threatening language of the Prince de Joinville, were largely unsuccessful. Their principal effect was to stimulate the technically more advanced British to develop their own steam

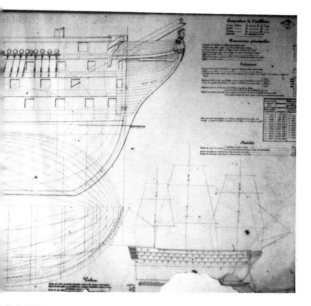

Outboard profile of the *Montebello* before the addition of a small engine made her a limited steam battleship.
Musée de la Marine

navy; not until *Le Napoléon* did the French build a steam warship that could be considered even a match for contemporary British designs. Dupuy de Lôme was a student of all that was best in British commercial shipbuilding. His visit of 1840 and his correspondence with John Scott-Russell were all used to advantage when he designed the pioneering *Le Napoléon* and *La Gloire*. These ships were the more

remarkable for having been built in France which did not have the powerful industrial base for marine technology that existed in Britain.

Louis Napoleon's Presidency of the Second Republic was marked by low naval estimates.[3] However a Parliamentary enquiry of 1851 recommended that the number of ships of the line afloat should be increased from 24 to 30. Soon afterwards all suitable sail of the line were ordered to be converted for the screw. Those building were speeded up, and further vessels after *Le Napoléon* were ordered. The last were intended to escort the army while on board the steam transports already built.[4]

The policy implemented after the founding of the Second Empire by the *coup d'etat* of December 1851 was governed by the need of the Bonapartist clique to gain popularity. During the last months of Louis Napoleon's Presidency it had been decided to spend far more money on the Navy, and it was this, rather than the technical stimulus provided by Dupuy de Lôme that brought the French into a construction race with Britain. One of Louis Napoleon's potential rivals for the Presidency had been the Prince de Joinville, son of King Louis Phillipe. Joinville had earned much public acclaim by his determined advocacy of naval expansion and the programme of 1851 was intended to use the obvious popularity of naval expenditure to help Louis Napoleon's cause. There was no strategic rationale for increasing the size of the French Navy, the new policy being no more than an electioneering device.

In the beginning of the new navy under the July Monarchy it was still largely an instrument of prestige, whose ambition was mere equality in numbers and superiority in technical skill to England.

Napoleon III further developed these characteristics; while French economic interests continued to expand, the prestige character of the navy developed even faster. The French had sold their liberties for prosperity and glory, and though the navy was a valuable accessory to the former, it became, under Napoleon III, the principal instrument of the latter.[5]

The French construction effort of the period 1851 to 1860 can be divided into three separate parts. Ten totally new steam battleships were built, the three-decker 130-gun *Le Bretagne* and eight more

*Napoléon*s. Four incomplete two-deckers were converted along the lines of *Le Napoléon*, while the remaining 25 ships were classed as *Vaisseau Mixte*, or auxiliary screw steamers. These inferior ships were essentially part of a numbers race that began in 1851 and was codified in 1855. Their conversions were not so comprehensive as those carried out on the large British ships and being smaller they offered less scope and consequently had to sacrifice part of their armament. Walker under-played this fact in his evidence for the Derby Committee, suggesting that the Symondite 80s he had converted were inferior to any of the French ships. In fact six of the French ships had started life as 00 gun ships no bigger than their British contemporaries although the French 90-gun ships had all been laid down as 100-gun sailing ships. They were regarded as cumbersome, ugly, old-fashioned and overcrowded by British seamen.[6]

By reproducing *Le Napoléon* the French dropped behind Britain in the overall performance of their steam battleships. The early British ships, such as the *Agamemnon*, were auxiliary steamers, while *Le Napoléon* was a sail-assisted steamer designed for the optimum performance under steam. Later British ships were fitted with more powerful machinery, but they were always designed with a view to preserving their sailing qualities and never matched the reported speed of ships like *L'Algesiras*, which was claimed to have exceeded 14 knots. However, as the bulk of both fleets was made up of slow converted ships the small extra speed of the French new construction was of little or no tactical value. Walker concentrated on improving the military qualities of his ships, providing additional space for working the guns, improved stowage and increased structural strength. His policy of only using the best materials and adopting a lengthy construction period gave his ships additional strength and longevity. Overall the British ships, both new and converted, were superior cruising and fighting men-of-war.

Napoleon III's naval policy was designed to fulfil a double function. He had decided that his uncle's great mistake had been to incur the undying enmity of Britain, and therefore he attempted to act in concert with the British. At the same time it was essential for the maintenance of his position in France that he was not seen to be submitting the will of France to her old rival. By building a large navy he could convince the French of his independence, and the British of his power. Like Tirpitz fifty years later he considered that he could make France so strong at sea that, in combination with one or two other powers she could equal Britain. If that were the case Britain would then be forced to pay heed to his will, the French Navy being a foe too dangerous to be challenged lightly.

In Britain the reaction was to approach panic on several occasions, notably in 1859. Throughout this

The *Charlemagne*, 1851.
Musée de la Marine

The *Castiglione*, 1860, a major conversion effected on the stocks to produce a similar ship to the *Algesiras* class new construction. *Musée de la Marine*

period Walker provided a consistent policy based on the need to keep the Royal Navy superior to the French. He considered that Napoleon would make a decisive bid for the command of the Channel that had eluded his uncle in 1805.[7] Good evidence to support this view came from the French policy of converting every seaworthy ship of the line, accepting major limitations on stowage that must have precluded operations outside European waters. The whole policy based on wooden steamships, made law in 1855, failed when Britain maintained equality in numbers and a decisive superiority in quality. No more wooden battleships were laid down after 1855.

While J P Baxter states that the French decision to build the first ironclad, *La Gloire*, taken by the Conseil de Travaux in February 1857 was a result of the new power of rifled artillery,[8] there were other factors of greater significance. By early 1857 the French attempt to build a wooden steam battlefleet to match that of Britain had failed. Despite the tremendous efforts of 1855 and 1856 the British remained ahead, and had far more new ships under construction. The French felt it necessary to continue the naval race, mainly to preserve the brilliant position secured at the Peace of Paris in 1856.[9]

Therefore it was essential that a new line be tried. Paixhans had advocated shell guns, and de Joinville steamships to give France the lead in naval affairs. Similarly opinion in France at this period favoured the ironclad. Yet even as he began his programme Dupuy de Lôme must have realised that this latest attempt would prove as chimerical as the last. The evolution of the ironclad in France, as befits the efforts of a technologically backward nation, was far less revolutionary than the response of Britain: *La Gloire* was still a wooden battleship, despite her armour plate, whereas the *Warrior* marked a clean break with the traditions of the wooden ship. In France the lack of foundry capacity enabled de Lôme to build only one iron-hulled ship, *La Couronne*; the others, like their 90-gun half-sisters, were built of unseasoned timber and decayed rapidly. In view of Britain's massive lead in iron shipbuilding experience and resources the introduction of the ironclad was to be even more of a disastrous naval policy than that of the race in wooden steam battleships.

Inboard profile, body plan and sections of the *Algesiras*.

Fig. 2

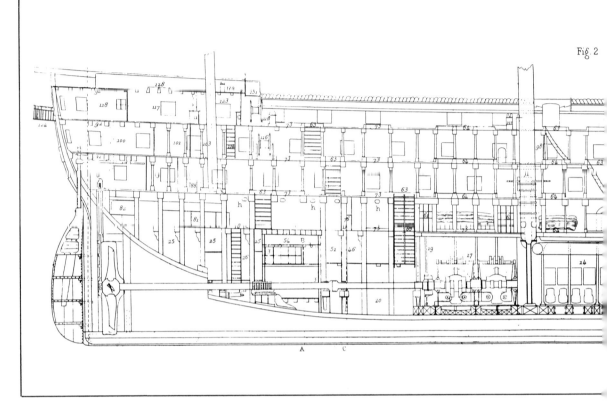

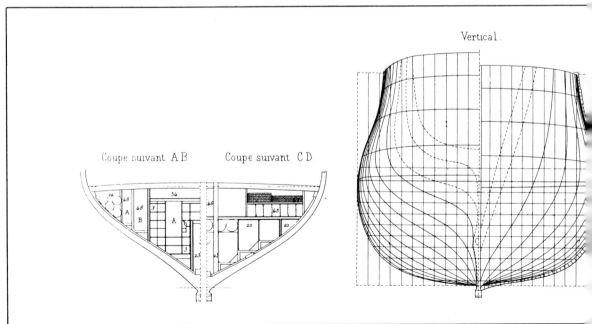

Vertical.

Coupe suivant A B   Coupe suivant C D

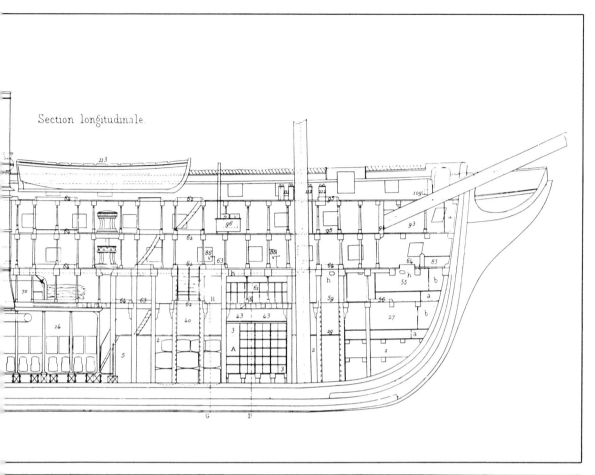

Section longitudinale.

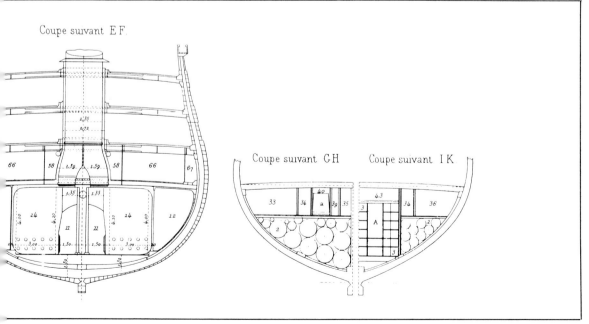

Coupe suivant E F.

Coupe suivant G H

Coupe suivant I K

Deck plans of the *Algesiras*.

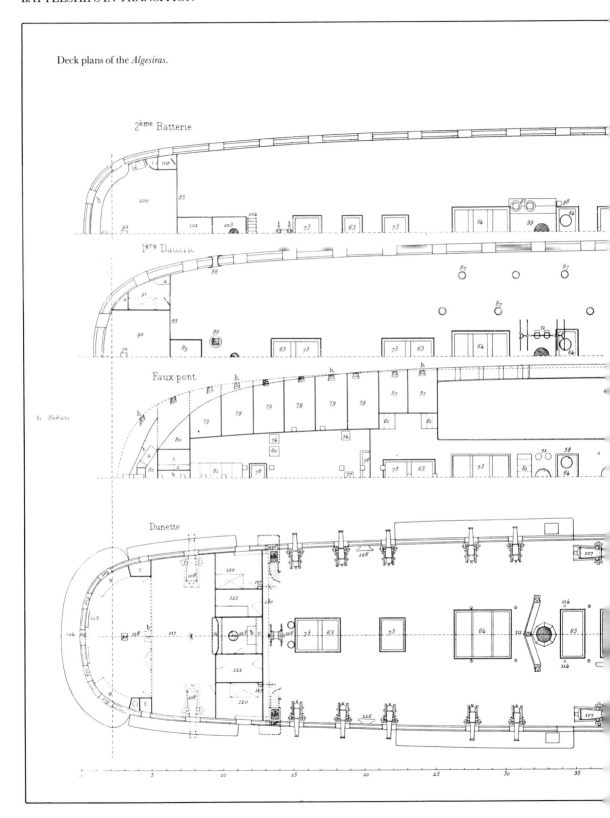

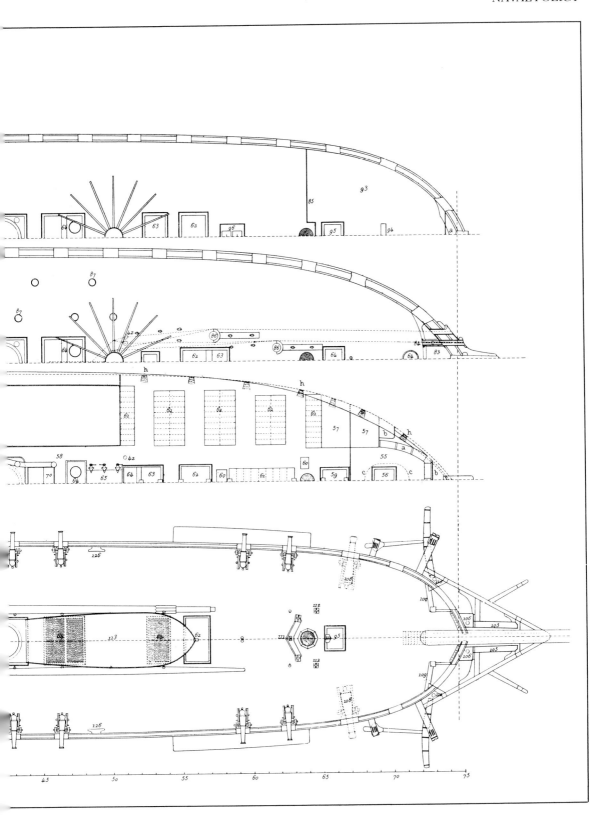

The machinery of the *Algesiras*: transverse and (following page) longitudinal sections.
'Algesiras' drawings from Admiral Paris' 'Souvenirs de Marine'

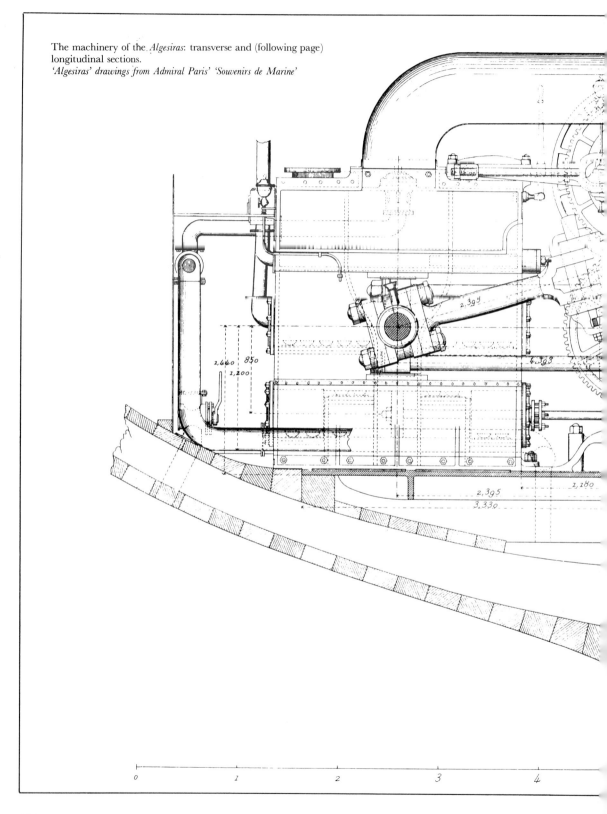

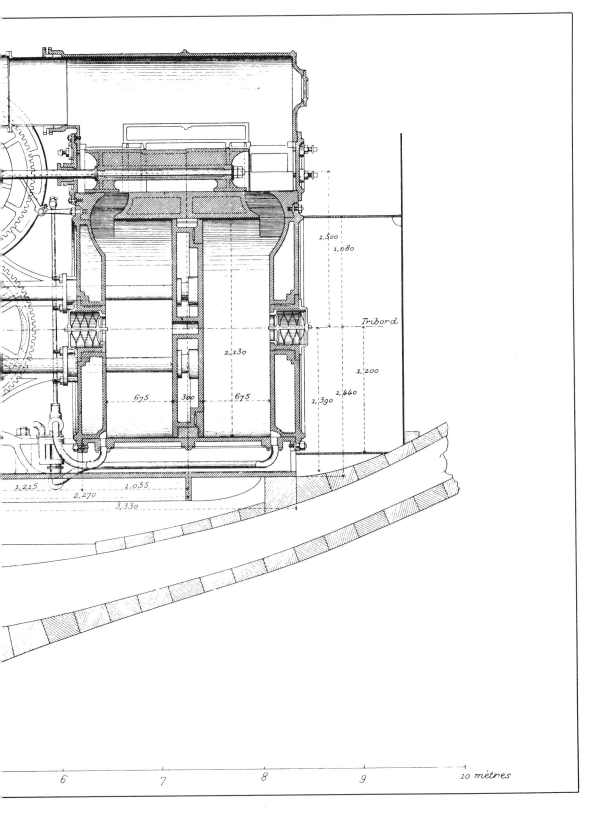

1,500
1,680

Tribord

2,130

1,200

675   300   675

1,440

1,390

1,215   1,055

2,270

3,330

6   7   8   9   10 mètres

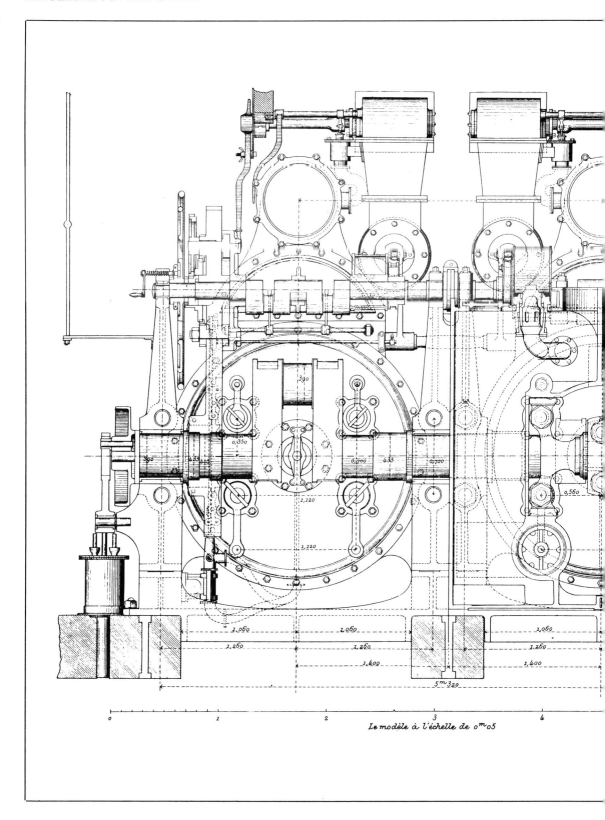

Le modèle à l'échelle de 0ᵐ05

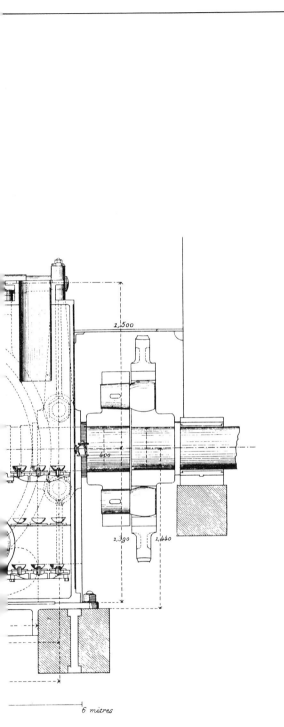

Toulon, le 1er Janvier 1855   Signe Dupuy de Lome.

The *Algesiras* as a training ship in 1885.
Musée de la Marine

Napoleon III's naval policy was hastily adopted, ill-considered and ultimately futile. Britain refused to be dictated to by any power, and almost the entire population considered the French Navy to be an affront to the dignity of the nation that must be answered. Therefore every French move was countered, the greater wealth and resources of Britain making Walker's policy of reacting rather than acting the ideal measure. The French had nothing left to counter the British, save some new technical innovation like the shell gun, the steam engine or armour plate, all of which had favoured Britain. France could not compete, and in view of his underlying policy Napoleon III's naval expansion was futile and counter-productive. Along with the whole Bonapartist prestige system that had nurtured it, the Navy declined in the last five years before the Franco-Prussian War of 1870–71 ended

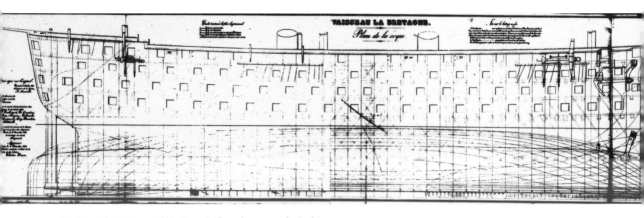

Profile of the *Bretagne*, 1855, the only French purpose-built three-decked steam battleship.
Musée de la Marine

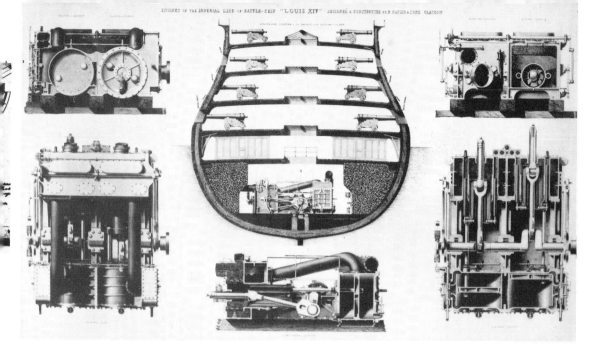

The machinery of the *Louis XIV* built by Robert Napier of Glasgow, a startling indication of the degree to which the French Navy was dependant upon outside sources of supply.
National Maritime Museum

The *Louis XIV* leaving Brest. The considerable tumblehome and old-fashioned stern galleries of this ship, laid down in 1811 can be seen and indicate a very limited conversion.
Conway Picture Library

the Empire.[10] The Second Empire spent three billion francs on the Navy between 1851 and 1869, much of it by extraordinary credit and Presidential decree. The underlying reasons for this were power, national prestige, imperial prestige and only lastly legitimate defence.[11]

THE REST OF THE WORLD

The rapid development and the even more rapid obsolescence of the wooden steam battleship were entirely due to the naval rivalry between Britain and France. The Russian War demonstrated the advantages of the type and the value of the ironclad that would replace them only five years later. In consequence the lesser naval powers had very little time in which to adopt the new type before it was overtaken by the more thorough ironclad revolution. While Britain and France prepared 100 steam battleships, between them the rest of the world could only muster 18: Russia had 9, Turkey 4, Sweden 2 and Austria, Denmark and Italy 1 each.

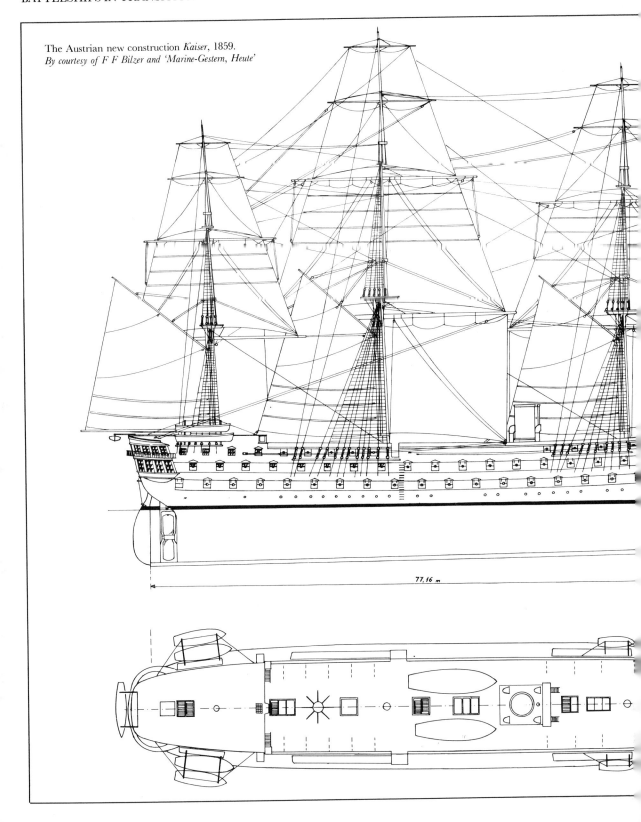

The Austrian new construction *Kaiser*, 1859.
By courtesy of F F Bilzer and 'Marine-Gestern, Heute'

77,16 m

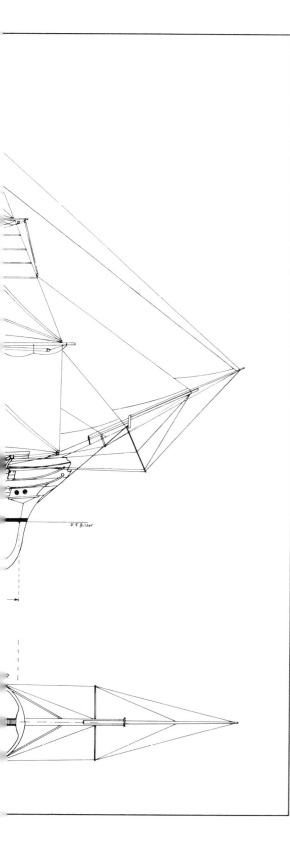

RUSSIA

The Russian Navy began work on screw battleships in 1852 with the conversion of the incomplete *Orel* and the older *Vyborg*. Hitherto the Russians had been able to maintain a large battlefleet in both the Baltic and the Black Sea, but their inability to produce efficient steam engines forced them to rely on outside assistance. Five of their nine completed ships had British-built machinery, the remainder being supplied by the foreign-owned firms of Nobel and Baird from their St Petersburg works (after two sets ordered from Robert Napier had been seized by the British Government on the outbreak of the war of 1854-56). The Russian attempt to build steam battleships was basically an imitation of British and French developments. The success of the Anglo-French invasion of the Baltic in 1854 and 1855 stimulated further work on the steam battlefleet. The *Vyborg* was completed in 1855 and did attempt to leave Cronstadt harbour, but was forced back by the British *Colossus* on 2 September.[12] Further ships were completed, and after the war British engines were once more available, but the whole policy was negated by the low quality of Russian design and shipbuilding. The ships were old-fashioned and built or modified with badly prepared timber. Consequently they were soon ravaged by dry rot and had very brief active careers, their machinery being removed and used in the early Russian ironclads. Under the terms of the Treaty of Paris (1856), the Black Sea was demilitarised. Russia was allowed to complete the two steam battleships then building at Nicolaiev, the three-deckers *Cesarevic* and *Sinop* and send them to the Baltic. These two ships were so badly constructed that even before reaching Cronstadt to receive their engines they were forced to put into Malta and Gibraltar respectively for emergency repairs, their hulls being strapped together with cables and their crews exhausted from constant pumping.[13]

The death of Csar Nicholas I in March 1855 removed the one man in Russia who believed in the battlefleet. His successor Alexander II left naval policy to his brother Grand Duke Constantine. After 1857 Constantine introduced a new policy based on coast defence ironclads and cruisers. He realised that a battlefleet trapped at the eastern end of the Baltic would always be as utterly useless as it had been in 1854-55 and concentrated on preparing for a campaign of long-range commerce raiding.[14] It was not until the 1890s that Russia built another battlefleet.

TURKEY

The Turkish fleet of the nineteenth century was not renowned either for its efficiency or its loyalty, although it had been restored to a relative degree of strength by Walker during his term as Commander in-Chief after the humiliations of 1840. During the Russian War the Turkish ships played an honourable part, displaying great courage at Sinope. After the war two Turkish ships were fitted with British engines, the *Peik-i-Zafer* at Devonport. Two more were built for the screw. With the disappearance of the Russian fleet from the Black Sea the exact purpose of these ships is uncertain, although the fact that British engines were used points to the great Turkish loan raised in Britain having been at least partly responsible for this new round of naval construction.

THE UNITED STATES

In the United States the wooden battleship had been considered outmoded even before the steam battleship was developed. American constructors in this period concentrated on extremely large frigates and corvettes with very heavy guns and some steam power. These experimental vessels were as large as British steam Second Rate 90-gun ships and could only have been justified by a speed in excess of any steam battleship and a battery capable of accurate fire at extreme ranges. In service the corvette *Niagara* and her half-sisters of the *Merrimack* frigate class made only 11 and 9½ knots respectively, while their heavy Dahlgren guns were almost impossible to use in a seaway.[15] Until the perfection of rifled artillery very long range fire was only useful for shore bombardment. Smooth bore shell-fire was inaccurate beyond 1200 yards, and that of solid shot outside 2000 yards, so therefore the best system for hitting a ship with smooth bore guns remained the heavy broadside of the battleship.

The design concept of the American ships was many years ahead of the technology necessary to bring it to perfection. Furthermore no reasonable explanation has been offered as to the design function of these ships. Bennett merely observed that they were the superior of any war vessel when

completed,[16] although he did not say whether he included steam battleships in this category. While the *Merrimack* impressed many British observers it was realised that she was only a large sailing ship, her engines being quite unequal to the task of driving her at combat speeds for any length of time.[17] Walker's reply, the *Mersey* and *Orlando*, were superior in every respect, but they too had no role: they were too fast for the line of battle and too powerful for cruising. The abject poverty of contemporary tactics must have precluded any attempt to use them as a fast division.

AUSTRIA

In 1848, faced with the challenge of Sardinia and the effective loss of Venice, the Austrian Navy had begun to be reconstructed on modern lines under the leadership of Archduke Ferdinand Max, later Emperor of Mexico. The new fleet was to be entirely steam-driven, the prototype frigate *Radetzky* being built at Wigram's yard on the Thames between 1852 and 1854. After visits to Britain in the autumn of 1853 and to the allied fleet off Constantinople in January 1854 the Austrians decided to build a steam battleship along the lines of the *Agamemnon*, which they regarded as the best ship in the world. At first the Austrians attempted to have the ship built in Britain, at a private yard on the Thames.[18] However nothing came of this, largely because in November 1854, when the approach was made, Walker was engaging all the spare capacity of the Thames yards to build gunboats. Attempts were then made to build the ship in New York, but in 1856 the Emperor called for the ship to be built at Pola.

The *Kaiser* was originally to be a copy of the *Agamemnon* in every detail. Plans of the British ship are supposed to have been obtained with the *Radetzky*, but it would appear more likely that they were handed over towards the end of the Russian War in an attempt to win Austrian help in finishing that struggle. Following the spectacular performance of the French new construction, especially the new *Algesiras*, which reputedly made 14 knots, the *Kaiser* was enlarged and fitted with engines of 800nhp on the Maudslay system in place of the 600nhp Penn type engines copied from the *Agamemnon*.

After initial signs of weakness caused by hurried completion the *Kaiser* proved to be a very durable

The *Stockholm* late in her career while serving as a training ship.
Statens Sjöhistoriska Museum

The *Carl XIV Johan*, a simple and unsatisfactory conversion.
Statens Sjöhistoriska Museum

ship, not only sustaining considerable damage at Lissa, but in 1870 she was converted into an ironclad and remained afloat until 1918. Her two claims to distinction were that she was the only wooden steam battleship to take part in a naval battle and that she was the only first class new construction built outside Britain and France.

The Austrians projected a half-sister for the *Kaiser* in 1859, but the 101-gun two-decker *Österreich* was never laid down.[19]

SWEDEN AND DENMARK

The Swedes and the Danes were very forcibly struck by the performance of the British steam battleships during the Baltic campaigns of 1854 and 1855. Realising that Russia would also prepare such ships they secured considerable technical assistance from Britain in late 1855, largely as a facet of the negotiations for an alliance against Russia that marked the last stages of the Russian War.

In Sweden the old *Carl XIV Johan* was converted into a blockship with engines of only 300nhp; she was unsuccessful and was demolished in 1867. The incomplete *Stockholm* was given a more thorough conversion and engines of 800nhp. However she was rapidly reduced to subsidiary duties.

The Danes converted the *Skjold*, but after service in the Schleswig-Holstein War of 1864 she was reduced to the reserve and laid up. In 1876 she was sold to a London shipbreaker. The battleships of the Scandinavian navies had always been built on very different lines to those of the British and French. They were generally smaller and proportionally shallower than ships intended to serve on the broad oceans. This hull-form was even less suitable for steam propulsion than that of Sir William Symonds' design. Furthermore the entirely defensive needs of both countries were better served by monitors, a type that all the Baltic navies adopted at a very early stage.

ITALY

The single Italian steam battleship, the *Re Galantuomo*, was laid down by the Neapolitan Navy as the sailing ship *Monarca*. After the conquest of Naples by Garibaldi she was converted into a screw steamer using plans already prepared by the Neapolitans. When the Kingdom of the Two Sicilies was annexed by the Kingdom of Italy she was renamed. On completion she was found to be capable of only 4 knots, although a four-bladed propeller pushed this up to 8. Despite numerous modifications she was never satisfactory, a point emphasized by a passage to New York in 1864. In the War of 1866 she was restricted to cruising the lower reaches of the Adriatic. The ship was broken up in 1875.

Like the majority of the conversions carried out by the minor navies the *Re Galantuomo* was ill suited to the demands of screw propulsion and her conversion was badly executed.

The Italian steam battleship *Re Galantuomo*.
Museo Storico Navale, Venice

Conclusion

The wooden steam battleship was an essential stage in the development of the modern warship that separated the ship of the line from the ironclad. The radical improvements in wooden shipbuilding introduced by Sir Robert Seppings released designers from the limitations hitherto set by the size of individual timbers and curved pieces. These had prevented any significant increase in the size of wooden battleships during the preceding two centuries. However the use of steam machinery placed new demands on the fabric of the ship, both by its weight and the vibration, and by the requirement for longer and finer hulls. While these problems were overcome it was at the cost of a marked increase in the amount of timber and iron worked into the later ships. This pushed up the weight of the ship and brought fresh demands for increased engine power. With the *Bulwark* class of 1859 the large wooden steamship reached its effective limits. There was no method of improving performance that would not be cancelled out by the additional weight penalty it imposed. The inability of the *Mersey* class frigates to maintain 14 knots when the best steam battleships exceeded 13 demonstrated the limits of the single-expansion and trunk engines then available. Furthermore the same technological revolution that provided the steam power for the wooden steam battleships also provided the rifled artillery, iron hulls and armour plate that ensured their rapid supercession.

Without the stimulus of the Russian War and the French challenge the type would not have progressed so quickly, or become obsolete so rapidly. Yet it is hard to see any direction in which the wooden battleship might have progressed beyond the *Bulwark*. The *Mersey* class frigates had already demonstrated that larger wooden ships were not practical. Similarly Walker and many others would not countenance any significant reduction in the number of guns carried by battleships. Walker built the *Mersey* and similar huge frigates to carry the new very heavy guns, keeping the battleships armed for a close-range action. Later Spencer Robinson was to suggest that if the *Caledonia* class ironclads were to fail they could be completed as heavily armed, but unarmoured, frigates. This suggestion was categorically rejected by the Admiralty.[1] The great frigates built in Britain, Russia and the United States proved to be short-lived and unsatisfactory. They were no faster than the best steam battleships and far more expensive to maintain. The iron-hulled *Inconstant* was superior in every respect.

Basically wood was no longer a suitable material for the construction of warships that had to carry a concentrated weight of engines and artillery. However the inevitable change was delayed until the adoption of armour because the hull of a wooden battleship was far better protection than the thin plating of an iron ship. The disastrous experience of the 1845 iron frigates convinced many that iron would never be used, and until the idea of fitting armour plates onto an iron hull with a substantial wooden backing was adopted, wooden-hulled ironclads proved far stronger than those built entirely of iron. After this breakthrough the iron hull quickly demonstrated its ability to support more armour than a similar wooden structure. The ease of internal subdivision was also an important factor. Furthermore, the Russian War and the invasion scares of the 1850s had consumed enormous quantities of good quality timber, so by 1860 timber prices were rising to levels that made iron ships considerably cheaper.

The British wooden steam battleship was essentially the creation of Captain Sir Baldwin Walker, Surveyor of the Navy from 1848 to 1861.

Walker was a conservative and methodical man, and in an age of dramatic innovation he remained firmly wedded to the doctrine of evolution rather than revolution in naval technology; and reaction rather than action in construction policy. Consequently the steam battleship developed toward a peak in Britain, whereas in France the genius of de Lôme produced *Le Napoléon* without any experience of large screw steamships. While the French were content to repeat their original design, Walker's later creations surpassed it in all save speed under steam. The construction policy adopted by Walker was to counter French moves, taking care not to initiate any new developments. He relied on the excellence of British construction methods and machinery to provide better ships, converting old ships to maintain equality in numbers rather than rush build new types.

On 11 March 1859 Captain Lord Clarence Paget spoke in the House of Commons, complaining of the wasteful alterations made to ships then building. This accusation was entirely without foundation: indeed only one steam battleship had been altered after being laid down, the *Howe* having an extra 15 feet worked into her bow at a cost of less than £100. Writing in *The Mechanic's Magazine* one week later Edward Reed declared that this was a personal attack on the Surveyor and defended him stoutly:

> Sir Baldwin Walker has really managed the Navy with unexampled judgement. We are quite aware that he has been most efficiently and constantly aided by a scientific staff of naval architects whose equals as a body are nowhere to be found out of Government service. None would, we believe, assert this more cordially than the Surveyor himself. And herein lies one of his greatest merits. Instead of thinking lightly of, and disregarding, the counsels of his scientific assistants, and enforcing crotchets of his own in place of their science – as ninety-nine Admirals out of a hundred would have done – he has given full scope to the skill of those gentlemen, and has anxiously supplemented it by his own great knowledge and experience as a seaman. The consequence is, we have a navy which, whatever defects it may possess, it superior to all the navies of the world – a navy which is, as we have before said, and as Sir Charles Wood repeated on Friday last, 'the embodiment of all such sound and well-tested improvements as have hitherto been found compatible with the purposes for which ships of war are designed'.

Coming from so brilliant and opinionated a man as Edward Reed that was praise of the highest order. Walker was no genius, but his solid administration of the Navy's *matériel* and his ability to win the political backing that was essential to carry out his programmes places him in the front rank of Admiralty administrators. His control of the steam battlefleet, both the overall policy and the development of the ships, and his direction of the nation's shipbuilding resources during the later stages of the Russian War were of the highest quality and enabled the Royal Navy to meet its most serious challenges between 1815 and 1906 and overcome them in the most comprehensive manner.

Of the First Lords of the period Auckland, Graham and Pakington were outstanding in their separate ways. Auckland was an early advocate of the steam battleship, and he selected Walker to carry through the necessary policy. Graham, for all his Benthamite parsimony with public funds, supported the gradual build up of the steam battlefleet by new construction, even at the height of the Russian War when such ships were considered irrelevant. Pakington had to stand against the leaders of his party, Derby and Disraeli, to win support for Walker's 1858–59 Emergency programme. Baring, Wood and Somerset were indecisive and politically weak. Wood at least had the good sense to leave Walker in control of a policy that he crippled by allowing the government to starve it of funds. Somerset by contrast listened to every naval 'expert' he could find, especially his Prime Minister, and in consequence had no naval policy worthy of the title.

It was Palmerston who dominated naval policy during his second administration. In 1859–60 he favoured achieving a two-power standard in wooden battleships, despite the fact that the French had not laid down any since 1855 and had ceased to consider such work after 1857. Once this had been obtained he shifted from merely advocating keeping pace with the French ironclad programme to creating a two-power standard in that class as well. He followed those policies with his great fortifications debate, which alienated both Gladstone and a large part of the Navy.

By late 1860 Walker was increasingly out of tune with Palmerston's government; he favoured further large ironclads while the Admiralty wanted smaller, and more economical ships. Somerset's weakness in the face of Paget's brusque advocacy forced Walker to build four inferior ships, the *Defence* and *Resistance*, *Hector* and *Valiant*. It must also have been largely responsible for Walker's resignation. Fortunately his successor, Spencer Robinson, was cast in a more combative mould and refused to let anyone interfere with his policies.

The invasion scare of 1859–60, was, as Cobden declared at the time, completely unnecessary. The French programmes were well known, having been established by the laws of 1855 and 1857. However the weak post-war administration of Sir Charles Wood had denied Walker the funds to maintain his programmes. This allowed the worst case analyses of 1858–59 to paint a grim picture. In fact the French were never capable of staging an invasion, and the figures given for their fleet were always far greater than the real force that they could deploy.

The British had ignored the French Navy for two years and were surprised by its advances, notably the completion of the Cherbourg Arsenal and Dockyard, the number of steam battleships available, and the pioneering moves toward an ironclad fleet. The panic was stimulated by fears of a Franco-Russian alliance. The French developments were answered by the 1858–59 emergency programme, the *Warrior* and 'Palmerston's follies'. The forts were quite unnecessary, given the obvious success of British construction policy in building up to a two-power standard in wooden ships while keeping pace with French ironclad developments.

Tables: Particulars of Wooden Steam Battleships

BRITISH NAVAL ARTILLERY

ARMSTRONG BREECH-LOADING RIFLES

100-pounder (later rated at 110-pounder): 7in bore, weight 82cwt, length 10ft.

40 pounder: 3¼in bore, weight 18cwt.

These guns were mounted on the upper decks of active battleships from 1860. They offered improved range and accuracy over the older guns. However they proved fragile in service and the larger gun could not match the shattering power of the 95cwt smooth bore gun, either against wooden or iron targets.

MUZZLE-LOADING SMOOTH BORES

68-pounder: solid shot gun, 8in bore, weight 95cwt, length 10ft. Used as a pivot gun on all larger battleships. The most powerful gun in service during the 1850s and still used well into the ironclad era.

32-pounder: 6in bore, weight 56 and later 58cwt, length 9ft 6in. The standard armament on the main decks of the wooden battleships from 1840 onward. Accurate up to 2000 yards.

32-pounder: 6in bore, weight 45 or 42cwt, length 8ft 6in or 8ft. A lighter pattern for the upper decks. Was less powerful but faster firing, due to the greater ease of handling a lighter gun. The shorter gun would be used on small or converted ships that lacked stability or displacement.

32-pounder: 6in bore, weight 25cwt, length 6ft. Upper deck guns for the *Duke of Wellington*, little better than the 17cwt carronades fitted to the *Royal George*. Not suitable for fleet action in the 1850s in view of the improved range and accuracy of the heavier solid shot guns and shell guns.

Note: all the 6in bore 32-pounders could also be used to fire shells.

10in shell gun: weight 84cwt, (later strengthened and increased to 85cwt and then 86cwt), length 9ft 4in. Used on the blockships. In service little more effective than the 8in gun.

8in shell gun: weight 65cwt, length 9ft. The standard gun deck armament of the 1850s, accurate up to 1200 yards. Like all shell guns of the period its destructive power was considerably over-rated and in service problems with the fuse prevented many shells from detonating.

8in shell gun: weight 52cwt, length 8ft. Used on the *Sans Pareil*; a lighter pattern for frigates, not very effective.

Note: all the shell guns could also fire 8in hollow shot, but these lacked the shattering power of solid shot and were only used against weak targets.

By the 1840s British advances in metallurgy, casting and boring ensured that these guns were generally superior to similar pieces cast abroad.

REGULATION ARMAMENT OF A FRENCH 90-GUN SHIP

Gun Deck	4–22cm (8.65in) shell guns of 73cwt.
	28–30-pounder (equivalent to 36-pounder in English weight) of 58cwt.
Main Deck	6–22cm of 73cwt.
	28–30-pounder of 49cwt.
Upper Deck	24–30-pounder of approximately 30cwt.

The armament of the French ships was inferior to that of their British contemporaries, most notably from their inability to carry effective long guns on the upper deck. The principal reason for this was their lack of beam. They sacrificed stability for the extra knot they could reach on trial while in the light condition. Furthermore they did not carry anything that could match the performance of the British 68-pounder 95cwt gun for range, accuracy or striking power. In 1855 the regulation armament was modified to include 18–36-pounders on the gun deck and 2–50-pounders on the upper deck in a total of 90 guns.

ABBREVIATIONS USED IN THE TABLES

Tonnage:	builder's old measurement figure used by the Royal Navy throughout the wooden steam battleship era.
Displacement:	the modern system of computation.
Dimensions:	oa=overall length, kl=length of keel for tonnage, ext=extreme breadth. The fourth figure is the depth in hold.
Machinery:	nhp=nominal horse power, ihp=indicated horse power, kts=knots.
Masts:	the figures are length from the main deck to the lower trestle trees and extreme diameter.
Armament:	GD=gun deck, MdD=middle deck (three-deckers only), MD=main deck, UD=upper deck.
Career:	TS=training ship.
Builder:	almost all British vessels were constructed in the royal dockyards, only a few of the early blockships being built in merchant yards; in these cases the company and location are given.

THE ROYAL NAVY (NEW CONSTRUCTION)

VICTORIA class *121 guns*

Tonnage:	*Victoria* 4116t, *Howe* 4236t
Displacement:	6959t (*Victoria*)
Dimensions:	260ft oa, 221ft kl x 60ft ext x 25ft 10in. Draught 23ft 7in fwd, 25ft 9in aft. (*Howe* 260ft, 222ft x 61ft 6in x 26ft 4in)
Machinery:	1000nhp. *Victoria* (Maudslay), trials in Stokes Bay 5.7.60, 4403ihp = 11.797kts. *Howe* (Penn), trials at Plymouth 1.6.61 (not masted or stored) 4564ihp = 13.565kts
Masts:	Main 67ft x 42in; Fore 61ft x 40in; Mizzen 51ft 6in x 26in
Armament:	GD 32–8in/65cwt; MdD 30–8in/65cwt; MD 32–32pdr/58cwt; UD 26–32pdr/42cwt, 1–68pdr/95cwt. Total 121 guns of 354 tons
Complement:	1000

Name	Builder	Ordered	Laid down	Launched	Cost
VICTORIA	Portsmouth	6.1.55	1.4.56	12.11.59	£150,578
HOWE	Pembroke	6.1.55	10.3.56	7.3.60	£147,465

Class. The original draught of an as yet unnamed ship dated November 1854. The altered dimensions of the *Howe* are dated April 1858 and were intended to improve her lines by lengthening and fining out the bow. Both ships were exceptionally fast. The machinery of these ships was unique among the British steam battleships. They had eight boilers, four more than was normal, which were arranged in fours on either side of the engines. Consequently they had two funnels, one on each side of the mainmast, and were the only British ships so fitted. The hulls were heavily strapped with diagonal iron riders 5in wide and 1in thick. The size of their machinery caused the mainmast to be stepped on the Orlop Deck.

Careers. *Victoria* 1860-64 Portsmouth. 1864 Flagship Mediterranean Fleet, Vice-Admiral Smart, Captain Goodenough; 1865 Rear-Admiral Lord Clarence Paget, Captain Gardner. 1867 paid off. Sold 31 May 1893.

Howe No sea service, in reserve at Plymouth. 1885 renamed *Bulwark*. 1886 became the *Impregnable*, TS at Devonport; 1919 renamed *Bulwark*. Sold 1921.

SAINT JEAN D'ACRE *101 guns*

Tonnage:	3200t
Displacement:	5499t
Dimensions:	238ft oa, 202ft 5in kl x 55ft 4in ext x 25ft. Draught 23ft 6in fwd, 25ft 3in aft
Machinery:	600nhp (Penn). Trials in Stokes Bay 3.12.53, 2136ihp = 11.199kts
Masts:	Main 67ft x 40in; Fore 61ft x 37in; Mizzen 51ft 6in x 27in
Armament:	GD 20–8in/65cwt, 16–32pdr/56cwt; MD 8–8in/65cwt, 28–32pdr/56cwt; UD 28–32pdr/42cwt, 1–68pdr/95cwt (17.1.53; later as *Conqueror*)
Complement:	930

Name	Builder	Ordered	Laid down	Launched	Cost
SAINT JEAN D'ACRE	Devonport	15.2.51	6.51	23.3.53	£107,561

Class. Stretched *James Watt*, a successful experiment at producing a more powerful two-decked ship. Originally ordered as an *Albion* class sailing ship, but suspended in 1845 before being laid down; materials subsequently used for this totally new design. Originally intended to fit the ex-*Simoom* engines that were eventually used in the *Duke of Wellington*. The *Saint Jean D'Acre* being a new ship the use of new machinery identical to that of the *Agamemnon* was a wise step. Very highly regarded.

Career. 1853 Western Squadron, Captain Henry Keppel. 1854 Baltic Fleet. 1855 Black Sea Fleet, 1855 Captain King. 1856 Particular Service (conveying Earl Granville to the Coronation of Csar Alexander II at St Petersburg). 1857 paid off. 1859 Mediterranean Fleet, Captain Thompson. 1861 paid off. 1875 sold to Castle's shipbreakers at Charlton.

CONQUEROR class *101 guns*

Tonnage:	3224t
Displacement:	5720t
Dimensions:	240ft oa, 204ft 10in kl x 55ft 4in ext x 24ft 5in. Draught (*Conqueror*) 24ft 8in fwd, 26ft 4in aft
Machinery:	800nhp (Penn). *Conqueror* trials at Plymouth 12.6.56, 2812ihp = 10.806kts. *Donegal* trials at Plymouth 16.7.59, 3103ihp = 11.912kts
Masts:	As *Saint Jean D'Acre*
Armament:	GD 36-8in/65cwt; MD 36-32pdr/56cwt; UD 28-32pdr/42cwt, 1-68pds/95cwt (26.10.55)
Complement:	930

Name	Builder	Ordered	Laid down	Launched	Cost
CONQUEROR	Devonport	19.10.52	25.7.53	2.5.55	£91,244
DONEGAL	Devonport	27.12.54	27.9.55	23.9.58	£105,265

Class. Slightly elongated *Saint Jean D'Acre* with more powerful engines; plans dated 2 December 1852. These ships followed *Saint Jean D'Acre* at Devonport, all three being built on the same slipway. Captain Broadhead's report on the *Donegal* stated that she 'sails fast, is stiff, weatherly and very easy, steers well, is sure in stays – though slow from her great length', 'carries her ports very high and steams very fast'. Overall they were outstanding ships.

Careers. *Conqueror* commissioned 1856 for the Baltic Fleet, later Mediterranean Fleet, Captain Hastings Yelverton. 1859 Captain Clifford. 1860 Channel Fleet, Captain Southeby. 1861 North America and West Indies. Wrecked on Rum Key 2 December 1861 by an error of navigation.

Donegal. 1859 Liverpool, Captain Glanville. 1860 Channel Fleet, Captain Broadhead. 1861 Captain Sherard Osborn VC, North America and West Indies. 1862 paid off. 1865 Coastguard at Liverpool. 1870 Portsmouth. 1886 *Vernon* Torpedo TS. Sold 18 May 1925.

DUNCAN class *101 guns*

Tonnage:	3715t
Displacement:	5950t
Dimensions:	252ft oa, 213ft 9¼in kl x 58ft ext x 25ft 6in. Draught (*Gibraltar* without masts or stores) 18ft fwd, 22ft 6in aft
Machinery:	800nhp. *Duncan* (Penn) trials in Stokes Bay 7.8.60, 3428ihp = 13.338kts. *Gibraltar* (Maudslay) trials at Plymouth 17.4.61 (not masted or stored), 3494ihp = 12.48kts
Masts:	As *Saint Jean D'Acre*
Armament:	As *Conqueror*
Complement:	930

Name	Builder	Ordered	Laid down	Launched	Cost
DUNCAN	Portsmouth	29.11.56	2.5.57	13.12.59	£132,697
GIBRALTAR	Devonport	31.3.55	10.58	16.8.60	£130,235

Class. Longer and broader version of the *Conqueror*; plans dated 6 January 1857. The final statement of the British design process. The *Bulwark* class were identical hulls. Noticeably faster than the *Conquerors*. The *Duncan* was considered for conversion into a raised breastwork monitor with similar upperworks to the *Cerberus*; plans drawn by Edward Reed, January 1867. This conversion was more detailed than Henwood's *Bulwark* proposal of 1866, but it was not carried out for economic reasons.

Careers. *Duncan* 1865 Flagship North America and West Indies,

Vice-Admiral Hope, Captain Gibson. 1868 paid off. 1868-69 Coastguard, Leith. 1870-90 Sheerness. 1890 renamed *Pembroke*. 1895 receiving ship Chatham. 1905 *Tenedos II*. Sold in October 1910 for £7525.

Gibraltar 1863 Commissioned at Devonport, Captain Prevost. Last wooden steam battleship to commission as a private ship. 1864 Mediterranean Fleet, Captain Coote, 1866 paid off. 1867 Devonport, 1871 Belfast TS Committee. 1889 renamed *Grampian*. Sold 16 March 1899.

JAMES WATT class *91 guns*

Tonnage:	3085t (*James Watt* 3074t, *Hero* 3127t)
Displacement:	4614t (*Hero* 4765t)
Dimensions:	230ft 3in oa (*Hero* 234ft 3in), 193ft 3in kl (*James Watt* 194ft 7¼in, *Hero* 199ft 1¾in) x 55ft 4in ext x 24ft 6in. Draught 22ft 8in fwd, 23ft 11in aft (*Agamemnon*), 24ft fwd, 24ft 6in aft (*Hero*)
Machinery:	600nhp. *Agamemnon* (Penn) trials Stokes Bay 3.5.53, 2268ihp = 11.243kts. *James Watt* (Boulton & Watt, ex-*Vulcan*, iron screw frigate rebuilt 1854-55) trials Stokes Bay 30.3.55, 1543ihp - 9.361kts. *Victor Emmanuel* (Maudslay) trials Stokes Bay 28.11.56, 2424ihp - 11.922kts. *Edgar* (Maudslay) trials Thames 27.6.59, 2475ihp = 11.371kts. *Hero* (Maudslay) trials Thames 5.11.58, 2662ihp = 11.707kts.
Masts:	As *Saint Jean D'Acre*
Armament:	GD 34-8in/65cwt; MD 34-32pdr/56cwt; UD 22-32pdr/45cwt, 1-68pdr/95cwt (3.7.52)
Complement:	860

Name	Builder	Ordered	Laid down	Launched	Cost
AGAMEMNON	Woolwich	25.8.49	11.49	8.52	£141,299
JAMES WATT	Pembroke	14.1.50	9.50	23.4.53	£79,837
VICTOR EMMANUEL (ex-*Repulse*)	Pembroke		16.5.53	27.9.55	£98,837
EDGAR	Woolwich		4.6.53	23.10.58	£103,807
HERO	Chatham		8.6.54	15.4.58	£93,106

Class. The original design was drawn up by John Edye in 1847 in direct response to the rumours of the ship laid down by Dupuy de Lôme that later became *Le Napoléon*. Originally an 80-gun ship; the *Agamemnon* plan is dated 28 June 1849, although at that stage she was intended to use secondhand engines of 780 or 400nhp. The final plan of the *James Watt* is dated 13 June 1850, and is still classed as an 80-gun ship. The high cost of the *Agamemnon* is a reflection of the exceptionally hurried nature of her construction. *Agamemnon* followed the *Ajax* and *Sans Pareil* in having her boilers abaft the mainmast, consequently she also had her funnel in this position. She was the only new construction so fitted and as a result steered badly when light forward. The *James Watt* was ruined by her unreliable machinery. Despite reconstructions during the winters of 1854-55 and 1855-56 it never equalled the performance of the new equipment fitted to her sisters.

The *Hero* was built to a modified draught with a finer bow and 4ft extra on the keel. The overall excellence of this design was confirmed by the retention of the same midsection for the enlarged *Renown* class.

Careers. *Agamemnon* Materials collected for an 80-gun ship, originally planned to be a sister of the *Cressy* from March 1842. Commissioned 1853, Captain T M C Symonds, son of the late Surveyor. 1854 Second Flagship Black Sea Fleet, Rear-Admiral Lyons, Captain Mends. Bombardment of Sebastopol. 1855 Captain Pasley as a private ship. 1857 laid the first (unsuccessful) Atlantic telegraph cable; selected because of her capacious fore

hold; 355 miles laid before it broke. 1858 July successful link up with the USS *Niagara* to complete the cable. 1859 Mediterranean Captain Hope. 1862 North America and West Indies. 1862 paid off. Sold 12 May 1870 for £10,181.

James Watt Originally materials collected for an 80-gun sailing ship, the *Audacious*, renamed 1847. 1854-55 Baltic Fleet, Captain Elliot. 1856 Devonport, Captain Anson, paid off. 1859 Channel fleet, Captain Codd. 1859 Mediterranean. 1862 paid off. Sold to Castle of Charlton 23 January 1875.

Victor Emmanuel Launched as the *Repulse*, but name changed on 4 December 1855 in honour of a visit to the ship by the King of Sardinia. 1858 Channel Fleet, Captain Willcox. 1859 Mediterranean Fleet, Captain Clifford. 1862 paid off. 1873-74 depot ship for the Ashanti campaign. 1875 receiving ship at Hong Kong. 1898 sold at Hong Kong.

Edgar 1858 Second Flagship Channel Fleet, Rear-Admiral Erskine, Captain Katon. 1859 Particular service. 1860 Channel Second Flagship, Erskine, Captain George Mends. 1862 Second Flagship North America and West Indies, Rear-Admiral Dacres. 1863 Second Flagship Mediterranean, Captain Foley. 1863 Flagship Channel Fleet, Captain Hornby. 1865 Captain Brandreth. 1866 paid off. 12 February 1870 engines removed, Quarantine ship at the Motherbank. 1904 sold for £5100.

Hero 1859 Channel Fleet, Captain George Seymour. 1860 Prince of Wales' visit to North America. 1861 Channel Fleet, Captain Ryder. 1862 North America and West Indies. 1862 paid off. Sold 20 June 1871 to Castle of Charlton for £10,416.

RENOWN class *91 guns*

Tonnage:	3318t
Displacement:	5500t
Dimensions:	244ft 9 in oa, 210ft kl x 55ft 4in ext x 24ft 6in. Draught 24ft fwd, 24ft 6in aft
Machinery:	800nhp. *Renown* (Penn) trials Stokes Bay 15.3.58, 3183ihp = 11.43kts. *Revenge* (Maudslay) trials Plymouth 14.2.60, 3249ihp = 11.53kts. *Atlas* (Penn) trials Thames 25.4.61 (not masted or stored), 3732ihp =13.022kts. *Anson* (Maudslay) trials Thames 24.6.61 (not rigged), 3,583ihp = 12.984kts
Masts:	As *Saint Jean D'Acre*
Armament:	GD 34–8in/65cwt; MD 36–32pdr/56cwt; UD 20–32pdr/45cwt, 1–68pdr/95cwt (19.12.56)
Complement:	860

Name	Builder	Ordered	Laid down	Launched	Cost
RENOWN	Chatham	7.12.54	20.12.54	28.3.57	£93,332
REVENGE	Pembroke	7.12.54	22.1.54	16.4.59	£98,583
ATLAS	Chatham	14.4.57	22.2.58	21.7.60	£115,860
ANSON	Woolwich	31.3.57	1.10.58	15.9.60	£121,086

Class. Originally to be of the *James Watt* class. First plan of the *Renown* and *Revenge* dated 7 December 1854. Walker had decided to lengthen the *James Watt* design both to improve the lines and to provide the space for more powerful machinery after his experience with the first new ships. The *Hero* marked the beginning of this development. The two active ships were always held in high regard. The delay between the commencement of the first and last pairs of ships can be explained by reference to the need to collect and season timber after the demands of the Russian War, and by the pressure of work in the royal dockyards. The *Atlas* and *Anson* were given a modified, finer stern run.

Careers. *Renown* 1857 fitted out at Sheerness, Captain Forbes. 1858 Channel Fleet, 1859 Mediterranean, 1861 paid off. Sold in 1870 to the Navy of the North German Confederacy as a gunnery TS and served until the 1890s; broken up in 1892.

Revenge 1861 Flagship of the Channel Fleet, Rear-Admiral Smart, Captain Fellowes. Second Flagship Mediterranean Fleet. 1863 Rear-Admiral Yelverton, Captain Foley. 1865 Coastguard, Pembroke. 1866 Coastguard, Devonport. 1869 Devonport. 1873 Flagship at Queenstown. 1886 TS at Queenstown. 1890 renamed *Empress* with Clyde Industrial TS Association. Sold 1 February 1923.

Atlas 1861–73 Sheerness. 1874 Chatham. 1884 Metropolitan Asylum District Hospital. Sold 1904.

Anson Renamed *Algiers* in 1883. Sold 1904.

The *Revenge* while flagship of the Channel Fleet 1861–62.
Imperial War Museum

DEFIANCE *91 guns*

Tonnage:	3475t
Displacement:	5700t
Dimensions:	254ft 9in oa, 219ft 11⅝in kl x 55ft 4in ext x 24ft 6in. Draught 24ft fwd, 24ft 6in aft.
Machinery:	800nhp (Maudslay). Trials Plymouth 5.2.62 (not masted or stored), 3550ihp = 11.884kts
Masts:	As *Saint Jean D'Acre*
Armament:	As *Renown*
Complement:	860

Name	Builder	Ordered	Laid down	Launched	Cost
DEFIANCE	Pembroke	17.6.55	20.9.58	27.3.61	£119,442

Class. Originally as *Atlas*; new plan prepared to show the lengthened bow 8 October 1858. From her trial speed this would appear to have been of no significant advantage, but her lack of sea service ensures that there can be no certainty in this matter.

The last ship to use John Edye's original *James Watt* midsection. **Career**. The last steam battleship to be launched in Britain. 1861 Devonport torpedo schoolship. Sold 20 June 1901.

BULWARK class *91 guns*

Dimensions:	As *Duncan*
Armament:	As *Renown* (except MD 36–32pdr/58cwt)
Complement:	860

Name	Builder	Laid down	Suspended	Converted	Cost
BULWARK	Chatham	8.3.59	7.3.61		
ROBUST	Devonport	31.10.59	12.3.61		
REPULSE	Woolwich	19.4.59		1866	
ZEALOUS	Pembroke	21.10.59		1864	
ROYAL ALFRED	Portsmouth	1.12.59		22.6.61	
ROYAL OAK	Chatham	1.5.60		3.6.61	
TRIUMPH	Pembroke	13.8.60		6.6.61	
OCEAN	Devonport	23.8.60		3.6.61	
CALEDONIA	Woolwich	1.10.60		6.6.61	

Class. As *Duncan* with a new timbering plan to suit the smaller armament, a reduction intended to improve the efficiency of each piece; plan dated 29 July 1858. The *Robust* was commenced as a *Duncan* class ship. Three further ships, the *Blake*, *Kent* and *Pitt* were ordered but never laid down and were finally cancelled in 1863. *Bulwark* and *Robust* were retained on the stocks in an advanced state of construction while the remaining seven ships were converted into ironclad 'frigates'. John Henwood proposed converting the *Bulwark* into a twin-turret monitor on the same principles as the *Royal Sovereign*. The plans are dated 5 July 1866 and show a limited conversion suitable for emergency use. When the value of such hasty measures had passed the *Bulwark* and *Robust* were broken up (in March 1873 and August 1872 respectively).

THE ROYAL NAVY (CONVERSIONS)

DUKE OF WELLINGTON class *131 guns*

Tonnage: As designed 3186t (*Wellington* 3759t, *Marlborough* 3853t)

Displacement: *Wellington* 5829t, *Marlborough* 6065t

Dimensions: As designed 210ft oa, 171ft 1in kl x 60ft ext x 24ft 8in. *Wellington* 240ft, 201ft 11⅛in x 60ft x 24ft 8in. Draught 23ft fwd, 24ft 5in aft. *Marlborough* 245ft 6in, 206ft 11⅛in x 60ft x 25ft 2in. Draught 25ft 5in, 27ft 3in.

Machinery: *Wellington* 700nhp (Napier, ex-*Simoom*, iron screw frigate), trials Stokes Bay 11.4.53, 1979ihp = 10.15kts. *Marlborough* 800nhp (Maudslay), trials Stokes Bay (not rigged) 12.5.56, 2683ihp = 11.886kts. *Royal Sovereign* 800nhp (Maudslay), trials Stokes Bay (not rigged) 12.8.58, 2796ihp = 12.253kts. *Prince of Wales* 800nhp (Penn), trials at sea (not rigged) 31.10.60, 3352ihp = 12.569kts.

Masts: As *Victoria*

Armament: GD 10–8in/65cwt, 25–32pdr/56cwt; MdD 6–8in/65cwt, 30–32pdr/56cwt; MD 38–32pdr/42cwt; UD 20–32pdr/25cwt, 1–68pdr/95cwt. Total = 131 guns of 382 tons. (*Wellington* 21.8.52; *Marlborough* was fitted with a similar 121-gun battery to that of the *Victoria*)

Complement: 1100

Name	Builder	Laid down	Converted	Launched	Cost
DUKE OF WELLINGTON (ex-*Windsor Castle*)	Pembroke	5.49	19.1.52	14.9.52	£130,886
MARLBOROUGH	Portsmouth	1.9.50	9.6.53	1.8.55	£123,564
ROYAL SOVEREIGN	Portsmouth	17.12.49	25.1.55	25.4.57	
PRINCE OF WALES	Portsmouth	10.6.48	27.10.56	25.1.60	£134,192

The *Prince of Wales* (foreground) as the training ship *Britannia* in the River Dart at the turn of the century. The teak-built sailing two-decker *Hindustan* was also a part of this establishment.
Author's Collection

Class. Originally ordered as ships of the *Queen* class; suspended by Cockburn in 1845 and modified by the 1846 Committee of Reference, primarily by the addition of 6ft at the bow and a finer entrance. Thereafter they were quickly built up to the launching stage, largely because the materials were already well seasoned. The *Duke of Wellington* was launched under her original name, *Windsor Castle*, but that day being the death of the victor of Waterloo she was renamed in his honour in the following month. The modification to the *Windsor Castle* for the screw was drawn up by John Abthell and Isaac Watts, dated 19 January 1852. It comprised the addition of 23ft amidships and 7ft at the stern; the *Royal Sovereign* was converted to the same plan. The *Marlborough* was given an extra 5ft at the bow, and the *Prince of Wales* also used this modified draught. The two active ships were held in high regard, both for their steaming and sailing qualities. The brief active career of the *Duke of Wellington* reflects the age of her secondhand machinery and the rapidity of her alteration for the screw.

Careers. *Duke of Wellington* 1853 Western Squadron, Commodore H B Martin. 1854 Flagship Baltic Fleet, Vice-Admiral Sir Charles Napier, Captain Gordon; 1855 Rear-Admiral R S Dundas, Captain Caldwell. 1856 Second Flagship Mediterranean Fleet. 1856 paid off. 1863 Receiving ship Portsmouth. Sold 1902.

Marlborough Took almost a month to launch, getting stuck on the ways. 1858 Flagship Mediterranean Fleet, Rear-Admiral Fanshawe, Captain Kerr; 1860 Vice-Admiral William F Martin, Captain Stewart; 1863 Rear-Admiral Smart, Captain Fellowes. 1864 paid off. Receiving ship at Portsmouth. Sold 1924; capsized off Brighton while on tow to the breakers.

Royal Sovereign No sea service as a wooden battleship. 1864 converted into an ironclad turret ship. Sold 1001. This ship had a most curious career, beginning life as a sailing ship, being converted into a steam battleship and then into the prototype of the modern armoured battleship.

Prince of Wales 3 March 1869 renamed *Britannia* to replace the original ship of that name as Boys' TS in the River Dart. 1909 hulked. Sold 13 September 1914.

ROYAL ALBERT *121 guns*

Tonnage:	As designed 3463t, as completed 3726t
Displacement:	As completed 5572t
Dimensions:	As designed 220ft oa, 185ft kl x 60ft 10in ext x 24ft 2in. As completed 232ft 9in, 193ft 6⅛in x 61ft x 24ft 2in. Draught 24ft 8in fwd, 27ft 4in aft
Machinery:	500nhp (Penn). Trials at sea 21.11.54, 1800ihp = 10.0kts
Masts:	As *Victoria*
Armament:	GD 32–8in/65cwt; MdD 32–32pdr/56cwt; MD 32–32pdr/42cwt; UD 24–32pdr/42cwt, 1–68pdr/95cwt (24.5.54)
Complement:	1050

Name	Builder	Laid down	Converted	Launched	Cost
ROYAL ALBERT	Woolwich	3.44	25.10.52	13.5.54	

Class. Designed by Oliver Lang senior, Master Shipwright at Woolwich, for Sir George Cockburn's Construction Board. When commenced was the largest ship of the line then planned. Having been nearly completed at the time she was selected for conversion (31 January 1852), it was at first proposed to fit her with the 700nhp engines from the iron frigate *Euphrates*. However Walker placed the whole issue of her conversion before a committee of Master Shipwrights who declared in favour of new engines of 400 and later 500nhp, allied to a complete reconstruction of the stern. The plans of the altered stern are dated 5 May 1853, those of the ship 20 July 1854. The conversion was hastened by the Russian War, and consequently was not entirely successful. The ship performed well, but her rudder snapped off early in 1855 and by 1861 she was so defective in the stern as to be unfit for further service. The rapid planking over of the remodelled stern timbers was the principal cause of this problem. The conversion of the *Royal Albert* was not as thorough, or as successful, as that of the *Duke of Wellington* class.

Career. 1854 Commissioned by Captain Pasley. 1855 Flagship Black Sea Fleet, Rear-Admiral Lyons, Captain Mends. 1856 Mediterranean Fleet. 1857 paid off. 1859 Flagship Channel Fleet Rear-Admiral Fremantle, Captain Rice. 1860 Captain Lacon. 1861 paid off. Sold 1883.

WINDSOR CASTLE *102 guns*

Tonnage:	3099t
Displacement:	?
Dimensions:	204ft oa, 166ft 5¼in kl x 60ft ext x 23ft 9in. Draught (not masted or stored) 18ft 8in fwd, 21ft 10in aft
Machinery:	500nhp (Maudslay). Trials Plymouth 7.5.59 (not masted or stored), 2052ihp = 10.955kts
Masts:	As *Saint Jean D'Acre*
Armament:	GD 30-8in/65cwt; MdD 30-32pdr/56cwt; MD 30-32pdr/42cwt; UD 10-32pdr/42cwt, 2-68pdr/95cwt (4.9.56)
Complement:	930

Name	Builder	Laid down	Converted	Launched	Cost
WINDSOR CASTLE (ex-*Victoria*)	Pembroke	5.44	3.10.57	26.8.58	

Class. Originally a *Queen* class 116-gun three-decked sailing ship. Laid down as the *Victoria*, name changed on 6 January 1855 to release that name for the new construction three-decker. This has given rise to much confusion, especially as the previous *Windsor Castle* had been renamed *Duke of Wellington*. The conversion was effected by cutting down the forecastle and quarterdeck, which was an unsuccessful attempt by Walker to retain the heavy battery of a three-decker while improving her stability. The poor seakeeping qualities she displayed on trials ensured that her sister, the *Royal Frederick* was cut down into a two-decker to form a separate class with the *Queen*.

Career. No sea service. 1869 *Cambridge* gunnery TS at Devonport. Sold on 24 June 1908.

ORION class *91 guns*

Tonnage:	As commenced 2600t, as completed 3232t
Displacement:	?
Dimensions:	As commenced 198ft oa, 161ft ¾in kl x 55ft 9in ext x 23ft 4in. As completed 238ft, 200ft 10¾in x 55ft 9in x 24ft. Draught 24ft 5in fwd, 26ft 10in aft
Machinery:	600nhp (Penn). *Orion* trials in the Thames 4.55, 2328ihp = 11.446kts. *Hood* trials in the Thames 24.11.59 (not masted or stored), 2385ihp = 11.722kts
Masts:	As *Saint Jean D'Acre*
Armament:	GD 34-8in/65cwt; MD 34-32pdr/56cwt; UD 22-32pdr/45cwt, 1-68pdr/95cwt (3.4.53)
Complement:	860

Name	Builder	Ordered	Laid down	Converted	Launched
ORION	Chatham	30.3.48	1.2.50	24.12.52	6.11.54
HOOD	Chatham	30.3.48	13.8.49	5.5.56	4.5.59

Class. Originally ordered as sailing ships of 80 guns, the *Orion* class were the last sail of the line commenced in Britain. The principal draught is signed by the Surveyor's assistants John Edye and Isaac Watts and dated 10 November 1848. It refers to a class of three ships: the third, *Edgar*, was never commenced, and this has led to some confusion in consequence of which the *Hood* is often referred to as the ex-*Edgar*. The conversion to steam followed plans dated 23 December 1852. The stern run of the *Hood* was improved according to alterations dated 30 December 1856, and this was the only difference between the ships. The *Hood* cost £105,478. The *Orion* was a fast ship and held in high regard. Her short career reflects the hasty completion caused by the Russian War and the resultant decay.

Careers. *Orion* 1855-6 Baltic Fleet, Captain Erskine. 1856 North America and West Indies. 1857 paid off. 1858 Flagship of the Channel Fleet, Vice-Admiral Fremantle, Captain D'Eyncourt. 1859 Mediterranean Fleet, Captain Frere. 1861 paid off. Sold 1867 to Castle of Charlton for breaking up. *Hood* 1872 torpedo company barracks at Woolwich. Sold 1888 for £5000.

CAESAR *91 guns*

Tonnage:	2767t
Displacement:	?
Dimensions:	208t oa, 170ft 7⅜in kl x 56ft ext x 23ft 4in. Draught 19ft 5in fwd, 22ft 8in aft
Machinery:	400nhp (Penn). Trials Stokes Bay 3.3.54, 1420ihp = 10.274kts
Masts:	As *Saint Jean D'Acre*
Armament:	GD 32–8in/65cwt; MD 32–32pdr/56cwt; UD 26–32pdr/42cwt, 1–68pdr/95cwt
Complement:	860

Name	Builder	Ordered	Laid down	Converted	Launched
CAESAR	Pembroke	18.10.48	8.48	22.11.52	8–10.8.53

Class. Designed by the Committee of Reference under Captain Lord John Hay. Marked an attempt to return to the moderate dimensions of the *Rodney* class prior to the *Albion* design and Seppings' timber plan rather than that of Symonds and Edye. Originally ordered at Portsmouth in June 1847, but cancelled. A new midship section was prepared and she was re-ordered at Pembroke to replace the *Algiers*. Despite some hogging (arching of the keel) caused by her hanging on the ways and requiring camels to launch her, the *Caesar* was a successful ship. She steamed and sailed well and was considerably more handy than the main competition.

Career. 1854 Baltic Fleet, Captain Robb. 1856 paid off. 1858 Channel Fleet, Captain Frederick. 1859 Mediterranean Fleet, Captain Mason. 1862 paid off. Sold to Mare on 9 April 1870 for £8893.

ALGIERS *91 guns*

Tonnage:	As commenced 3136½t, as completed 3346t
Displacement:	As completed 4730t
Dimensions:	As commenced 210ft oa, 170ft kl x 60ft ext x 24ft 5in. As completed 218ft 7in, 179ft 9in x 60ft x 24ft 5in. Draught (Fairbairn engines) 24ft 6in fwd, 25ft 7in aft; (Maudslay engines, not masted) 19ft 7in, 22ft 7in
Machinery:	450nhp (Fairbairn, ex-*Megaera*, iron screw frigate). Trials at Plymouth 1.6.54, 1117ihp = 9.0kts. This machinery was removed and scrapped at Portsmouth between 12.1.57 and 21.8.57 and replaced by 600nhp (Maudslay). Trials Stokes Bay 18.2.58 (not masted), 2516ihp = 12.191kts
Masts:	As *Saint Jean D'Acre*
Armament:	As *Caesar*
Complement:	850 (860 after re-engining)

Name	Builder	Ordered	Laid down	Converted	Launched
ALGIERS	Devonport	1847	7.48	27.9.52	26.1.54

Class. John Edye's expansion of the *Albion* drawn after the departure of Symonds. Plan dated 19 November 1847. Originally ordered at Pembroke, but replaced there by the *Caesar*. Design related to the *Albion* as the *Duke of Wellington* did to the *Queen* before conversion to steam. However she was very badly reported on, her rolling being in the typical Symondite pattern. This would indicate that the extra 5ft and later 8ft were insufficient to cure this problem, unlike the 5ft and later 30ft added to the *Duke*. Her first commission was ruined by her cumbersome, inefficient and unreliable engines.

Career. 1854 trooping run to the Baltic, Captain Talbot. 1855 Black Sea. 1856 Baltic Fleet, gunboat depot ship, Captain Codrington. 1856 Trooping run to the Crimea. 1857 paid off for re-engining. 1859 Channel Fleet, Captain O'Callaghan. 1861 Mediterranean Fleet, Captain Rice. 1862 paid off. Sold 26 January 1870 for £10,675.

The *Hannibal* on her arrival at Castle's Shipbreaking yard at Charlton in April–May 1904. She, along with the *Duke of Wellington*, *Edgar*, *Anson* and *Atlas*, was sold to the firm on 12 April of that year.
Topham Picture Library

PRINCESS ROYAL class *91 guns*

Tonnage:	As commenced 2695t, as completed 3114t
Displacement:	As completed 4540t
Dimensions:	As commenced 208ft oa, 170ft 7⅜in kl x 58ft ext x 24ft. As completed 217ft, 179ft 1¾in x 58ft x 24ft. Draught 23ft 6in fwd, 26ft 6in aft
Machinery:	*Princess Royal* 400nhp (Maudslay), trials Stokes Bay 2.11.53, 1491ihp = 11.031kts. *Hannibal* 450nhp (Scott & Sims, ex-*Greenock*, iron screw frigate), trials at the Nore 12.4.54 (with the launching cleets still in place), 1071ihp = 8.6kts
Masts:	As *Saint Jean D'Acre* with a lighter mainmast
Armament:	GD 32-8in/65cwt; MD 34-32pdr/56cwt; UD 24-32pdr/42cwt, 1-68pdr/95cwt (*Hannibal* 17.4.54)
Complement:	850

Name	Builder	Laid down	Converted	Launched
PRINCESS ROYAL	Portsmouth	2.41	30.10.52	23.6.53
HANNIBAL	Deptford	12.48	23.9.52	31.1.54

Class. Ordered as *Albion* class ships in 1840; *Princess Royal* originally commenced as the *Prince Albert*, name changed on 26 March 1842. The *Hannibal* commenced at Woolwich but her keel was taken up in 1842 to make room for the *Royal Albert*. On 9 December 1844 all large Symondite ships were suspended. The *Princess Royal* was modified by the 1846–47 Committee of Reference to the 'as commenced' figures above; re-ordered 19 March 1847, *Hannibal* on 14 June 1847. Edye's new plan dated 30 June 1847. The *Hannibal*'s materials were then transferred to Deptford from 10 July 1847 and she was laid down again.

They were ordered to convert to steam on 30 October and 23 September respectively. The more advanced *Princess Royal* completed first. These ships were generally well regarded, the low speed of the *Hannibal* being entirely due to her elderly and inefficient engines. They were more successful than either the unmodified *Albion* class, or the lengthened *Algiers*, the new midsection having cured the heavy rolling of the original design.

Careers. *Princess Royal* 1853 Captain Lord Clarence Paget. 1854 Baltic Fleet. 1855 Black Sea, later Captain Giffard. 1856 Portsmouth. 1857 Mediterranean Fleet. 1858 Captain Baillie. 1860 paid off. 1864 Flagship East Indies and China, Rear-Admiral King, Captain Jones. 1865 Flagship China. 1867 paid off. Sold to Castle 1872 for £58,500.

Hannibal 1854 trooping run to the Baltic, Commodore Frederick Grey. 1855 Second Flagship Black Sea, Rear-Admiral Houston Stewart, Captain Hay. 1856 paid off. 1858 guardship of the Portsmouth Ordinary, Captain Gordon. 1859 Second Flagship Mediterranean Fleet, Rear-Admiral Mundy, Captain Connolly. 1860 Captain Farquahar. 1862 paid off. 1884 hulked, machinery removed. Sold 12 April 1904.

RODNEY class *91 guns*

Tonnage:	As built 2590t (*London* as converted 2626t, *Rodney* 2770t)
Displacement:	?
Dimensions:	As built 205ft 6in oa, 170ft 4in kl x 54ft 6in ext x 23ft. *London* 210ft 3in (*Rodney* 214ft oa), 175ft 11in x 54ft 6in x 23ft 2in. Draught (*Nile*) 23ft 6in fwd, 26ft 5in aft
Machinery:	500nhp. *Rodney* (Maudslay), trials in the Thames 3.7.60 (not masted or stored), 2246ihp = 11.479kts. *Nile* (Seaward and Capel, ex-*Euphrates*, iron screw frigate), trials off Plymouth, early 1854, 928ihp = 6.854kts; in April 1859 fitted with new boilers and steam pipe, trials at sea 7.4.60, 1247ihp = 8.2kts. *London* (Miller and Ravenhill), trials at Plymouth 15.12.58 (not masted or stored), 1804ihp = 11.522kts
Masts:	As *Saint Jean D'Acre*
Armament:	GD 32-8in/65cwt; MD 34-32pdr/56cwt; 24-32pdr/42cwt, 1-68pdr/95cwt (*Rodney* 21.10.58)
Complement:	850

Name	Builder	Laid down	Launched	Converted	Completed
RODNEY	Pembroke	0.27	10.0.00	10.0.50	11.1.00
NILE	Devonport	10.27	28.6.39	14.12.52	30.1.54
LONDON	Chatham	10.27	28.9.40	14.1.57	13.5.58

Class. Designed by Sir Robert Seppings; original plan dated 17 November 1826 in response to American ships of similar force. The *Nile* and *London* were considered for conversion into large blockships in 1847. The conversion of the *Nile* into a steam battleship was ordered on 24 November 1852, and undertaken at Devonport. It was largely experimental, the ship was not lengthened and an inferior set of secondhand engines were fitted. The *London* was lengthened and fitted with new machinery, and her performance was so outstanding that she was used as the model for the subsequent conversion of the *Rodney* and the *Caledonia* class three-deckers. *London* converted at Devonport, *Rodney* at Chatham.

These ships benefitted from the strong hull construction methods employed by Seppings, and in the case of the last pair, from a very lengthy building period. At sea they were stable gun platforms and fine sailers; along with the *Caledonia*s they were the most satisfactory conversions effected on ships already afloat.

Careers. *Rodney* 1860 trials. 1867 Flagship China Station, Vice-Admiral Sir Henry Keppel, Captain Heneage. 1870 paid off. The last wooden steam battleship in full commission in the Royal Navy.

Nile 1854 Baltic Fleet, Commodore Henry Byam Martin, 1855 Captain George Mundy. 1856 North America and West Indies. 1858 Flagship Queenstown, Rear-Admiral Henry D Chads, Captain H D Chads. 1859 Rear-Admiral Talbot, Captain Wilmott. 1860 Flagship North America and West Indies, Rear-Admiral Alexander Milne, Captain Barnard. 1864 paid off. 1876 engines removed, became TS *Conway* in the Mersey. Removed to Anglesey in 1940, wrecked in the Menai Straits, April 1953. Constructive total loss, burnt during breaking up 31 October 1956. The last survivor of the wooden steam battlefleet.

London 1859 Mediterranean Fleet, Captain H D Chads. 1863 paid off. 1874 depot ship at Zanzibar for the anti-slavery patrol. Broken up 1884.

NELSON *91 guns*

Tonnage:	Originally 2619t, as converted 2736t
Displacement:	?
Dimensions:	Originally 205ft oa, 170ft 7in kl x 53ft 8¾in ext x 24ft. As converted 216ft 3in, 180ft (approx) x 54ft 6in x 24ft. Draught (not masted or stored) 17ft 6in fwd, 21ft 10in aft
Machinery:	500nhp by (Miller and Ravenhill). Trials Stokes Bay 21.6.60 (not masted or stored), 2102ihp = 11.533kts
Masts:	As *Saint Jean D'Acre*
Armament:	GD 32-8in/65cwt; MD 34-32pdr/56cwt; UD 22-32pdr/42cwt, 1-68pdr/95cwt (21.10.59)
Complement:	850

Name	Builder	Laid down	Launched	Converted
NELSON	Woolwich	12.09	4.7.14	Portsmouth 10.3.59-7.2.60

Class. Originally a 120-gun ship designed by the Surveyor's Office as an improvement on the *Caledonia* (plan dated 13 October 1806); sisters *Howe* and *St Vincent*. Cut down and lengthened along the lines of the *London*. As sailing ships this class were considered inferior to the *Caledonia*.

Career. No sea service as a sailing or steamship. October 1867 fitted out as a schoolship for the Government of New South Wales. Sold 1898; broken up 1928.

The *Royal George*, after her second reconstruction, as a steam battleship. At this stage she was an 86-gun two-decker, although she was never lengthened like the other *Caledonia* class three-deckers that were transformed into steamships.　　*Royal Naval Museum*

ROYAL GEORGE class *89 guns*

Tonnage:	Originally 2695t
Displacement:	?
Dimensions:	205ft 5½in oa, 170ft 6in kl x 53ft 6in ext x 23ft 2in. *Prince Regent* 218ft oa, 183ft (approx) x 55ft. Draught (*Royal George* 4.5.64) 22ft 6in fwd, 24ft 2in aft
Machinery:	*Royal George* 400nhp (Penn), trials at Plymouth 4.5.64, 1417ihp = 8.65kts. *Prince Regent* 500nhp (Watt), no trials figures
Masts:	As *Saint Jean D'Acre*
Armament:	GD 8-8in/65cwt; 24-32pdr/56cwt; MdD 4-8in/65cwt, 30-32pdr/50cwt; MD 34-32pdr/42cwt; UD 6-32pdr/45cwt 14-32pdr/17cwt (*Royal George* as a 120-gun ship; as a 102-gun ship UD 2-68pdr/95cwt; as 89-gun ships both armed as *Nelson*)
Complement:	830 as two-deckers

Name	Builder	Laid down	Launched	Converted
PRINCE REGENT	Chatham	17.7.15	12.4.23	Portsmouth 8.2.60–27.5.61
ROYAL GEORGE	Chatham	6.23	22.9.27	Chatham 1.11.52–18.12.53

Class. *Caledonia* class ships of 120 guns. Not as successful as the original, the *Prince Regent* being so crank that she had to be cut down into a two-decker 92 between 6 March 1841 and 30 September 1847 at a cost of £53,815. This greatly improved her sailing, at the same time an extra 1ft of beam was added by doubling.

Royal George converted without any major structural alterations into a steam 120; plans dated 19 April 1852. She was rendered unbearably crank and her poop and forecastle were removed in December 1854 leaving her as a 102-gun ship. Even this was not entirely successful as the modified upperworks decayed rapidly. She was then cut down into a two-decker, still without being lengthened, to a plan dated 12 April 1860. The *Prince Regent* was adapted for screw propulsion on the lines of the *London*.

Careers. *Prince Regent* no sea service as a steamship. Broken up in 1873.
Royal George 1854 Baltic Fleet, Captain Codrington. 1856 Captain Robert Spencer Robinson. 1856 paid off. 1865 Coastguard service. 1875 broken up.

SAINT GEORGE class *89 guns*

Tonnage:	Originally 2694t, *Royal William* as converted 2849t
Displacement:	?
Dimensions:	Originally 205ft 5½in oa, 170ft 11in kl x 54ft 6in ext x 23ft 2in. *Royal William* 216ft 9in, 180ft (approx) x 55ft 7in x 23ft 2in. Draught (*Saint George*) 23ft 4in fwd, 24ft 7in aft.
Machinery:	500nhp. *Saint George* (Miller and Ravenhill), trials at Plymouth 8.8.59, 1730ihp = 10.933kts. *Royal William* (Napier), trials at Plymouth 11.12.60 (not masted or stored), 1763ihp = 10.581kts. *Neptune* (Miller and Ravenhill), trials Stokes Bay 18.6.59 (not masted or stored), 1910ihp = 11.242kts. *Waterloo* (Miller and Ravenhill), trials at the Nore 17.4.63, 2048ihp = 9.934kts. *Trafalgar* (Maudslay), trials in the Thames 12.7.59, 2275ihp = 10.908kts.
Masts:	As *Saint Jean D'Acre*
Armament:	As *Nelson*
Complement:	830

Name	Builder	Laid down	Launched	Converted
SAINT GEORGE	Devonport	5.27	27.8.40	Devonport 21.8.58–12.6.59
ROYAL WILLIAM	Pembroke	10.27	2.4.33	Devonport 31.3.59 9.8.60
NEPTUNE	Portsmouth	1.27	27.9.32	Portsmouth 10.8.58–7.3.59
WATERLOO	Chatham	3.27	18.6.33	Chatham 1.4.59–12.11.59
TRAFALGAR	Woolwich	12.29	22.6.41	Chatham 16.8.58–14.8.59

Class. Broadened *Caledonia*s; all five ships converted to follow the *London*. Officially rated as 86-gun ships. Not outstanding seaboats after conversion, but powerfully armed and strongly built. They provided a valuable reinforcement for the battlefleet at a time when new construction had fallen seriously in arrears.
Careers. *Saint George* 1860 North America and West Indies, Captain Egerton. 1862 Channel Fleet. 1863 Mediterranean Fleet. 1864 Coastguard at Falmouth, Captain Rice. 1870 mobilised for the Reserve Fleet cruise. Sold 1883.
Royal William no sea service as a steamship. 1885 TS *Clarence* in the Mersey. 1899 burnt at her moorings.

Neptune 1859 particular service, Captain Sir William Hoste, Bart. 1860 Mediterranean Fleet, Captain Campbell, 1861 Captain Geoffrey Hornby. 1862 paid off. Sold 1875.
Waterloo 1862 renamed *Conqueror*. 1864 China, Captain Luard. 1866 paid off. 1877 renamed *Warspite* as TS at Greenhithe/Woolwich. 1918 burnt.
Trafalgar 1859 Channel fleet, Captain Fanshawe. 1861 Captain Dickson. 1863 Mediterranean, Captain Baillie. 1863 Captain Mason. 1864 Coastguard at Queensferry, Captain Schomberg. 1869 converted to a boys' TS at Portsmouth. 1873 renamed *Boscawen* as TS at Portland. Sold 10 July 1906.

The *Trafalgar* and *Neptune*.
Imperial War Museum

ALBION class *91 guns*

Tonnage:	3109t
Displacement:	4300t
Dimensions:	204ft oa, 166ft kl x 60ft 2¼in ext x 23ft 8in. Draught 24ft fwd, 24ft 9in aft
Machinery:	400nhp. *Albion* (Humphreys & Tennant), trials at Plymouth 21.3.62 (not masted or stored), 1835ihp = 10.986kts. *Aboukir* (Penn), trials at Plymouth 13.11.58 (not masted or stored), 1533ihp = 9.55kts. *Exmouth* (Maudslay), trials at sea 21.4.58, 1252ihp = 9.1kts.
Masts:	As *Saint Jean D'acre*
Armament:	GD 32-8in/65cwt; MD 32-32pdr/56cwt; UD 26-32pdr/42cwt, 1-68pdr/95cwt
Complement:	830

Name	Builder	Laid down	Launched	Converted
ALBION	Devonport	13.8.39	6.9.42	Devonport 4.4.60–21.5.61
ABOUKIR	Devonport	8.40	4.4.48	Devonport 8.10.56–1.1.58
EXMOUTH	Devonport	13.9.41	–	Devonport 20.6.53–12.7.54

Class. With the *Queen* the *Albion* was at the centre of the controversy as to the merits of the Symondite hull-form. Capable of great speed in light winds she tended to roll heavily in adverse conditions. Being large and heavily built they were suitable for conversion, but the addition of heavy machinery and coal only increased their tendency to roll. The *Aboukir* was considered by her Captain to 'roll excessively', while the Captain of the Channel Fleet observed that all the Symondites rolled much worse than they had done as sailing ships. On trials the *Exmouth* rolled so quickly that she could not clear herself of the water that was being shipped aboard. Captain Pelham considered her 'too heavily loaded, not at all easy'. Even in moderate seas she shipped large quantities of water, a fault common to all Symondites.

Being largely complete on the stocks at the time of the suspensions of 9 December 1844 and 20 March 1847, both *Aboukir* and *Exmouth* were not modified on the lines of the *Princess Royal*. The *Aboukir* was launched, but *Exmouth* remained on the stocks. Her conversion was effected without lengthening the stern, as ordered on 30 October 1852. The limited nature of these conversions, and the small engines used reflected Walker's low regard for the Symondite form.

Careers. *Albion* never completed for sea. Held in reserve at Devonport until broken up in 1884.

Aboukir 1859 Channel Fleet, Captain Schomberg. 1860 Captain Curry. 1861 Captain Shadwell. 1862 North America and West Indies. 1862 converted into a depot/floating battery at Jamaica. 1867 receiving ship Jamaica. Sold 1878.

Exmouth 1854 commissioned, Captain Thomas Pelham. 1855 Second Flagship Baltic Fleet, Rear-Admiral Seymour, Captain King-Hall. 1856 Devonport, Captain Eyres. 1858 Guardship of the Ordinary at Devonport, Captain Robert Spencer Robinson. 1859 Mediterranean, Captain Stopford. 1860 Captain Paynter. 1862 paid off. 1877 loaned to the Metropolitan Asylum as a TS for pauper boys. Sold 4 April 1905 and replaced by a steel ship of the same dimension.

QUEEN class *86 guns*

Tonnage:	Originally 3240t
Displacement:	As converted 4502t
Dimensions:	*Queen* 204ft oa, 166ft 5¼in kl (*Frederick William* 165ft 11in) x 60ft ext x 23ft 9in. Draught (*Queen*, not rigged or stored) 22ft fwd, 23ft 7in aft
Machinery:	500nhp (Maudslay). *Queen* trials in the Thames 6.9.59 (not rigged or stored), 2283ihp = 10.578kts. *Frederick William* trials Stokes Bay 29.11.60 (not rigged), 2276ihp = 11.777kts
Masts:	As *Saint Jean D'Acre*
Armament:	GD 30-8in/65cwt; MD 32-32pdr/56cwt; UD 22-32pdr/42cwt, 2-68pdr/95cwt (21.10.59)
Complement:	830

Name	Builder	Laid down	Launched	Converted
QUEEN	Portsmouth	11.33	15.5.39	Sheerness 23.8.58–30.10.59
FREDERICK WILLIAM (ex-*Royal Frederick*)	Portsmouth	7.41	–	Portsmouth 28.5.59–24.3.60

Class. Symonds' alteration of a *Caledonia* class ship, the *Royal Frederick* was ordered on 29 October 1827 (plan drawn 2 September 1833), using frame timbers already prepared. Original *Royal Frederick* renamed *Queen* when launched. *Windsor Castle* also originally of this class. *Royal Frederick* renamed on 28 January 1860, the wedding day of the Princess Royal to Crown Prince Frederick William of Prussia. These ships were converted as simply as possible, following the unhappy experience with the *Windsor Castle* and other Symondites. They were cut down, but

The *Queen* as a screw ship of 86 guns cut down from a sailing three-decker of 116. She was not lengthened and served to illustrate the unsatisfactory results that were produced by converting Symonds' ships.
Imperial War Museum

the *Queen* was still an exceptionally bad seaboat.

Careers. *Queen* 1860 Mediterranean Fleet, Captain Hillyar. 1864 paid off. Sold 1871.

Frederick William 1864 Coastguard service at Portland. 1865 Queenstown. 1868 River Shannon. Renamed *Worcester* on 19 October 1876 and became TS at Greenhithe for the Thames Marine Officers Training Society. 1948 sold. 30 August 1948 foundered. Raised in May 1953 and broken up at Tennant & Herne of Grays.

CRESSY *80 guns*

Tonnage:	2537t
Displacement:	3707t
Dimensions:	198ft 5in oa, 162ft 1½in kl x 55ft ext x 21ft 8¼in. Draught 23ft 7in fwd, 25ft 8in aft
Machinery:	400nhp (Maudslay). Trials at sea 12.5.58, 1076ihp = 7.2kts
Masts:	Main 64ft 6in x 37in; Fore 59ft x 36in; Mizzen 54ft 6in x 24in
Armament:	GD 10–8in/65cwt, 18–32pdr/56cwt; MD 4–8in/65cwt, 24–32pdr/50cwt; UD 24–32pdr/42cwt (6.12.52)
Complement:	750

Name	Builder	Laid down	Converted	Launched
CRESSY	Chatham	4.46	29.11.52	21.7.53

Class. Ordered by the Admiralty on 23 April 1844, and designed by Read, Creuze and Chatfield, stalwarts of the old School of Naval Architecture. Part of the reaction to the Symondites instigated by Cockburn, but considered to be old-fashioned, having too much tumblehome and using more curved timber than any post-1815 ship. Like all the small converted ships she was not outstanding under either steam or sail.

Careers. 1854 Baltic Fleet, Captain Warren. 1857 paid off. 1858 Guardship of the Ordinary at Sheerness, Captain E P Halstead. 1859 Mediterranean Fleet, Captain Elliot. 1861 paid off. Sold to Castle of Charlton 1867 for £6100.

MAJESTIC class *80 guns*

Tonnage:	2889t (*Brunswick* 2484t)
Displacement:	?
Dimensions:	190ft oa, 155ft 3in kl x 56ft 9in ext x 23ft 4in (*Brunswick* 154ft 4¾in ext x 55ft 9in). Draught 23ft 7in fwd, 25ft 3in aft
Machinery:	400nhp. *Goliath* (Penn), trials in the Thames 14.8.58 (not masted or stored), 1438ihp = 9.16kts. *Collingwood* (Rennie), trials in the Thames 26.1.62 (not masted or stored), 1424ihp = 10.46kts. *Centurion* (Miller & Ravenhill), trials at Plymouth 14.4.56, 1255ihp = 8.5kts. *Mars* (Maudslay), no trials figures available. *Lion* (Penn), trials at Plymouth 18.7.61 (not masted or stored), 1771ihp = 10.911kts. *Majestic* (Maudslay), trials at sea 24.6.58 (not masted or stored), 1191ihp = 8.783kts. *Meeanee* (Penn), trials at sea 17.2.58, 1384ihp = 10.44kts. *Colossus* (Penn), trials Stokes Bay 16.10.54, 1458ihp = 9.312kts. *Brunswick* (Miller & Ravenhill), trials at Plymouth 29.3.56, 1438ihp = 7.742kts. *Irresistible* (Penn), trials in the Thames 22.5.60, 1669ihp = 10.01kts
Masts:	As *Cressy*
Armament:	GD 10–8in/65cwt, 18–32pdr/56cwt; MD 4–8in/56cwt, 24–32pdr/50cwt; UD–32pdr/42cwt (*Colossus* 7.4.54)
Complement:	750

Name	Builder	Laid down	Launched	Converted
GOLIATH	Chatham	2.34	25.7.42	Chatham 16.10.56–30.11.57
COLLINGWOOD	Pembroke	9.35	17.8.41	Sheerness 23.3.60–13.7.61
CENTURION	Pembroke	7.39	2.5.44	Devonport 28.9.54–12.11.55
MARS	Chatham	12.39	1.7.48	Chatham 7.3.55–20.6.56
LION	Pembroke	7.40	29.7.47	Devonport 1.2.58–17.5.59
MAJESTIC	Chatham	2.41	–	Chatham 29.11.52–17.5.53
MEEANEE	Bombay	4.42	11.11.48	Sheerness 6.12.56–31.10.57
COLOSSUS	Pembroke	10.43	1.6.48	Portsmouth 26.1.54–27.6.55
BRUNSWICK	Pembroke	30.8.47	–	Pembroke 7.8.54–27.6.55
IRRESISTIBLE	Chatham	1.1.49	–	Chatham 1.5.55–27.10.59

Class. *Vanguard* class ships of 80 guns designed by Symonds. *Brunswick* built to a modified draught dated 14 October 1847. Considered too small and too fine-lined for any full-scale conversion; Walker always looked on them as second class ships hardly fit to lay in the line of battle. *Majestic* was the prototype for all the subsequent conversions.

Careers. *Goliath* no sea service as sail or steam. 22 December 1875 burnt while serving as a TS for the Forest Gate School Ships Committee at Grays.

Collingwood never completed for sea. Sold 1866 for £8361 to Castle of Charlton.

Centurion 1856 Baltic Fleet, Captain Fanshawe. 1857 Mediterranean Fleet. 1858 Captain Broke. 1859 Captain Patey. 1860 Channel Fleet, Captain Rogers. 1862 paid off. Sold 1870.

Mars 1859 Channel Fleet, Captain Strange. 1861 Mediterranean Fleet. 1863 paid off. Sold 1929.

Lion 1864 Coastguard at Greenock, later TS with the *Implacable*.

Sold 1905.

Majestic 1854 Baltic Fleet, Captain Hope. 1856 Mediterranean. 1857 paid off. 1860 Coastguard at Liverpool, Captain Mends. Sold 1867 for £7160.

Meeanee 1862 Mediterranean Fleet, Captain Wodehouse. 1865 paid off. Sold 1906.

Colossus 1855 Baltic Fleet, Captain Robert Spencer Robinson. 1856 gunboat depot ship, Captain Henry Keppel. 1856 paid off. 1860 Coastguard at Portland, Captain Scott. 1861 Captain Patey. 1863 Captain Carnegie. Sold 1867 for £6865.

Brunswick 1856 Baltic Fleet, gunboat depot ship, Captain Hastings Yelverton. 1856 Black Sea trooping run, Captain Broadhead. 1857 North America and West Indies, Captain Ommaney. 1858 Channel. 1859 Mediterranean. 1860 paid off. Sold 1867 for £6990.

Irresistible 1865 Coastguard at Southampton, Captain Dickson. 1869 depot at Bermuda. Sold 1891 at Bermuda.

BOMBAY *81 guns*

Tonnage:	Originally 2255t, as converted 2783t
Displacement:	?
Dimensions:	Originally 193ft 10in oa, 160ft 2½in kl x 52ft 4½in ext x 22ft 6in. As converted 233ft 9in, 197ft 9¼in kl x 52ft 4½in ext x 23ft. Draught 20ft 8in fwd, 24ft aft
Machinery:	400nhp (Humphreys & Tennant). Trials in the Thames 26.3.64, 1688ihp = 10.157kts
Masts:	As *Cressy*
Armament:	GD 10-8in /65cwt, 24-32pdr/56cwt; MD 4-8in/65cwt, 30-32pdr/50cwt; UD 12-32pdr/42cwt, 1-68pdr/95cwt. (31.10.60)
Complement:	750

Name	Builder	Laid down	Launched	Converted
BOMBAY	Bombay	5.26	17.3.28	Chatham 23.5.60–25.6.61

Class. Seppings' modifications applied to the lines of the ex-French *Canopus* captured at the Nile as the *Franklin*. Built in India of teak, renowned for its longevity, this class were also considered superior sailers to their famous model. Converted to plans dated 1 January 1860 for 'an 81 gun ship of the old class', her sister the *Powerful* was originally selected but when stripped out she was found to be defective and the *Bombay* was substituted.

Career. 1864 Flagship South Coast of America. Destroyed by fire and explosion off Montevideo 22 December 1864.

SANS PAREIL *70 guns*

Tonnage:	Originally 2242t, as converted 2339t
Displacement:	As converted 3800t
Dimensions:	Originally 193ft oa, 158ft 11½ kl x 52ft 1in ext x 22ft 8in. As converted 200ft, 165ft 11½in x 52ft 1in x 22ft 8in. Draught 22ft 8in fwd, 25ft 8in aft
Machinery:	Originally 350nhp (Boulton & Watt, intended for one of the 1845 frigate blockships), 622ihp = 7.05kts. Replaced in early 1855 by 400nhp (James Watt & Co), trials off Plymouth 12.8.55, 1471ihp = 9.3kts
Masts:	As *Cressy*
Armament:	GD 30-32pdr/56cwt; MD 24-32pdr/45cwt, 6-8in/52cwt; UD 8-32pdr/25cwt, 2-32pdr/56cwt
Complement:	626 as a 70-gun ship

Name	Builder	Laid down	Launched	Converted
SANS PAREIL	Devonport	1.9.45	–	Devonport 3.1.49–18.3.51

Class. Originally ordered to be built after the lines of the old ex-French *Sans Pareil* captured in 1794; one of the ships ordered by Sir George Cockburn in 1845. Lengthened by 7ft at the stern as a first attempt to produce a seagoing steam battleship. Basically a failure on account of her weak and unreliable machinery and lack of stowage and stability. Used for subsidiary duties from 1855 until the end of her career.

Career. 1853 Mediterranean Fleet, Captain Dacres. 1854 Black Sea. 1855 munitions transport, Captain Williams. 1856 Baltic Fleet depot for gunboats, Captain Astley Cooper-Key. 1856 China. 1858 Captain Maguire. 1859 paid off. 1860 Flagship at Queenstown, Rear-Admiral Talbot, Captain Wilmott. 1861 Particular service (Marines to Veracruz and troops to China), Captain Bowyer. 1863 East Indies and China. 1864 paid off. Sold March 8 1867 for £6620.

BLENHEIM class *60-gun blockships*

Tonnage:	Originally 1741t, *Blenheim* and *Hogue* 1832t
Displacement:	?
Dimensions:	Originally 176ft oa, 145ft 1in kl x 47ft 6in ext x 21ft. *Blenheim* and *Hogue* 181ft 2$\frac{7}{8}$in, 150ft x 48ft 6in x 21ft. Draught 21ft 2in fwd, 23ft 10in aft
Machinery:	450nhp. *Ajax* (Maudslay), trials Stokes Bay 6.8.49, 846ihp = 7.147kts. *Blenheim* (Seaward & Capel), trials Stokes Bay 5.6.49, 938ihp = 5.816kts. *Edinburgh* (Maudslay), trials Stokes Bay 25.5.52, 962ihp = 8.873kts. *Hogue* (Seaward & Capel), trials Stokes Bay 18.12.50, 797ihp = 7.328kts.
Masts:	On the scale of a 46-gun frigate, except the mizzen which was a full size 74-gun ship mast
Armament:	GD 28–32pdr/56cwt; MD 26–8in/52cwt; UD 2–68pdr/95cwt, 4–10in/67cwt.
Complement:	600

Name	Builder	Laid down	Launched	Converted
AJAX	Perry & Co Blackwall	8.07	2.5.09	Portsmouth 17.11.45–28.9.48
BLENHEIM	Deptford	8.08	31.5.13	Sheerness 12.11.45–27.10.47
EDINBURGH	Brent, Rotherhithe	11.07	26.1.11	Portsmouth 11.8.46–19.8.52
HOGUE	Deptford	4.08	31.10.11	Sheerness 1.12.45–28.7.49

Class. Originally *Armada* class 74s, they became the pioneer screw battleship conversions. *Blenheim* and *Hogue* given a lengthened and fined stern, the other pair being adapted without major structural alteration. *Blenheim* and *Hogue* had a single funnel before the mainmast, the other pair had two side by side abaft the mainmast. The *Ajax* was noted for her poor performance under steam or sail.

Careers. All four served in the Baltic fleet 1854–56 and were thereafter reduced to subsidiary functions and sold between 1864 and 1866.

CORNWALLIS class *60-gun blockships*

Tonnage:	1741t (*Cornwallis* 1788t, *Hawke* 1738t)
Displacement:	?
Dimensions:	176ft oa, 145ft 1in kl x 47ft 6in ext x 21ft. *Cornwallis* 177ft 1in, 145ft 11in x 48ft x 21ft 1$\frac{3}{4}$in. *Hawke* 176ft, 144ft 9$\frac{7}{8}$in x 47ft 6in x 21ft. Draught (*Cornwallis*) 20ft fwd, 22ft 4in aft
Machinery:	200nhp (all trials Stokes Bay). *Cornwallis* (Penn) 1.5.55, 787.4ihp = 7.188kts. *Hastings* (Maudslay) 5.4.55, 597.3ihp = 6.702kts. *Hawke* (Penn) 26.4.55, 500ihp = 6.525kts. *Pembroke* (Maudslay) 7.4.55, 572ihp = 7.602kts. *Russell* (Penn) 27.4.55, 578ihp = 6.68kts
Masts:	Any serviceable secondhand equipment that was available
Armament:	GD 24–32pdr/56cwt, 4–8in/65cwt; MD 26–32pdr/50cwt; UD 2–68pdr/95cwt, 4–10in/85cwt (14.10.54)
Complement:	600

Name	Builder	Laid down	Launched	Converted
CORNWALLIS	Bombay	1812	2.5.13	Devonport 9.10.54–25.4.55
HASTINGS	Calcutta	Bought 22.6.1818		Portsmouth 11.11.54–12.5.55
HAWKE	Woolwich	5.15	16.3.20	Chatham 10.10.54–20.5.55
PEMBROKE	Wells & Co, Blackwall	3.09	27.6.12	Portsmouth 10.10.54–24.5.55
RUSSELL	Deptford	8.14	22.5.22	Sheerness 7.10.54–6.6.55

Class. Stopgap conversions intended to be used as batteries to attack Russian forts in the Baltic. Secondhand materials used wherever possible. Machinery of the same type as the gunboats.

Careers. All five served with the Baltic fleet 1855–56. *Cornwallis* 1865 became part of Sheerness jetty, sold 1957. *Hastings* sold 1886. *Hawke* sold 1866. *Pembroke* sold 1904. *Russell* sold 1865.

MERSEY class *40-gun frigates*

Displacement:	5643t
Dimensions:	336ft oa x 52ft ext x 21ft 6in
Machinery:	1000nhp. *Mersey* (Maudslay) 3691ihp = 12.58kts. *Orlando* (Penn) 3617ihp = 13.00kts.
Masts:	Main 64ft 6in x 37in; Fore 59ft x 36in; Mizzen 54ft 6in x 24in
Armament:	28-10in/85cwt, 12-68pdr/95cwt
Complement:	600

Name	Builder	Laid down	Launched	Completed
MERSEY	Chatham	12.56	13.8.58	3.59
ORLANDO	Pembroke	11.56	12.6.58	12.61

Class. A direct response to the United States *Merrimack* class, but superior in every respect. The hull was even more wall-sided than the two-deckers, but otherwise similar: especially noticeable were the heavy iron straps. However the combination of extreme length and heavy machinery put tremendous strain on the hull structure. After crossing the Atlantic in 1863 the *Orlando* was discovered to have opened some of her seams by up to 9in. As a result they were not kept in service for very long, being broken up in 1875 and 1871 respectively.

FRENCH NAVY (NEW CONSTRUCTION)

LA BRETAGNE *130 guns*

Displacement:	6770t
Dimensions:	265ft 8in oa x 59ft 4in ext
Machinery:	1200nhp by Indret

Name	Builder	Laid down	Launched	Fate
LA BRETAGNE	Brest	1.53	17.2.55	TS 1866

LE NAPOLÉON class *90 guns*

Displacement:	5040t
Dimensions:	233ft 8in oa x 53ft 1in ext
Machinery:	900nhp by Indret (by Toulon in *Algesiras*, by Cherbourg in *Ville de Nantes*)

Name	Builder	Laid down	Launched	Fate
LE NAPOLÉON	Toulon	1.48	16.5.50	Stricken 1876
ARCOLE	Cherbourg	1853	20.3.55	Stricken 1870
REDOUTABLE	Rochefort	3.53	25.10.55	Stricken 1869
ALGESIRAS	Toulon	4.53	4.10.55	Transport 1869
IMPERIAL	Brest	8.53	15.9.56	Hospital ship 1869
INTREPIDE	Rochefort	9.53	1864 as transport	Renamed *La Borda* 1890, stricken 1914
VILLE DE NANTES	Cherbourg	6.54	7.8.58	Stricken 1872
VILLE DE BORDEAUX	L'Orient	6.54	21.5.60	Stricken 1879
VILLE DE LYON	Brest	6.54	26.2.61	Stricken 1883

FRENCH NAVY (MAJOR CONVERSIONS, RATED VAISSEAUX RAPIDES)

FRIEDLAND *114 guns*

Displacement: 5170t
Dimensions: 229ft 1in x 53ft 8in (originally 207ft 4in oa)
Machinery: 600nhp by Marseilles

Name	Laid down	Launched	Converted	Fate
FRIEDLAND	5.12	14.4.40	1858 at Cherbourg	Hospital ship 1865

Class. This conversion, reported in 1858, was never in fact carried out.

EYLAU *90 guns*

Displacement: 4920t
Dimensions: 225ft 5in x 55ft 1in (originally 205ft oa)
Machinery: 900nhp by M Cave

Name	Builder	Laid down	Launched	Fate
EYLAU	Toulon	4.33	15.5.56	Stricken 1877

ALEXANDRE class *90 guns*

Displacement: 4920t (*Castiglione* 5093t, *Masséna* 5267t)
Dimensions: 236ft 6in x 53ft 10in (*Castiglione, Masséna* 239ft 6in x 53ft 5in)
Machinery: 800nhp (*Castiglione, Masséna* 900nhp)

Name	Builder	Laid down	Launched	Fate
ALEXANDRE	Rochefort	5.48	1857	Stricken 1877
CASTIGLIONE	Toulon	10.35	1860	Stricken 1881
MASSÉNA	Toulon	9.35	1860	Stricken 1879

FRENCH NAVY (MINOR CONVERSIONS, RATED VAISSEAUX MIXTES)

AUSTERLITZ *90 guns*

Displacement: 4430t
Dimensions: 230ft 7in x 55ft 1in (originally 204ft 3in x 53ft 1in)
Machinery: 500nhp by Indret

Name	Builder	Laid down	Launched	Fate
AUSTERLITZ	Cherbourg	8.32	15.9.52	Stricken 1872

LOUIS XIV class *114 guns (ex-120-gun sailing ships)*

Displacement:	4920t (*Souverain* 5094t, *Ville de Paris* 5302t)
Dimensions:	209ft 7in x 57ft 1in (*Souverain* 205ft 5in x 56ft 11in, *Ville de Paris* 226ft 6in x 56ft 4in)
Machinery:	600nhp by Marseilles (*Louis XIV* by Napier)

Name	Builder	Laid down	Launched	Converted	Fate
LOUIS XIV	Rochefort	4.11	28.4.54	1857 at Brest	Stricken 1880
SOUVERAIN	Toulon	1813	25.8.19	1854 at Toulon	Stricken 1882
VILLE DE PARIS	Rochefort	6.07	5.10.50	1857 at Toulon	Stricken 1882

MONTEBELLO *114 guns (ex-120-gun sailing ship)*

Displacement:	4920t
Dimensions:	207ft 4in x 56ft 2in
Machinery:	140nhp by Indret

Name	Laid down	Launched	Converted	Fate
MONTEBELLO	10.10	6.12.22	1852	Stricken 1867

DUGUAY-TROUIN class *90 guns (ex-100-gun sailing ship)*

Displacement:	4530t (*Fleurus* 4509t, *Navarin* 4562t, *Tage* 4707t, *Ulm* 4493t, *Wagram* 4508t, *Turenne* 4554t)
Dimensions:	203ft 2in x 55ft 1in (*Fleurus* 203ft 7in x 55ft 8in, *Navarin* 203ft 5in x 55ft 5in, *Tage* 209ft 1in x 55ft 0in, *Ulm* 204ft 5in x 56ft 1in, *Wagram* 206ft 2in x 55ft 8in, *Turenne* 212ft 11in x 55ft 1in)
Machinery:	*Duguay-Trouin* and *Tage* 500nhp by Napier; the remainder 650nhp by Le Creuzot (except *Ulm*, by Indret and *Turenne*, by Marseilles)

Name	Builder	Laid down	Launched	Converted	Fate
DUGUAY-TROUIN	L'Orient	9.22	21.3.54	1857 at L'Orient	Stricken 1872
FLEURUS	Toulon	4.25	2.12.53		Stricken 1869
NAVARIN	Toulon	5.32	26.7.54		Transport 1873
TAGE	Brest	8.24	15.4.47	1857 at Brest	Transport 1875
ULM	Rochefort	6.25	13.5.54		Hospital ship 1867
WAGRAM	L'Orient	2.33	12.6.54		Stricken 1867
TURENNE	Rochefort	1827	1854	1859 at Brest	Stricken 1867

PRINCE JÉRÔME *90 guns*

Displacement:	4490t
Dimensions:	206ft 3in x 55ft 8in
Machinery:	650nhp by Le Creusot

Name	Builder	Laid down	Launched	Fate
PRINCE JÉRÔME (ex-*Annibal*)	L'Orient	9.27	2.12.53	Transport 1872

BAYARD class *80 guns (ex-90-gun sailing ships)*

Displacement:	4230t (*Breslaw* 4289t, *Donawerth* 4093t, *Fontenoy* 4051t, *Charlemagne* 4124t)
Dimensions:	204ft 5in x 53ft 5in (*Donawerth* 198ft 6in x 53ft 5in, *Charlemagne* 197ft 2in x 53ft 4in, *Saint Louis* 198ft 5in x 53ft 5in)
Machinery:	450nhp by Mazeline (except *Charlemagne* by La Ciotat, *Breslaw* by Brest, *Fontenoy* by Toulon; *Tilsitt* 500nhp by Brest)

Name	Builder	Laid down	Launched	Converted	Fate
BAYARD	L'Orient	7.27	28.8.47	1860 at Cherbourg	Stricken 1872
DUGUESCLIN	Rochefort	3.23	4.5.48	1859 at Brest	Wrecked 14.12.59
BRESLAW	Brest	5.27	31.7.48	1856 at Brest	Stricken 1872
DONAWERTH	L'Orient	7.27	15.2.54	1858 at L'Orient	Stricken 1880
FONTENOY	Toulon	7.27	31.7.48	1857 at Toulon	Transport 1881
CHARLEMAGNE	Toulon	12.33	16.1.51		Transport 1867
SAINT LOUIS	Brest	7.48	25.5.54	1858 at Cherbourg	TS 1881
TILSITT	Cherbourg	3.32	30.3.54	1856 at Brest	Stricken 1872

DUQUESNE class *80 guns*

Displacement:	4556t (*Tourville* 4565t)
Dimensions:	201ft 5in x 55ft 5in
Machinery:	650nhp by Mazeline

Name	Builder	Laid down	Launched	Fate
DUQUESNE	Brest	8.47	2.12.53	Hospital ship 1867
TOURVILLE	Brest	8.47	31.10.53	Stricken 1872

JEAN BART *70 guns*

Displacement:	4070t
Dimensions:	199ft 5in x 53ft 4in
Machinery:	450nhp by Indret

Name	Builder	Laid down	Launched	Fate
JEAN BART	L'Orient	1.49	14.9.52	Stricken 1869

THE IMPERIAL RUSSIAN NAVY

Note that all dates are old style.

IMPERATOR NICOLAI I *111 guns*

Displacement: 5426.9t
Dimensions: 237ft 9in oa x 58ft 3½in
Machinery: 600nhp (Humphreys & Tennant) = 11.0kts
Complement: 1020

Name	Builder	Laid down	Launched	Deleted
IMPERATOR NICOLAI I	New Admiralty, St Petersburg	23.6.55	30.5.60	26.1.74

Class. Originally named *Imperator Alexsander I*.

SINOP class *135 guns*

Displacement: *Sinop* 5585t, *Cesarevic* 5563t
Dimensions: *Sinop* 248ft oa x 59ft 6in, *Cesarevic* 247ft 3in oa x 60ft ext
Machinery: 800nhp (Maudslay) = 11.0kts
Complement: 1130

Name	Builder	Laid down	Launched	Deleted
SINOP	New Admiralty, Nicolaiev	29.10.52	26.9.58	26.1.74
CESAREVIC	New Admiralty, Nicolaiev	3.8.53	29.10.57	26.1.74

Class. Under the terms of the Treaty of Paris, 1856, these ships had to leave the Black Sea, which they did on 2 December 1858. Both were forced to put into British harbours in the Mediterranean, *Cesarevic* at Malta and *Sinop* at Gibraltar, for emergency repairs. Fitted out with their machinery at Cronstadt. *Sinop* laid down as *Bosfor*, but name changed to honour the Russian victory of November 1853. Machinery had six boilers.

VYBORG *74 guns*

Displacement: 3505t
Dimensions: 215ft x 51ft 8in
Machinery: 450nhp (Robert Napier) = 7.5kts
Complement: 827

Name	Builder	Launched	Converted
VYBORG	Ochta Admiralty, St Petersburg	30.7.41	Cronstadt 1853–21.5.54

Class. The first Russian steam battleship. Deleted 7 December 1863.

RETVIZAN *84 guns*

Displacement:	3823t
Dimensions:	215ft 10in x 52ft 8in
Machinery:	500nhp (Nobel of St Petersburg) = 9.5 kts
Complement:	840

Name	Builder	Laid down	Launched	Deleted
RETVIZAN	New Admiralty, St Petersburg	17.9.54	17.9.55	22.11.80

Class. Design lengthened from an old 84-gun sailing ship.

OREL *84 guns*

Displacement:	3717t
Dimensions:	206ft 8in x 51ft 6in
Machinery:	450nhp (Baird of St Petersburg) = 9.5kts
Complement:	827

Name	Builder	Laid down	Launched	Deleted
OREL	New Admiralty, St Petersburg	14.6.51	12.8.54	7.12.63

Class. Laid down as a sailing ship, plans altered in 1852. Her original machinery was ordered from Robert Napier, but this was seized by the British Government on the outbreak of the Russian War.

KONSTANTIN *74 guns*

Displacement:	3697t
Dimensions:	214ft x 53ft 2in
Machinery:	450nhp (Humphreys & Tennant) = 10.5kts
Complement:	827

Name	Builder	Launched	Converted
KONSTANTIN	Ochta Admiralty, St Petersburg	24.8.37	Cronstadt 1854–26.10.56

Class. Original machinery by Napier seized by Britain in 1854. Deleted 8 February 1864.

GANGUT *84 guns*

Displacement:	3814t
Dimensions:	211ft 3in x 53ft 8in
Machinery:	500nhp (Nobel of St Petersburg) = 9.0kts
Complement:	840

Name	Builder	Launched	Converted
GANGUT	Glavnoe Admiralty, St Petersburg	19.10.25	Cronstadt 24.9.56

Class. Present at the Battle of Navarino in 1827. Twice rebuilt before being converted. Deleted 26 August 1871.

VOLA *84 guns*

Displacement:	3814t
Dimensions:	215ft 10in x 53ft 8in
Machinery:	500nhp (Nobel of St Petersburg) = ?
Complement:	840

Name	Builder	Launched	Converted
VOLA	New Admiralty St Petersburg	30.7.37	Cronstadt 26.10.59

Class. This vessel was deleted on 26 August 1871.

In addition to above ships the Russian Navy also intended to complete a new 90-gun ship at William Webb's Yard at New York. This ship, the *Imperatrica Maria*, was ordered in 1856, but re-ordered as the 70-gun frigate *General Admiral* in 1857.

An unnamed 1000nhp ship of the line was listed as planned to build at the New Admiralty Yard, St Petersburg, but was cancelled before being laid down.

The sailing 84-gun ship *Prochor*, identical to the *Orel*, was ordered to convert to steam in 1861 but this plan was cancelled in 1862 and the ship was then hulked.

THE TURKISH NAVY

KOSOVO *110 guns*

Displacement:	3464t
Dimensions:	307ft 9in x 58ft $8\frac{5}{8}$in x 24ft $10\frac{1}{3}$in
Machinery:	700nhp (Maudslay) = 12.0kts
Complement:	863

Class. Built at Constantinople (1826?), three-decker, engined in 1858. Deleted about 1880.

PEIK-I-ZAFER *90 guns*

Displacement:	3125t
Dimensions:	218ft 5in x 55ft 8in x 29ft
Machinery:	600nhp (Napier) = ?
Complement:	800

Class. Built at Ghemlik in 1850, engined by Napier at Devonport in 1857. Deleted 1880.

FETIYE class *94 guns*

Displacement:	3526t
Dimensions:	227ft 8¼in x 56ft 3¼in x 26ft 11⅝in
Machinery:	700nhp (Napier) = ?

Class. *Fetiye* Laid down at Constantinople, *Sadiye* at Ismid, both completed 1856–57. *Fetiye* served as a TS until 1913, *Sadiye* deleted about 1880.

In addition the Turkish Navy laid down another screw battleship, the *Selimiye*, in 1858–59, but she was completed as a large frigate.

OTHER NAVIES

The Austrian Navy launched the *Kaiser* of 91 guns on 4 October 1858 at Pola Navy Yard (5194t, 242ft 10in x 53ft 2in, 800nhp machinery). She was converted into an ironclad in 1870, and although her ultimate fate is unknown, she was still afloat as a hulk in 1918.

The Danish Navy converted the 64-gun *Skjold* at Christianhaven from 29 July 1858 to 8 August 1860 (2550t, 2065t burden, 193ft 7in x 47ft 2in, 300nhp machinery by Baumgarten and Burmeister). She was originally a sailing ship launched at Copenhagen on 3 May 1856; broken up 1876. A similar ship, the *Dannebrog*, was converted from sail into an ironclad frigate in 1864.

The Italian Navy launched the 66-gun *Re Galantuomo* at Naples in 1861 (3669t, 191ft x 50ft 8in, 450nhp machinery). She was broken up in 1875.

The Swedish Navy operated two steam line of battleships: the 68-gun *Carl XIV Johan*, launched at Stockholm in 1824 and converted 1852–54 (2608t, 176ft 11in x 48ft 2in, 300nhp machinery), was deleted in 1867; the 66-gun *Stockholm* was launched at Stockholm in 1856 (2846t, 185ft 8in x 50ft 6in, 350nhp machinery) and broken up in 1922.

The conversion of *Scandanavien* and *Gustav den Store* (both 76 guns) was ordered on 31 January 1855 and cancelled in 1858.

Tables: The Disposition of the British and French Fleets

THE ROYAL NAVY, 1854
BLACK SEA
Steam battleships. *Agamemnon, Sans Pareil*
Sailing ships. *Britannia, Queen, Trafalgar, Albion, London, Rodney, Vengeance, Bellerophon*

BALTIC FLEET
Steam battleships. *Duke of Wellington, Royal George, St Jean d'Acre, Princess Royal, Caesar, James Watt, Nile, Cressy, Majestic, Edinburgh, Ajax, Hogue, Blenheim*
Sailing ships. *Neptune, St George, Prince Regent, 1 Monarch, Cumberland, Boscawen*

THE ROYAL NAVY, 1855
BLACK SEA
Royal Albert, St Jean d'Acre, Agamemnon, Princess Royal, Hannibal, Algiers

BALTIC FLEET
Duke of Wellington, Royal George, Orion, James Watt, Caesar, Nile, Exmouth, Cressy, Majestic, Colossus, Edinburgh, Ajax, Hogue, Blenheim, Cornwallis, Hastings, Hawke, Pembroke, Russell

THE ROYAL NAVY, DECEMBER 1857
MEDITERRANEAN FLEET
Royal Albert, Conqueror, Centurion, Princess Royal

HOME PORTS
Renown

NORTH AMERICA AND WEST INDIES
Brunswick

EAST INDIES AND CHINA
Sans Pareil

THE ROYAL NAVY, JUNE 1859
MEDITERRANEAN FLEET
Marlborough, Hannibal, Agamemnon, Brunswick, Centurion, Conqueror, Cressy, Exmouth, London, Orion, Princess Royal, Renown, St Jean d'Acre, Victor Emmanuel

CHANNEL FLEET
Royal Albert, Edgar, Algiers, Caesar, Hero, James Watt

HOME PORTS
Aboukir, Neptune, Trafalgar, Nile

THE FRENCH FLEET, JULY 1859
ACTIVE AT TOULON
Bretagne, Algesiras, Redoutable, Alexandre, Arcole, Imperial, Ville de Paris, Fontenoy, Breslaw

AT LEGHORN
Donawerth

ADRIATIC
Eylau, Napoléon

BREST
Tage, Duquense

CHERBOURG
St Louis, Tourville

RESERVE AT TOULON, FITTING OUT
Fleurus, Navarin, Prince Jérôme, Charlemagne

THE ROYAL NAVY, SEPTEMBER 1861
MEDITERRANEAN FLEET
Marlborough, Hannibal, Agamemnon, Algiers, Caesar, Exmouth, James Watt, London, Mars, Neptune, Orion, Queen, Victor Emmanuel

CHANNEL FLEET
Revenge, Edgar, Aboukir, Centurion, Conqueror, Donegal, Hero, Trafalgar

NORTH AMERICA AND WEST INDIES
Nile, St George

COASTGUARD SERVICE
Colossus, Majestic

PARTICULAR SERVICE
Sans Pareil

FRENCH BATTLESHIPS USED AS TROOP TRANSPORTS FOR THE MEXICAN ADVENTURE OF 1862

Eylau,	*Fontenoy,*	*Navarin,*
Imperial,	*Tilsitt,*	*Wagram*
Masséna,	*Duquense,*	
Ville de Lyon,	*Tourville,*	
Ville de Bordeaux,	*Breslaw,*	
Souverain,	*Ulm,*	
Turenne,	*St Louis,*	

Appendices

APPENDIX I

AN ANONYMOUS LETTER TO SIR CHARLES WOOD (Received 25 May 1857).

Sir,

It cannot be doubted that you have at heart the honour of the Royal Navy over the administration of which you preside and the safety of the Country, which to a great extent is entrusted to your hands.

Our naval glory was, (under God), gained, and it must be maintained, by the bravery and skill of our Officers and Seamen. But they ought to be supplied with the best ships possessing the most powerful armaments. Gunboats will be useful in their way and place, but are not likely to supersede line of battle ships and frigates. It is a matter of congratulation therefore, that you have not been influenced by the assertions of *The Times* and of other parties as to the probable inutility of these larger ships, and that you have ordered to be constructed such a frigate as the *Mersey*. One only hopes that you will go further in the same direction, and order to be built two or three line of battle ships of proportionate dimensions. As compared with the *Niagara*, our *Duke of Wellington*, *Royal Sovereign* and *Marlborough*, seem unfit to be our First Rates. Close alongside, or at a reasonable distance, they will doubtless speedily give a good account of these Americans, should there ever unfortunately be a war between the two countries; but could they not come within fair range, I should fear for our three-deckers. Their 68-pounders of 65cwt would not go for much against guns weighing 7 tons and discharging shells weighing 130lb. Could our line of battle ships carry eight or ten 95cwt guns on the lower deck, which it is likely they could (the experiment, at all events might be tried), their power and efficiency of armament would be much enhanced. Could not the *Shannon* also and other frigates of her class have been tried with from six to eight of these guns?

Line of battle ships are certainly necessary and especially three-deckers. In the long war with France our Second Rates of 98 guns very soon settled the finest and most heavily armed two-decked ship of the French; and it is not at all unlikely that such a ship as the *Princess Charlotte*, at *close quarters*, would be more than a match for any two-decker we have. It will always be the duty of an English Captain to lay his ship alongside the enemy, if he can; but in the event of his not being able to do so, he would be in a predicament in the presence of an adversary's ship armed with guns of greater calibre and longer range. It seems that for the future the plan should be something like this:

To give our ships fewer guns, but those fewer to be able to propel shot and shell further; and to build our ships with greater tonnage and capacity, without their drawing, at the same time, more water, but even less, than our present ships do. Our three-deckers might mount 104 guns, our Second Rates 74 guns, and our Third Rates 64 guns – all these to be of the line. Our First Class frigates to mount 42 guns, and our Second Class 36; our corvettes to be of 26 and 20 guns; our sloops of 14 and 8 guns. These line of battle ships would be of far greater dimensions than any we now have; but so scientific an officer as Sir Baldwin Walker would be at no loss how to construct them, and to turn them out superior to all that has yet been seen of the kind. I have ventured to enclose certain hints as to the tonnage & armament of ships to be built.

> I am, Sir
> your obed't serv't
> J.R.

After all, will not Armstrong's Rifled Cannon soon take the place of our smooth-bored ordnance, and a 32-pounder gun of his construction throw further and with more certain aim and do more mischief than the 7-ton guns of the *Niagara*? Armstrong should be noticed.

FIRST RATE OF 104 GUNS
Length of keel for tonnage: 300ft
Breadth for tonnage: 66ft
Burden in tons: 6947
Horsepower: 1200

Armament
Lower deck: 30 guns
10-10in guns, 160cwt = 80 tons
20-8in guns, 95cwt = 95 tons. Total = 175 tons
Middle deck: 30 guns
10-8in guns, 95cwt = 47½ tons
20-8in guns, 84cwt = 65 tons. Total = 131½ tons
Main deck: 30 guns
10-8in guns, 95cwt = 47½ tons
20-8in guns, 65cwt = 65 tons. Total = 112½ tons
Quarterdeck & forecastle: 14 guns
2-10in pivot guns, 200cwt = 20 tons
12-8in guns, 55cwt = 33 tons. Total = 53 tons
Total weight of 104 guns = 472 tons
Total weight of 131 guns, in *Duke of Wellington* = 318 tons, which is more in proportion to her tonnage

SECOND RATE OF 74 GUNS
Length of keel for tonnage: 285ft
Breadth for tonnage: 60ft
Burden in tons: 5547
Horsepower: 1200

Armament

Lower and main decks: as above [Lower and middle decks]
Quarterdeck & forecastle: 14 guns
2–10in pivot guns, 200cwt = 20 tons
12–8in guns, 65cwt = 39 tons
Total weight of 74 guns = 365½ tons
Total weight of 91 guns in *Renown* = 260 tons

THIRD RATE OF 64 GUNS

Length of keel for tonnage: 280ft
Breadth for tonnage: 56ft
Burden in tons: 4670
Horsepower: 1000

Armament

Lower deck: 26 guns
6–10in guns, 160cwt = 48 tons
20–9in guns, 94 = 94 tons. Total = 132 tons
Main deck: 26 guns
6–8in guns, 95cwt = 28½ tons
20–8in guns, 65cwt = 65 tons. Total = 93½ tons
Quarterdeck & forecastle: 12 guns
2–10in guns, 200cwt = 20 tons
10–8in guns, 55cwt = 27½ tons. Total = 47½ tons
Total weight of 64 guns, = 273 tons

FIRST CLASS FRIGATE OF 42 GUNS

Length of keel for tonnage: 300ft
Breadth for tonnage: 52ft
Burden in tons: 4315
Horsepower: 1200

Armament

Main deck: 28 guns
28–8in guns, 95cwt = 133 tons
Quarterdeck & forecastle: 14 guns
2–10in guns, 160cwt = 16 tons
12–10in guns, 84cwt = 51 tons. Total = 67 tons
Total weight of 42 guns, = 200 tons

APPENDIX II

WALKER TO THE BOARD OF ADMIRALTY (11 DECEMBER 1858)

Observations on an anonymous paper calling for enlarged battleships.

1st. That I do not consider that sufficient experience has been obtained either as regards the practicability of using the heavy guns referred to under all the circumstances in which a ship of war should be able to use her guns, or as to whether the topsides of ships as presently constructed are capable of withstanding for any considerable length of time, the increased strain which such heavy guns would occasion, to justify their general introduction into the Navy for the purpose of substituting the lighter guns placed on the upper decks of ships of the line and frigates.

With reference to the former point I would beg to call their Lordship's attention to the report of the Committee composed of Admiral, then Captain, Chads as Chairman which assembled at Portsmouth in the year 1847 to investigate this subject.

In opposition to which report we have only the opinion of the Captain of the *Diadem* formed after a very limited experience of that vessel and who not withstanding his earnest desire to arrive at the correct conclusions can hardly be regarded as competent for want of more extensive experience at sea than he has yet had to decide so important a question.

2ndly. With reference to increasing the distance between the ports to afford better quarters I would remark that the distance apart of the ports must be regulated to a certain extent by the timbers which compose the frame of the ship. The usual distance between the ports of ships of the line is 8ft 6in and if this distance is not sufficient it must be made at least 11ft 6in at which distance apart

the broadside ports of the *Bulwark*, 90-gun ship 252 feet in length, would be reduced on the lower deck from 36 to 28 and on the main deck from 36 to 30 and the total armament from 90 to about 74 guns.

3rdly. To obtain the necessary elevation for long range with 68-pounders of 95cwt the port must be increased in depth either by lowering the lower sill and placing the gun on a lower carriage, or by cutting up the upper sill. The former would be inadvisable on the lower deck of ships of the line inasmuch as the height of the sill above the sea would thereby be reduced and the ship would in consequence be less able to keep her ports open in a sea and in the latter case *viz*, cutting the ports up, the decks would have to be raised with everything on them and connected with them – by which means the ships stability might be seriously injured.

Hence the only feasible course would be to place these heavy guns on the main deck the ports of which might without serious objection be made of sufficient depth, in ships to be hereafter built to afford the requisite elevation of the guns and on which they might be used at all times when frigates could use their main deck guns, which would not be the case if they were placed on the lower deck, the ports of which could not be open when there is much sea.

4thly. In the case of ships already built or far advanced in their construction it would be attended with considerable expense both as regards labour and materials to reduce the number of ports and increase the distance between them inasmuch as the topsides would have to be entirely stripped and a considerable portion of the timbers and inboard work altered and the time for the completion of the ships now being converted would in consequence have to be deferred.

5thly. To increase the sizes of the different classes of ships as herein proposed is a matter deserving of serious consideration on account of the great additional outlay it would occasion in their construction and subsequent repairs.

Reasons may be given for increasing their length in some cases to a moderate extent in order to give them finer lines to enable them to attain high speed by means of great power but there can be no good reason given, it is conceived for increasing their breadth beyond what is necessary for their armament and to give the requisite amount of stability, and excess of which occasions quick motion and uneasy rolling and difficulty and uncertainty in the use of the guns.

In the annexed table the dimensions of some of the ships now built or building are inserted in red [in italics] underneath those proposed, some of which of the smaller classes it should be observed would not have sufficient breadth to carry their proposed armament.

I think it worthy of their Lordship's serious consideration whether alterations which will entail large expense and great delay should be entertained at the present moment before the results of the experiments are known relative to the newly invented gun by Armstrong which it is believed will not only be more efficient but much lighter than the guns now in use.

	LOA	Keel	Beam	Tons	HP	Draught
100-gun First Rate	333ft	288ft	64ft	6274	1000	28ft
Victoria	*260ft*	*221ft*	*59.2ft*	*4113*	*1000*	*26.3ft*

Guns

	Lower deck	Middle deck	Main deck	Quarterdeck	Weight
100-gun First Rate	28–68pdr	28–10in/86cwt	28–8in/65cwt	14–32pdr/56cwt, 2–10in/160cwt	400 tons
Victoria	*32–8in/65cwt*	*30–8in/65cwt*	*32–32pdr/58cwt*	*26–32pdr/42cwt, 1–68pdr*	*354 tons*

	LOA	Keel	Beam	Tons	HP	Draught
74-gun Second Rate	322ft	280ft	60ft	5361	1000	26.6ft
Bulwark	*252ft*	*213.9ft*	*57.2ft*	*3716*	*800*	*25.9ft*
64-gun Third Rate	300ft	260ft	58ft	4652	800	25.6ft

Guns

	Lower deck	Main deck	Quarterdeck	Weight
74-gun Second Rate	26–8pdr	28–10in/86cwt	16–8in/65cwt, 2–10in/160cwt	323 tons
Bulwark	*36–8in/65cwt*	*36–32pdr/58cwt*	*18–32pdr/42cwt 1–68pdr*	*264 tons*
64-gun Third Rate	26–68pdr	26–8in/65cwt	10–32pdr/56cwt, 2–10in/160cwt	254 tons

Notes

CHAPTER ONE

1. Brown D K, 'The Structural Improvements to Wooden Ships Instigated by Sir Robert Seppings', *The Naval Architect*, May 1979, pp103-4
2. Byam-Martin Mss, BL Add 41,396, letter of 25 July 1826
3. Sharp, James A, *Memoirs of the Life and services of Rear-Admiral Sir William Symonds*, London 1858
4. Construction Board to Admiralty, 15 November 1845, ADM 3/263
5. Napier to Lord John Russell, undated 1849, in Sir C Napier, *The Navy*, London 1851, pp188-192
6. Auckland to Napier, 6 February 1848, Nap Mss BL, Add 40,022, f 275
7. Walker before the Committee on Marine Engines, PP 1859 xv p48
8. Auckland to Napier, 7 September 1848, Nap Mss, BL, Add 40,023, f278
9. Baring to Sir William Parker, 24 August 1848, Parker Mss NMM PAR/157B
10. Osbon, G A, 'Paddle wheel Fighting Vessels of the Royal Navy', *The Mariner's Mirror*, 68, 1982
11. Biographical details of John Edye, undated MLN 155/4
12. Committee of Reference to Admiralty, 5 November 1847, ADM 87/18
13. Brown, D K, 'The First Steam Battleships', *The Mariner's Mirror*, 63, 1977, pp327-333
14. Testimony of Hay before the Select Committee on Naval and Military Estimates, 6 April 1848, PP 1847-8 xxi pp1943-4
15. *ibid* pp2049, 2060, 2000 & 1943
16. Philimore, Sir A, *The Life and Letters of Sir William Parker*, London 1878-80, vol ii; and Williams, HN, *The Life and Letters of Sir Charles Napier* London 1917 pp220-239
17. Testimony of Walker, 6 April 1847, PP 1847-8 xxi pp2064-2088
18. Instructions to the Surveyor of the Navy, 2 June 1848, Walker Mss NMM, WWL/10

CHAPTER TWO

1. King-Hall, L, *Sea Saga*, London 1935, p93
2. Laughton, Sir J, *Dictionary of National Biography*, entry on Walker
3. O'Byrne, *Naval Biographical Dictionary*, London 1848, vol ii, p1236
4. Auckland to Napier, 6 February 1848, Nap Mss, BL Add 40,022, f 275
5. Admiralty to Surveyor, 2 June 1848, WWL/10
6. Reed, Sir, E J, *On the modifications which the Ships of the Royal Navy have undergone in the present Century*, London 1859
7. Testimony of Edye, 10 April 1848, PP 1847-8 xxi p2560 & Symonds to Admiralty, 22 November 1848, WWL/11
8. Auckland to Napier, 7 September 1848, Nap Mss BL Add 40,023, ff 272-8
9. Wallin, F W 'The French Navy during the Second Empire', unpublished PhD thesis, Berkeley 1953, p9
10. Admiralty to Surveyor, 12 June 1848, ADM 12/197
11. Brown, D K, 'The first Steam Battleships', *The Mariner's Mirror*, 63, 1977
12. Brown, D K 'Thomas Lloyd CB', *Warship*, 20, October 1981
13. Testimony of Walker, 6 April 1846, PP 1847-8 xxi pp2066 & 2088
14. Admiralty to Surveyor, 23 January 1849, ADM 12/512
15. See generally ADM 87/35 which is taken up with the detailed reports of the sailing and steaming trials of the Squadron
16. Martin, W F, to Admiralty 30 November 1850, ADM 87/35
17. Board Minute 6 December 1850, ADM 87/35
18. Bartlett, C J, *Great Britain and Seapower, 1815-53*, Oxford 1963, p223
19. Surveyor to Admiralty, 20 February 1851, ADM 87/36
20. Halstead, Captain E P, *The Screw Fleet of the Navy*, London 1850, p143
21. Hoseason, Commander J C, *The Steam Navy*, London 1853, pp64-6
22. Evidence of Walker before the Committee on Marine Engines, PP 1859 xv, p24
23. Admiralty to Surveyor, 15 February 1851, ADM 87/36
24. Martin to Surveyor, 18 August 1851, ADM 87/37
25. Admiralty to Surveyor, 20 September 1851, ADM 87/42, f 5617
26. Admiralty to Ordnance, 18 September 1850, ADM 87/45, f3100
27. Surveyor to Devonport, 7 April 1854, ADM 87/48, f 7379
28. Baring to Lord John Russell, undated but clearly early 1852, Russell Mss, PRO 30/22/10
29. Pasley, L, *Life of Sir Thomas S Pasley*, London 1900, p155
30. Admiralty to Surveyor, 19 January 1852, ADM 87/39
31. Pasley, P155
32. *Ibid*, pp157-8; and Admiralty to Surveyor, 30 September 1852, ADM 87/42, f8503
33. Committee to Surveyor 23 October 1852, ADM 87/42, f 8901
34. Mr Robb (Consul at Algiers) to the Surveyor, 20 October 1852, WWL/1
35. Surveyor to Admiralty, 19 October 1852, WWL/1
36. Surveyor to Admiralty, 30 October 1852, WWL/1
37. Board Memorandum to the Surveyor 25 October 1852, Milne Mss, NMM MLN 142/1/2
38. Surveyor to Admiralty, 2 November 1852, WWL/1
39. Surveyor to the Dockyards, 10 November 1852, ADM 12/561
40. Admiralty to Penn & Maudslay's, 22 November 1852, ADM 12/561
41. Undated Memo by the Surveyor, late 1852, WWL/1
42. See papers in WWL/2
43. Vincent, J, *The formation of the British Liberal Party*, London 1966, p80
44. Blake, R, *Disraeli*, London 1966, pp320-322 & 394

45. Briggs, Sir J, *Naval Administrations 1827–1898*, London 1898, p107
46. Graham to Sir Charles Wood, Halifax Mss A4/70
47. Martin, T B to Graham, 11 June 1853, Martin Mss, BL Add 41,370, ff 210-234
48. Graham to Aberdeen, 29 May 1853, BL Add 43,191

CHAPTER THREE

1. Eardley-Wilmot, Captain S, *The Life and Letters of Vice-Admiral Lord Lyons*, London 1898
2. Admiralty to Surveyor, 17 January, 23 June & 10 August 1854, ADM 87/47, f6200 87/49 ff9232, 8597
3. Admiralty to Surveyor, 27 December 1854, ADM 87/50, f11519
4. Admiralty to Surveyor, 6 January 1855, ADM 87/51, ff175 & 209
5. Graham to Wood, Halifax Mss, Borthwick Institute, York A4/70
6. Surveyor to Sir John Pakington, 11 February 1859, WWL/3
7. *The Times*, 16 & 17 May 1854
8. Surveyor's Estimate, September 1854, ADM 1/5632 and Graham to Gladstone, 6 October 1854, Gladstone Mss, BL Add 44,163, f153
9. Hamilton, C I, 'Sir James Graham, the Baltic Campaign and War Planning at the Admiralty in 1854', *The Historical Journal*, 1976, pp89–112
10. Admiralty to Napier, 10 November 1854, Napier Mss, BL Add 40,026, f257
11. Berkeley to Wood, 1 November 1855, Halifax Mss, BL Add 49,532
12. Earl Clarendon (Foreign Secretary) to Earl Cowley (Ambassador to Paris), 17 March 1855, Cowley Mss, PRO FO 519/171 ff218–220
13. Raglan to Dundas, 13 October 1854, Dundas Mss, NMM Vol II
14. Hamley, Sir E, *The Crimea*, London 1899, p99
15. Eardley-Wilmot, p241
16. General Memorandum 17 October 1854, Dundas vol II
17. Laird-Clowes, Sir W, *A History of the Royal Navy*, London 1903, vol vi, p142
18. Dewar, Captain A C, *The Russian War 1854, Black Sea*, Navy Records Society, London 1943, p336
19. *ibid* p227
20. Douglas, General Sir Howard, *A Treatise on Naval Gunnery*, London 1860 (5th edition), pp350-3, 377 & 616
21. Sulivan, H N, *Life and Letters of Admiral Sir B J Sulivan*, London 1896, p262
22. Surveyor to Sheerness Dockyard, 3 October 1854, ADM 87/49 f10,007; and Admiralty to Surveyor, 12 January 1855, ADM 87/51, f377
23. Eardley-Wilmot, pp261-7; and Baxter, J P, *The Introduction of the The Ironclad Warship*, Cambridge, Mass 1933, pp63–80
24. Palmerston to Clarendon, 8 November 1855, Clarendon Deposit Bodleian Library, Oxford, C31, ff627-9
25. Wood to Keppel, 30 November 1855, Halifax Mss BL Add 49,565, f18
26. Admiralty to the Medical Director, 24 January 1856, ADM 2/1682, f332
27. Admiralty to Surveyor, 19 February 1856, ADM 2/1682, f434
28. Journals of Rear-Admiral Sir RS Dundas, ADM 50/338
29. List of Vessels, 23 April 1856, ADM 87/60, f11391
30. Surveyor to Portsmouth Dockyard, 11 June 1856, ADM 87/60, f11848

CHAPTER FOUR

1. Brodie, B, *Seapower in the Machine Age*, New York 1941, p73
2. Wood to Milne, 5 August 1856, Milne Mss, MLN 165/13
3. Surveyor to Charles Wood, 3 March 1858, WWL/1
4. Evidence set before the Derby Committee 1858, WWL/8
5. Parkes, O, *British Battleships*, London 1958
6. Sheerness Dockyard to Surveyor, 15 September 1855; ADM 87/55, f4967
7. Dockyards to Surveyor, 17 January 1856 re *Brunswick*, 4 February re *Orion*, 4 & 5 May re *Conqueror* and *Centurion*, ADM 87/57, f7851, 87/58, f8394; 87/60, f10916 & 10937
8. Chatham Dockyard to Surveyor, 9 October 1857, ADM 87/66, f4547 re *Renown*
9. Woolwich Dockyard to Surveyor, 28 May 1860, ADM 87/75, f3428
10. Portsmouth Dockyard to Surveyor, 8 June 1860, ADM 87/75, f3754
11. Bartlett, p223
12. Surveyor's evidence before the Committee on Marine Engines, PP 1859 xv p40
13. Osbon, G A, 'The First of the Ironclads', *The Mariner's Mirror*, 50, 1964, p196
14. Digest cut for 1855, ADM 12/608 cut 91
15. Letter of 13 May 1854, ADM 12/593 cut 91
16. Report of the Committee on Marine Engines, PP 1859 xv
17. Devonport Dockyard to Surveyor 13 December 1855, ADM 87/56, f6950
18. Surveyor to Ordnance Board, 24 March 1854, ADM 87/48, f7243
19. Anonymous to Surveyor, 11 December 1858, WWL/1; and anonymous to Wood, 25 May 1857, ADM 87/66, f6036. See Appendix I
20. Surveyor to Admiralty in reply to above letter, 11 December 1858, WWL/1. See Appendix II
21. Admiralty to Surveyor, 18 December 1858, ADM 87/69, f6122
22. Captain Hewlett to Admiral Sir George Seymour, 24 May 1858, ADM 87/68, f2566
23. Surveyor to Admiralty, 10 June 1858, ADM 87/68
24. Admiral W F Martin to the Duke of Somerset, 1862, Martin Mss, BL Add 41,441, f17
25. Surveyor to Admiralty, 22 June 1858, printed in the Report of the Select Committee on the Board of Admiralty, Sessional Papers 1861 v pp231-3
26. Chatham Dockyard to Surveyor, 14 April 1855, ADM 87/53, f2249
27. Devonport Dockyard Surveyor, 24 August 1855, ADM 87/55, f4633
28. Portsmouth Dockyard to Surveyor, 27 October 1853, ADM 87/46, f4857
29. Napier to Walker, 30 May 1854, Napier Mss, PRO 30/16/12, f323
30. Napier to Admiralty, 24 April 1854, ADM 1/5624 Ha 71
31. Admiralty marginalia on the above
32. Standing Order, 6 April 1854, Napier Mss, PRO 30/16/17, f34
33. Milne to Napier, 13 April 1854, Napier Mss, BL Add 40,024, f137
34. Standing Order, 13 April 1854, Napier BL Add 40,024, f137
35. Milne to Napier, 20 June 1854, Napier BL *loc cit* f316
36. Telegraph from Admiralty to Buchanan, Minister at Copenhagen, 1 July 1854, MLN/169/5
37. Papers on the supply of coal, MLN/154
38. Admiralty Order, 9 April 1854, ADM 1/5675

39. Bonner-Smith, D, *The Russian War 1855: The Baltic*, Navy Records Society, London 1945, pp382-398
40. Memorandum on War readiness 1858, MLN 142/1
41. Milne to R S Dundas, 26 June 1859, MLN 142/3/5
42. Surveyor before the Committee on Marine Engines, PP 859 xv p47
43. Auckland to Napier, 25 October 1847, Napier Mss, NMM NAP/1
44. Report on the Channel Fleet, June 1860, ADM 87/75, f3912
45. Report on the Mediterranean Fleet, November 1860, ADM 87/77, f7055
46. Sulivan p132
47. Hornby to his wife, 9 June 1863, in Egerton, F, *Admiral Sir G P Hornby*, London 1896, p101
48. Surveyor to Admiralty, 28 September 1860, ADM 87/77, f6016
49. Parkes, pp21 & 63
50. Portsmouth Ship... to Surveyor, 9 November 1860, ADM 87/69, f5475
51. Report of the Channel Fleet, Captain Lacon of the *Royal Albert*, ADM 87/75, f3912
52. Pembroke Dockyard to Surveyor, 3 December 1860, ADM 87/77, f7355
53. Papers of May/June 1860, ADM 87/75 ff3557-3694
54. Surveyor before the Derby Committee, WWL/8
55. Papers prepared for the Derby Committee 1858, WWL/1
56. Brodie, pp157-8
57. Laird-Clowes, G S *Sailing Ships*, London 1932, vol i, p96

CHAPTER FIVE

1. Pakington to W F Martin, 27 February 1858, Martin Mss, BL Add 41,409, f7
2. The Queen to Derby, 2 August 1858, in Benson & Esher, *The Letters of Queen Victoria 1837-62* London 1908, vol iii, p298
3. Blake, *Disraeli*, p394
4. Derby to Disraeli, 12 October 1858, in Jones, W D, *Lord Derby and Victorian Conservatism*, London 1956
5. Speech by Pakington, 24 February 1859, Hansard 3rd series, CL11 col 779
6. Surveyor to Devonport Dockyard, 10 August 1858 re *St George* & *Trafalgar*, ADM 91/21, f554
7. Cobden, Richard, *The Three Panics*, London 1862, p70
8. Report on the Channel Fleet, June 1860, ADM 87/75, f3912
9. Surveyor to the relevant Dockyards, 27 July
10. Surveyor to Portsmouth Dockyard, 11 August 1858, men from *Duncan* to *Neptune*, ADM 91/21, f557; and Surveyor to Chatham Dockyard, 11 December 1858, men from *Atlas*, to *Trafalgar*, ADM 91/21, f718
11. Memorandum regarding the Surveyor's programme for 1858-59, 13 November 1858, MLN 142/2/4
12. 'Report of a Committee appointed by the Treasury to inquire into the Navy Estimates from 1852 to 1858 and into the comparative state of the Navies of England and France', published 4 April 1859, PP 1859 xiv
13. Surveyor to Admiralty, 27 July 1858, Martin Mss, BL 41,410 f1202
14. Brodie p74
15. Milne's reply to the three Questions put by the Queen, MLN 142/1
16. Cabinet Minute of 1 December 1858
17. See footnote 11
18. See footnote 12
19. Admiralty to Surveyor, 27 June 1859 and 17 January 1860, ADM 87/73, f8231 and 87/72, f491
20. Pitcher to Surveyor, 2 September 1856, ADM 87/61, f1385
21. Vincent, J R ed, *The Political Journals of Lord Stanley*, London 1979
22. Palmerston to Somerset, 25 September 1859, Palmerston Mss BL Add Mss 48,581, f40; and Palmerston to Gladstone, 29 November 1859, Palmerston Mss BL Add Mss 48,581, f50
23. Somerset to Palmerston, 27 May 1860, Somerset Mss, in Baxter, C F
24. Statement by Somerset, April 1862, Hansard CLXVI col 430-444; and Somerset to Palmerston, 25 February 1861, Palmerston Mss, Broadlands
25. 1860-61 Programme, dated 6 February 1860, ADM 1/5749
26. Baxter, Colin Frank, 'Admiralty Problems during the Second Palmerston Administration', unpublished PhD thesis, University of Georgia 1965
27. Stanmore, Lord, *Sidney Herbert*, London 1906, vol ii, pp201-2
28. Surveyor to Admiralty, 22 June 1858, published in the Derby Committee report
29. Kennedy, Paul, *The Rise and Fall of British Naval Mastery*, London 1976, p173
30. Stanmore, vol ii, pp289-90
31. Palmerston to Gladstone, 15 December 1859, Palmerston Mss, BL Add 48,581, f66
32. Stanmore, p277
33. Gladstone to Palmerston, 25 November 1859, in Guedalla, P, *Gladstone and Palmerston*, london 1928, p113
34. Palmerston to Gladstone, 29 November 1859, in Guedalla, p114
35. Speech by Sir C Napier, 7 March 1859, Hansard CLI col 1411
36. Stanmore, p277
37. Palmerston to Somerset, 14 November 1859, Palmerston Mss, BL Add 48,581
38. Palmerston to Somerset, 8 May 1860, *ibid*
39. Palmerston to Somerset, 27 March 1861, in Baxter, C F
40. Cobden, p127
41. Controller to Admiralty, 8 May 1861, in Parkes p49
42. Burns, Commander K V, *Plymouth's Ships of War*, London 1972, p110
43. Controller to Admiralty, 22 November 1863, ADM 1/5842, f1714
44. Papers relating to Henwood's proposal, MLN 161/14
45. Controller to Admiralty, 1 April 1862, ADM 1/5802, f1714; and Reed, Edward, *Our Ironclad Ships*, London 1869
46. Controller to Admiralty, 2 March 1863, ADM 1/5840
47. Controller to Admiralty, 13 December 1864, MLN 143/2
48. Admiralty Memorandum October 1865, MLN 143/2
49. Admiralty Memorandum November 1867, MLN 143/2
50. Memorandum by the First Lord, 2 December 1867, MLN 143/2
51. Programme of the 1867 Review, MLN 164/4
52. W F Martin to Admiralty, 4 July 1860, Martin Mss, BL Add 41,436, f51
53. Controller to Admiralty, 17 May 1861, ADM 1/5774
54. Sources in MLN 116 (letters), MLN 117 (Standing Orders) and MLN 119/1 (Returns of Foreign Vessels)
55. Wadia, R A, *The Bombay Dockyard and the Wadia Master Builders*, Bombay 1955

CHAPTER SIX

1. Admiralty Standing Order, 23 March 1854, Napier Mss, PRO 30/16/12, f32
2. Napier Standing Order, 6 April 1854, *ibid*, f34
3. Codrington to Lady Bourchier, 29 June 1854, in Bourchier ed, *The Life and Letters of Admiral Sir Henry Codrington*, London 1880, p397
4. Egerton, p81
5. *ibid*, p80
6. Douglas, Sir Howard, *On Naval Warfare Under Steam*, London 1858
7. Biddlecombe, G, *Naval Tactics and Sailing Trials*, London 1850
8. Wilson, H W, *Ironclads in Action*, London 1898, vol 1, p240
9. Bartlett, C, p324 (based on Auckland to Napier, 26 December 1847, Napier Mss, BL Add 40,022, f231)
10. Wilson, p240
11. Baxter, J P, p69
12. Douglas, *Gunnery*, p343
13. Admiralty Order, 28 February 1854, ADM 2/1565
14. Photograph dated 4 April 1857, ADM 87/66, f6034
15. War Office to Surveyor, 26 April 1858, ADM 87/71, f2094
16. Milne to W F Martin, July 1858, Martin Mss, BL Add 41,417, f104
17. Hewlett to C-in-C Portsmouth, 18 July 1860, ADM 87/76, f5018
18. Query by Captain John Moore in *The Mariner's Mirror*, 66, 1980, p267
19. Brown, D K 'Shells at Sebastopol', *Warship* 10, April 1979, pp74-9
20. Scott-Russell, J, *The Fleet of the Future*, London 1861, p28

CHAPTER SEVEN

1. Captain T M C Symonds to Commodore W F Martin, 2 August 1851, Martin Mss, BL Add 41,417, f10

2. Papers by John Edye concerning Sir William Symonds, October 1847, MLN 155/4
3. Baxter, C F, p7
4. Douglas, Sir H, *A Treatise on Naval Gunnery*, London 1855 (4th edition), p558
5. Ropp, T, 'The Development of a Modern Navy', unpublished PhD thesis, Harvard 1937, p8
6. Sulivan, H N, p143
7. Reed, E, letter to *The Times*, 10 January 1859
8. Baxter, J P, p92
9. Ropp, p9
10. *ibid*, p14
11. Baxter, C F, p70
12. Rear-Admiral Sir M Seymour to Rear-Admiral Sir Richard Saunders Dundas, 3 September 1855, Melville Castle Muniments, Scottish Record Office, GD 51/1008/2, f19
13. Busk, Hans, *The Navies of the World*, London 1859, p101
14. Rodger, N A M, 'British Belted Cruisers', *The Mariner's Mirror*, 64, 1978, p23; and Mitchell, D, *A History of Russian and Soviet Seapower*, London 1974, pp176-8
15. Busk, pp106-110
16. Bennet, F M, *The Steam Navy of the United States*, Pittsburgh 1896, p141
17. Wood to Palmerston, 9 October, 1856, Broadlands Mss, GC/WO 85/90
18. Admiralty Digest, 24 November, 1854, ADM 12/593 cut 91
19. Bilzer, F, '*Kaiser*, Linienschiff und Kasemattschiff der K u K Kriegsmarine', *Marine – Gestern, Heute*, December 1983

CONCLUSION

1. Controller to Admiralty, 13 May 1861, ADM 1/5774

Bibliography

UNPUBLISHED PAPERS

Public papers held at the Public Record Office
Admiralty Papers, particularly:
ADM 1. Secretary's In Letters
ADM 2. Secretary's Out Letters
ADM 3. Special Minutes
ADM 12. Digest
ADM 50. Admiral's Journals
ADM 84. Steam Department
ADM 87. Surveyor's Department
ADM 91. Materiel, Departments: Out Letters
ADM 92. Surveyor's Submission Book
ADM 180. Progress Book

Public Papers held at the National Maritime Museum
Admiralty Papers
Ship's Draughts

Private Papers
ABERDEEN MSS, British Library Add Mss
CODRINGTON MSS, National Maritime Museum
COWLEY MSS, Foreign Office Papers, Public Record Office
CLARENDON DEPOSIT, Bodleian Library Oxford.
DUNDAS, ADMIRAL SIR JAMES WHITLEY DEANS, National
Maritime Museum
DUNDAS, ADMIRAL SIR RICHARD SAUNDERS, Scottish Record
Office
GLADSTONE MSS, British Library Add Mss
GRAHAM MSS, Microfilm at Cambridge University Library
HALIFAX MSS, British Library Add Mss; and Borthwick
Institute, York
KEPPEL MSS, National Maritime Museum
MARTIN MSS: ADMIRAL SIR THOMAS BYAM; ADMIRAL SIR
WILLIAM FANSHAWE; ADMIRAL SIR HENRY BYAM: all British
Library Add Mss
MILNE MSS, National Maritime Museum
NAPIER MSS, British Library Add Mss, Public Record Office, and
National Maritime Museum
PALMERSTON MSS, Broadlands Mss at the National Register of
Archives, and British Library Add Mss
PARKER MSS, National Maritime Museum
RUSSELL MSS, Public Record Office
WALKER MSS, National Maritime Museum (now only
available on microfilm)

PUBLISHED DOCUMENTS

Great Britain: Parliament
Parliamentary Papers, particularly:
1847–8 vol xxi
1852–3 vol ix
1856 vol xi
1859 vols xiv & xv
Hansard's Parliamentary Debates 1845–1863

Journals and letters
STANLEY, LORD The Political Journals of Lord Stanley, edited by
John Vincent, London 1979
VICTORIA, QUEEN The Letters of Queen Victoria: A Selection from Her
Majesty's correspondence between the years 1837 and 1861

Publications of the Navy Records Society
BONNER-SMITH, DAVID The Russian War 1854 – The Baltic,
London 1943
BONNER-SMITH, DAVID The Russian War 1855 – The Baltic,
London 1944
CORBETT, SIR JULIAN STAFFORD Fighting Instructions 1530 – 1816,
London 1905
CORBETT, SIR JULIAN STAFFORD Signals and Instructions, 1776 –
1794, London 1909
DEWAR, CAPTAIN A C The Russian War 1854 – the Black Sea,
London 1943
DEWAR, CAPTAIN A C The Russian War 1855 – the Black Sea,
London 1945
HAMILTON, ADMIRAL SIR R VESEY Letters and Papers of Sir T Byam
Martin, London 1899, 1900 & 1903
LAMBERT, ANDREW D 'Captain Sir Henry Keppel's account
Capture of Bomarsund – August 1854', in The Naval Miscellany IV,
edited by N A M Rodger, London 1984

SECONDARY SOURCES

Books
(The major relevant books are marked*)

ALBION, R G Forests and Seapower, Harvard 1925
ANDERSON, OLIVE A Liberal State at War: English Politics and
Economics during the Crimean War, London 1967
ANDERSON, R C Naval Wars in the Baltic during the Sailing Ship
Epoch, 1522 – 1850, London 1910
ANDERSSON, INGVAR A History of Sweden, London 1956
BALLARD, ADMIRAL SIR G The Black Battlefleet, London 1980
BANBURY, PHILIP Shipbuilders of the Thames and Medway, Newton
Abbot 1971
BAPST, GERMAIN Le Marechal Canrobert, Souvenirs d'un Siècle, 6 vols,
Paris 1898 – 1913
BARFLEUR Naval Policy, London 1907
*BARTLETT, C J Great Britain and Seapower, 1815 – 53, Oxford 1963
BAXTER, J P The Introduction of the Ironclad Warship, Cambridge,
Mass 1933
BONNETT, S The Price of Admiralty, London 1968
BIDDLECOMBE, GEORGE Naval Tactics and Sailing Trials, London
1850
BLAKE, ROBERT Disraeli, London 1966
BENNETT, F M The Steam Navy of the United States, Pittsburgh 1896
*BOURCHIER, LADY Selections from the Correspondence of Sir Henry
Codrington, London 1880
BOURNE, K and WALT, D C Studies in International History, London
1967

BRIERLEY, OSWALD *The English and French Fleets in the Baltic, 1854*, London 1858

BRIGGS, SIR JOHN *Naval Administrations 1827 – 92*, London 1897

BRIGHT, PHILIP *Diaries of John Bright*, London 1930

BRODIE, BERNARD *Seapower in the Machine Age*, New York 1941

BURROWS, MONTAGUE *Memoir of Admiral Sir H D Chads*, Portsea 1867

*BUSK, HANS *Navies of the World*, London 1859

BURNS, K V *Plymouth's Ships of War*, London 1972

CHAPELLE, HOWARD I *The American Sailing Navy*, New York 1947

CHESNEY, KELLOW *A Crimean War Reader*, London 1960

CHEVALIER, E *Histoire de la Marine Francais*, vol 5, Paris 1905

CLAPHAM, J H *An Economic History of Modern Britain*, vol I, Cambridge 1926

CLARKE, SIR GEORGE SYDENHAM, *Fortification*, London 1890

CLARKE, SIR GEORGE SYDENHAM *Russia's Seapower*, London 1898

CLARKE, SIR G S and THURSFIELD, I *The Navy and the Nation*, London 1897

COBDEN, RICHARD *Political Writings*, 2 vols, London 1868

COLOMB, ADMIRAL PHILIP H *Naval Warfare* (2nd Edition), London 1898

CONACHER, J B *The Aberdeen Coalition 1852 – 55*, Cambridge 1968

CONACHER, J B *The Peelites and the Party System: 1846 – 52*, Newton Abbot 1972

*CORBETT, SIR JULIAN STAFFORD, *Some Principles of Maritime Strategy*, London 1911

CLOWES, SIR WILLIAM LAIRD *Sailing Ships*, London 1932

CLOWES, SIR WILLIAM LAIRD *The Royal Navy*, vol 6, London 1903

CRAUFORD, *The Russian Fleet in the Baltic in 1836*, London 1837

CURTISS, JOHN SHELTON *Russia's Crimean War*, Ithaca 1979

DOLBY, E T *Sketches in the Baltic*, London 1854

*DOUGLAS, GENERAL SIR HOWARD *A Treatise on Naval Gunnery*, London (various editions, 1855, 1860 etc)

*DOUGLAS, GENERAL SIR HOWARD *Naval Warfare Under Steam*, London 1857

EARDLEY-WILMOT, CAPTAIN S *The Life of Lord Lyons*, London 1898

EARLE, EDWARD MEADE *Makers of Modern Strategy*, Princeton 1942

EARP, G BUTLER *The History of the Baltic Campaigns of 1854*, London 1857

EGERTON, MRS F *Admiral Sir Geoffrey Phipps Hornby*, London 1896

ELERS-NAPIER, GENERAL G *The Life and Correspondence of Admiral Sir Charles Napier*, 2 vols, London 1862

EMMERSON, G S *John Scott-Russell*, London 1977

FINCHAM, J *A History of Naval Architecture*, London 1851

FITZGERALD, ADMIRAL P *Memoirs of the Sea*, London 1913

FITZMAURICE, LORD E *The Life of Granville George Leveson Gower, Second Earl Granville KG 1815 – 1891*, 2 vols, London 1905

GARDINER, R et al *Conway's All the World's Fighting Ships 1860 – 1905*, London 1979

GIFFARD, ADMIRAL SIR GEORGE *Reminiscences of a Naval Officer*, Exeter 1892

GOOCH, B D *The New Bonapartist Generals in the Crimean War*, The Hague 1959

GOOCH, G P *The later Correspondence of Lord John Russell*, 2 vols, London 1925

GORSHAKOV, ADMIRAL SERGEI *The Seapower of the State*, London 1979

GLEASON, J H *The Genesis of Russophobia in Great Britain*, London 1950

GRAHAM, G S *Empire of the North Atlantic*, London 1950

*GRAHAM, G S *The Politics of Naval Supremacy*, London 1965

GRAHAM, G S *Great Britain in the Indian Ocean 1810 – 1850*, Oxford 1967

GRAHAM G S *The China Station*, Oxford 1979

GUEDALLA, PHILIP *Gladstone and Palmerston*, London 1928

HALLENDORF, C and SCHUCK, A *A History of Sweden*, New York 1970

HAMILTON, ADMIRAL SIR R VESEY *Naval Administration* 1897

HOGG, IAN *Coast Defences of England and Wales, 1856 – 1956* Newton Abbot 1974

HORSEFIELD, JOHN *The Art of Leadership in War*, London 1980

HOSEASON, COMMANDER J C *The Steam Navy*, London 1853

HOVGAARD. W *A Modern History of Warships*, London 1928 (reprinted 1971)

IMLAH, A H *Economic Elements in the Pax Britannica*, London 1958

IREMONGER, L *Lord Aberdeen*, London 1978

JANE, F T *The Imperial Russian Navy*, London 1904 (reprinted 1983)

JANE, F T *Heresies of Seapower*, London 1907

JENKINS, E H *A History of the French Navy*, London 1974

JONES, W D *Lord Derby and Victorian Conservatism*, London 1956

KEMP, P *The Oxford Companion to Ships and the Sea*, Oxford 1976

KEMP, T *Industrialisation in Nineteenth Century Europe*, London 1969

KENNEDY, PAUL *The Rise and Fall of British Naval Mastery*, London 1976

KEPPEL, ADMIRAL SIR HENRY *A Sailor's Life under Four Sovereigns*, 3 vols, London 1899

KINGLAKE, A W *The Invasion of the Crimea*, 9 vols, London 1877

KINGSLEY-MARTIN B *The Triumph of Lord Palmerston*, London 1924

KING-HALL, L *Sea Saga*, London 1935

KREIN, DAVID *The Last Palmerston Administration*, Iowa 1978

LAUGHTON, JOHN KNOX *Memoirs of the Life and Correspondence of Henry Reeve*, 2 vols, London 1898

*LAVERY, BRIAN *The Ship of the Line*, vol I, London 1983

LEWIS, MICHAEL *The Navy of Britain*, London 1948

*LEWIS, MICHAEL *The Navy in Transition 1814 – 1864*, London 1965

LINCOLN, W BRUCE *Nicholas I*, London 1978

LLOYD, CHRISTOPHER *The British Seaman*, London 1978

MARTIN, THEODORE *Life of His Royal Highness the Prince Consort*, 5 vols, London 1879

MITCHELL, D *A History of Russian and Soviet Seapower*, London 1974

MORESBY, ADMIRAL SIR J *Two Admirals*, London 1909

*NAPIER, ADMIRAL SIR CHARLES *The Navy*, London 1851

NAVY LIST, Various dates

*OTWAY, A *Autobiography and Journals of Admiral Lord Clarence Paget*, London 1896

O'BYRNE, J *Naval Biographical Dictionary*, 2 vols, London 1849

PARKER, C S *Life and Letters of Sir James Graham 1792 – 1861*, 2 vols, London 1907

PASLEY, L *Life of Admiral Sir T S Pasley*, London 1900

PHILIMORE, A *Life of Sir William Parker*, 3 vols, London 1876   80

PREST, J M *Lord John Russell*, London 1972

PRESTON, A and MAJOR, J *Send a Gunboat*, London 1967

RANFT, BRYAN *Technical Change and British Naval Policy 1860 – 1939*, London 1977

RASOR, E *Reform and the Royal Navy*, Connecticut 1976

*REED, EDWARD *On the Modifications which the Ships of the Royal Navy have undergone in the present Century*, London 1859

*REED, EDWARD *Our Ironclad Ships*, London 1870

RICHMOND, ADMIRAL SIR H *Statesmen and Seapower*, London 1946

ROBERTSON, F C *The Evolution of Naval Armaments*, London 1967

RODGER, N A M *The Admiralty*, Lavenham 1979

ROLT, L T C *Isambard Kingdom Brunel*, London 1957

SCOTT-RUSSELL, JOHN *The Fleet of the Future*, London 1861

SCHROEDER, PAUL W *Austria, Great Britain and the Crimean War*, New York 1972

SCHURMAN, D M *The Education of a Navy*, London 1965

SCHURMAN, D M *Sir Julian Stafford Corbett 1856 – 1922*, London 1981

SETON-WATSON, H *The Russian Empire 1801 – 1917*, Oxford 1967

SETON-WATSON, R W *Britain in Europe*, London 1938

*SHARP, JAMES A *Memoirs of Rear Admiral Sir William Symonds*, London 1858

SIMPSON, F A *Louis Napoleon and the Recovery of France 1848 – 1856*, London 1923

SMITH, E I *A Short History of Naval and Marine Engineering*, Cambridge 1938

*SOUTHGATE, D *The Most English Minister*, London 1966

SPROUT, H and M *The Rise of American Naval Power 1776 – 1918*, Princeton 1939

STUART, VIVIAN *Beloved Little Admiral*, London 1967

SULIVAN, H N *Life and Letters of Admiral Sir B J Sulivan*, London 1896

SUMNER, B H *A Survey of Russian History*, London 1947

TAYLOR, A J P *The Struggle for Mastery in Europe 1848 – 1918*, Oxford 1954

TEMPERLEY, H M V *England and the Near East: the Crimea*, London 1936

TUNSTALL, BRIAN *Flights of Naval Genius*, London 1930

VINCENT, JOHN *The Formation of the British Liberal Party 1857 – 1866*, London 1966

WADIA, R A *The Bombay Dockyard and the Wadia Master Shipbuilders*, Bombay 1955

WARD, J T *Sir James Graham*, London 1967

WILLIAMS, H N *The Life and Letters of Admiral Sir Charles Napier*, London 1917

WILSON, H W *Ironclads in Action*, 2 vols, London 1896

WOODWARD, E *The Age of Reform*, Oxford 1962

Articles

BILZER, FRANZ '*Kaiser*, Linienschiff und Kasemattschiff der KuK Kriegsmarine', *Marine, Gestern – Heute*, December 1983

BROWN, D K 'The First Steam Battleships', *The Mariner's Mirror*, 63, 1977

BROWN, D K 'Shells at Sebastopol', *Warship*, 10, April 1979

BROWN, D K 'The Structural Improvements to Wooden Warships instigated by Sir Robert Seppings', *The Naval Architect*, May 1979

BROWN, D K 'Thomas Lloyd CB' *Warship*, 20, October 1981

LAING, E A M 'The Introduction of the Paddle Frigate into the Royal Navy' *The Mariner's Mirror*, 66, 1980

OSBON, G A 'The First of the Ironclads', *The Mariner's Mirror*, 50, 1964

OSBON, G A 'Paddlewheel Fighting Ships of the Royal Navy', *The Mariner's Mirror*, 68, 1982

PACKARD, J J 'Sir Robert Seppings and the Timber Problem', *The Mariner's Mirror*, 64, 1978

RODGER, N A M 'The Design of the *Inconstant*' *The Mariner's Mirror*, 61, 1975

VINCENT, JOHN 'The Parliamentary Dimension of the Crimean War', *Transactions of the Royal Historical Society*, 1981

Unpublished Dissertations

BAXTER, C F 'Admiralty Problems during the Second Palmerston Administration', University of Georgia 1965

LAMBERT, ANDREW D 'Great Britain, the Baltic and the Russian War, 1854 – 1856', University of London 1983

MACMILLAN, D F 'The Development of British Naval Gunnery, 1815–1853', University of London 1967

ROPP, T 'The Development of a Modern Navy', Harvard 1937

WALLIN, FRANKLIN 'The French Navy during the Second Empire', University of California 1953

Index